Sell Your House and Buy a Sailboat
Then Sail Halfway Around the World

Ray Emerson

Copyright 2014

Pack Lite Travel for

Ray Emerson

Judy Emerson

1-15 To mK

Acknowledgements

Special thanks to those that helped this dream evolve.
Robert Maury for his book *Tinkerbelle*.
John Hefner for the 14.5 foot Windmill class boat we built.
Jim Kilroy for passage on his 76' racing ketch, *Kealoa II*.
Son Ross for directing me to the right boat for ocean cruising.
Edd and Judi Claire for our first passage.
Latitude 38 for the confidence building '*puddle jump*'.
Daughter Taylor and family for providing safe haven in the US.
Stephanie Mitchell for excellent editing and keeping my voice.
Mark Boyd for his encouragement, patience, production of this book, including cover design and associated website.
It was a team effort…thank you all for being on the team!

Dedication

This book is dedicated to my wife Judy who made this adventure a joy and a dream come true. Her initial agreement was for two years with a smile, but ended up being an eight year adventure of a lifetime.

Table of Contents

Prologue

Part 1: Pacific Ocean

    Chapter 1: Passage to Marquesas Islands
                  Judy's Observations

Part 2: South Pacific Islands

    Chapter 2: Marquesas

        Headin South
        Checking the Anchor
        Water on the Islands
        Rite of Passage
        Judy and the Pirates
        Mexican and Marquesans Cultures
        Marquesan Heart

    Chapter 3: Tuamotus

        Passage to the Tuamotus
        Treasures of Cruising
        The Intruder
        Ross and the Walkers
        Church in Makemo
        No Mechanic in Makemo
        Our Friend the Grouper
        Diving with the Young Men
        Good Naked and Bad Naked

    Chapter 4: Tahiti

        Sunday in Tahiti
        A Time to Dance
        Getting to Know You

Drums and Hips
Making Things Happen
The French Connection
Departure Withdrawal
Home Wreckers

Chapter 5: Moorea and Bora Bora

Batten Down the Hatches
Meet the Rays
Dead Animals
Bon Appétit at Sea
Moment of Truth
Bora Bora
Ladies Rite of Passage
Molly
Sea Monsters

Chapter 6: Beverage Reef and Niue

Atypical Eight Days at Sea
Beverage Reef
Niue Ugas
Lost and Found

Chapter 7: Tonga

King's Men in Black
Mammal to Mammal
Flag Man
Jenny to Jenny
Bugs
Night Lights

Part 3: Down Under

Chapter 8: New Zealand

New Zealand Crossing
Crossing with the King
Opua at Night
Rugby, A Man's Game
Return to Kiwi Land
"On the Hard"
New Zealand Goodbye

Chapter 9: New Caledonia

Fast Passage to New Caledonia
"He is Coming in Again"
French Desserts and Visual Treats

Chapter 10: Australia

Bird on the Boom
Breasts, Thighs, and Small Dinghies
Lizard Island (Cook's Look)
One Tree, Two Leaf Blowers
Go Deep! Go Deep!
Top of My Game
Sensory Realignment
Darwin Passage (Summary)
Tipperary Waters Marina
Kakadu National Park
Return to Darwin
Decision to Return
The Fall
Humping the Hostess
Byron Bay R&R
Pining Away in Darwin
Darwin Side Shows

Part 4: SE Asia

Chapter 11: Indonesia

>Leaving Australia
>Jurassic Park, Rindja Island
>*Selat* – For or Against
>Grounded High and Dry
>Bali Marina – The Slip
>"I am Hindu, I am Lucky"
>Kodak Moment in Lombock
>"Keep the Change"
>Bawean Burkas
>Mounted on Lord's Mantle
>Tanker, Tug and Bad Guys

Chapter 12: Malaysia

>Traveling with the Big Boys
>Marina Hopping in SE Asia
>The Rally
>Surgery in Penang
>Penang: World Food Court
>Circle of Life
>Zonation
>Backpacker Suite
>Tomorrow I Will Do Something
>Mr. Din
>Two Ladies from Kazakhstan
>Roast Beast

Chapter 13: Thailand

>Romeo Lost and Found
>Thailand in the Heat
>Chiang Mai
>Ant Wars
>Mindfulness

Silent Movie – Observation from Judy
Conning the Duffers
Walking the Dog

Part 5: Homeland and Side Trips

Chapter 14: USA

R&R in San Francisco
R&R in Spokane
Number 24
Team Effort at 1.25 People
Kindergarten Science I
Kindergarten Science II
Pit Bulls and Sushi
Parking Lot Slip
Sudoku and Opera
For All the World to See
No Pets Allowed
Changing Priorities

Chapter 15: China

Gathering, Gasping, Pushing
Flavors of Beijing
Blossom's Suitcase

Chapter 16: Cambodia and Viet Nam

Golden Temple
Trains, Buses, Boats, Rickshaws
Kalashnikov AK–47
"Only One Dollar" – *Teacun*
Grasshopper
Tunnels, Mines and a Pot Hole
Two Flags – One Vietnam

Chapter 17: France and Ireland

>   Paris (Bonaparteville)
>   French River Cruise
>   Dublin Duffers

Chapter 18: Italy and Greece on the *Princess*

>   The Crown Princes
>   Rome, Athens and Beyond
>   Table Talk
>   Champagne Trail w Blanco
>   Special Moments

Epilogue

Glossary

Prologue

The idea for this sailing adventure was planted with *Tinkerbelle*, a book by Robert Manry about a solo voyage across the Atlantic Ocean in a thirteen-and-a-half-foot sailboat, which I read in 1967. That seed lay dormant for thirty-six years, until the one day when I came home from my job as a marine biologist.

"Raymond," my darling wife, Judy, said, "I have spent twenty-five years here. This is my last winter in Alaska. I am leaving." She paused. "I hope you will come with me."

I considered her words and, after a few moments, said, "Yes." I then asked, "Would you live on a sailboat?"

She quietly considered my question then replied, "Yes."

It was as simple as that—the rest is history.

It was soon after this conversation, in December 2002, that we purchased a forty-foot sailboat in Bellingham, Washington, and moved from a 3,200-square-foot home to a space forty feet by twelve feet that tapered at each end to a useable space of about 200 square feet. Much of the stuff we had accumulated over the years was dispersed like it would be at an estate sale, as if someone had died. In a sense, we had died, but as the stuff went away we began to feel reborn. My gun collection was toughest to part with. In Alaska, everyone has guns. It took three trips to the gun shop before I could bring myself to take them into the store to be sold. Judy does not collect stuff, so the transition to our smaller space was easier for her. If something has no further function or usefulness to her it is dumped. I am always concerned the same standard will someday apply to me.

When we decided to sell the house, it was a two-month crash course in relocating our stuff. We donated to local service organizations and took advantage of the garage sale, which provided the added bonus of meeting some interesting people and giving the answer to their usual question.

"Why are you moving?"

"We bought a sailboat and plan to sail around the world."

This was especially effective since we had a nice house and the appearance of having all we would want in life right there. It seemed to give people some renewed insights into their lives. To date, one of the neighbors has sold their house and bought an RV and another booked passage on a thirty-day sailing adventure in the Bahamas. Several folks met with us to find out more about how to go about what we were doing. Our son, Ross, and his new bride, Laura, sold their holdings and purchased a similar boat. They planned to sail with us.

Along with our favorite books, cooking utensils and some select tools, we decided to bring Romeo, our faithful feline of almost fourteen years. We agonized over bringing him, but now know it was the right thing to do. We gave him the forward cabin and some alternative sleeping places in the salon and the cockpit. Since he spends about eighty percent of his time sleeping, these were important decisions on his behalf. He would have his scratching pole, cat box and designated feeding area.

The first night in his new home on the water went well, but the next morning the water was glassy smooth, and he jumped off the boat. He flew out of the water onto the dock with eyes blazing and wet trail dragging. He only made that mistake once.

Judy and I had had little experience sailing before this great adventure at sea. We started in 1963 and spent several summers on Lake Folsom, near Sacramento, California, with a fourteen-foot Windmill-class sloop I had built with a friend. It was magical to move silently through the water with only the power of the wind. Judy did not particularly enjoy sailing, but liked being towed on an air mattress behind the boat. She really didn't like the boat, or the water for that matter, but the air mattress was okay as long as she didn't get too wet.

My next sailing experience came many years later, while in graduate school at the University of Southern California. Jim Kilroy, a successful real estate developer and ocean-racing skipper, came to the campus looking for two graduate students to accompany and assist the crew of his seventy-nine-foot racing ketch, the *Kealoa II*, across the Pacific from Hawaii to Australia for the Sydney Hobart Race. He interviewed about twenty graduate students, all of whom made the mistake of talking only about their research.

"I want to sail around the world someday, but I've only sailed a small fourteen-foot boat," I informed him.

"The principles of sailing are the same for any size sailboat," he replied.

I was later selected and asked to select the second graduate student. Judy did not go on this trip, but hoped it would get this "sailing-around-the-world thing" out of my system, and it did. The crews on the smaller boats that came into the harbors along the way looked badly weathered and tired, I assumed from being at the wheel, since we always had someone at the wheel on the big ketch. The concept of an autopilot was unknown to me then.

My third sailing experience came when Ross and I rented a sailboat complete with a skipper for a ten-day cruise of the San Juan Islands, off the coast of Washington. The rental included sailing lessons. We must have done okay, because the skipper left us midweek to finish on our own. I was at the wheel of the Peterson 36 as we motored out of the harbor that first day, and I knew right then I wanted more of this someday. When we returned from our successful sailing trip, Ross pointed out a Valiant 40 to me.

"Dad," he said, "if you ever do decide to sail around the world that is the kind of boat you want."

Less than two months later, I purchased that very same boat.

Buying a sailboat to go ocean cruising is in no way the same as buying a car. First, a boat is not just a transportation conveyance. It is also a house, with all of its appointed comforts and maintenance requirements. We had the requisite survey. However, there were many surprises that needed to be attended to before we could launch. We bought the boat December 4, 2002, on Judy's birthday, but it would be ten months before we moved aboard our new home on the water. Those ten months were packed with transitions and decisions. We retired from our jobs—Judy was a dental hygienist—sold our house, dealt with medical issues and were part of our son's wedding.

Next, we moved onto the boat and lived there for sixteen months, adjusting to marina life and meeting other cruisers. I took a navigation class, got my ham radio license, and prepared our new home for the open sea. The decision to head south came unexpectedly when Edd and Judi Claire, experienced cruisers we had become friends with, announced they wanted to leave right then.

"February is about the worst time of year to be on the West Coast in a sailboat," Judy and I reminded them.

"We agree," they replied, "but we are anxious to get going and don't want to wait."

We had undergone months of repairs and refurbishing while in Port Townsend, Washington, and the *Nereid* was deemed ready to head down the West Coast to Mexico and cross the Pacific. Ross expressed deep concern that we were taking off at this time of year with only limited experience and how-to books under our belts, but we felt ready and were eager to begin. Also, we trusted our boat and we trusted Mr. Edd.

And so it was that, sixteen months after moving onto the boat and with limited sailing experience, we found ourselves headed south following *Claire de Lune*, a Valiant 40 just like ours with skipper Edd and his wife Judi at the helm. We were off!

There was a farewell dinner and long goodbyes the night before we left, but it was with little fanfare that we cast off at first light. The early hour was timed to catch the morning tidal boost. It would be more than a year before I would be able to acknowledge in any detail that momentous occasion. With Judy at the bow and me at the helm, we slowly motored out of Point Hudson, through the morning mist, headed for the somewhat restricted sea entrance. As we watched the marina slip away behind us, there was a sudden terrified scream from the bow. I turned to find Judy standing with one hand over her mouth and the other hand pointing and shaking frantically.

"Oh #$%*," I said.

We were headed directly for the pilings on the starboard side of the entrance.

We braced for the impact, as it was too late to avoid a crash. We hit the pilings with a glancing blow that took out some of the piling timber and left an unsightly deep scratch in the decorative blue strip, the trademark of

Valiant yachts. Assessment of the damage to the pier and the boat came down to small amounts of displaced timber and fiberglass but huge amounts of ego and self-confidence lost, as this had been our "we are ready to go" moment. Now there was the big question—what in the name of all that is sacred were we about to do if we couldn't even get out of the harbor safely?

We were continually reminded of the incident, as the ugly scratch on our bow would always draw a comment.

"What happened there? Wow, you really had an accident!"

"Boy, somebody whacked you good!"

"We were boarded by the Coast Guard in the Straights of Juan de Fuca and, with the currents, you know how those young kids in the Coast Guard can be…" I would say, skirting around the truth.

"You know you can bill them for dinging your boat," was usually the reply.

"Too much trouble," I would say.

Well, it is now time to fess up and apologize to the boys in white and set the record straight.

Fortunately, there were no witnesses to our incident, but it always reminds me of the scene in *The Caine Mutiny* when the crazy captain brings his minesweeper into port with cheering fans and takes out a section of the dock. The fans, having escaped with their lives, quickly turn and begin yelling obscenities and shouting comments about the Chinese Navy and so forth. I don't think our fans would have turned on us had they been up—at least not so we could hear them.

In the Straits of Juan de Fuca, the Coast Guard really did hail us down while *Claire de Lune* sailed on. We were anxious when the big cutter approached and broadcast over the horn they wanted to have a boarding party. The seas were rough, but it was only a few minutes before we had three young men aboard the *Nereid* and a fourth person holding their inflatable alongside. They were very young boys—we could have been their parents. I showed one of them below deck, where we counted fire extinguishers and flares.

Judy entertained the other two men in the cockpit with her paperwork. She had everything nicely organized in a binder: documentation of ownership, insurance, radio license, ham license, and all of the rest. They said it was the nicest presentation they had seen. I think they were as taken by her as I was and still am.

Between Judy's attention to detail and our having a few extra fire extinguishers and flares, we received a whopping 100 points, a perfect score.

"So why did you stop us?" Judy asked.

"We needed something to do," they replied.

The next day we met up with *Claire de Lune* in Neah Bay, our last stop before heading into Oregon waters. All was well until we sailed out of the harbor at daybreak. We had just made our left turn when the boat steerage was challenged by high winds and a strong current. The vessel was rocking, the boom and mainsail began thrashing and making loud popping sounds as if they were breaking up.

"We don't know what we are doing, this is way too dangerous. We don't know what we are doing, this is way too dangerous." This was Judy's mantra that I would hear many times in the months to come.

"Push the boom out!" Edd yelled above the noise and confusion. "Push the boom out!"

Moments passed before I did as he ordered, though I had no idea why I should push out the boom. Instantly, everything was calm and beautiful. We were back on our plan and all was well. We hoped Mr. Edd felt the same. True, we didn't know what we were doing, but we have always been quick learners.

Heading south, we found the Oregon coast was true to its reputation. Judy was concerned about the deteriorating weather conditions, but I kept quiet, preferring not to share my own concern and reinforce her uncertainty. At about midnight, I came up from a brief nap to check on Judy, who was on watch. Water was flying overhead as we blew through a wave.

"Seems a little rough out here!" she said.

I wanted to say, "No kidding! This is terrible! We shouldn't be out in this mess!" Instead I pretended it was what we had expected all along. "Nothing to worry about," I said.

I had used this line once before, in Alaska, when we were about to launch our inflatable into a wild rushing river. This same sweet voice had said, "Seems a little fast."

About this time, there was a problem with some gear on the bow that needed to be secured. We were in our foul-weather gear and still getting wet but tethered to the jack line, I went forward. It was there in the bow area with water hitting me from every angle I had my first real wakeup call to what we were undertaking. I was mentally preparing to lose the game, just like on an Alaska hunting trip some years earlier when stranded on a mountainside. My hunting partner and I couldn't move up or down the mountain.

"I don't think I'm going to see my little boy again," my hunting partner had said.

At that moment, we knew we had to stop that line of thinking and focus on getting off the mountain. Remembering that mindset, I took a deep breath, finished securing the gear and crawled back to the cockpit. Although Judy didn't know it at the time, it was our darkest hour.

Following another boat in rough weather conditions is somewhat hypothetical. Two vessels start out together, then lose sight of each other almost immediately and, after a while even the VHF radio is out of range. It's not the greatest insurance policy. Neither boat is in a position to assist the other. It's more of a psychological lift just knowing someone else is enduring the same thing. Or at least we think they are.

The *Nereid* caught up with *Claire de Lune* in the morning light; they had waited for us. For days with more reasonable weather we followed their stern light during the night passages. Edd and Judi called Judy every hour when they knew she was on watch to make sure she was okay. It was reassuring to have company.

As we were leaving Eureka, California, we had another visit from the Coast Guard. This time a cutter pulled alongside us, and a crewman, using only a hand signal, directed us to head back to the harbor to wait for better weather. They circled the *Nereid* and *Claire De Lune* like we were two lost sheep needing directions to the barn. The conditions eventually improved and continued to improve all the way to Puerto Vallarta, our point of departure to cross the Pacific.

We parted company with *Claire De Lune* in San Francisco after long goodbyes and many thanks. They planned to spend some time with friends and relatives in the East Bay. Our daughter also lives in the Bay Area with her family, and we wanted to spend some time with them and show off *Nereid*. We took them sailing to demonstrate our new boat and sailing skills. It was one of those perfect days, clear sunny skies, warm light breeze, about 10 knots. The six of us set sail for the far side of Angel Island. The trip over went smoothly. Our grandkids were delighted to pull sails and help with anchoring. We had a picnic lunch, made driftwood art and played in the water. Calling it a perfect day, we raised the anchor and headed back to the marina. Unfortunately, as we rounded the island we had some high-crosswind excitement, which has my son-in-law still refusing to go sailing again—at least with his father-in-law.

After a few months, we were joined by Ross and Laura on *New Dawn,* and our two Valliant's were headed out through the Golden Gate and turning left on our way to Mexico. The trip south into Mexico was uneventful and much smoother than our one-day family sailing experience in San Francisco Bay.

We were in Puerto Vallarta, Mexico, for about three months enjoying the tacos, doing some minor repairs and provisioning. We did prefer getting out and mingling with the local people. On these outings, we would usually find a crowded street-side taco stand. On one occasion, the fellow next to me had a lovely foursome of tacos, and we followed his lead with our order. They were delicious, and after a second order, we noticed the menu on the wall. We evidently had ordered the second entrée on the list. I didn't recognize any of the words but made some notes, which later translated into some exciting news like lips, brain, tongue and something to do with the digestive tract. Anyway, the tacos looked and tasted good and resulted in no digestive disruptions.

Our son Ross departed with about twenty-five other boats as scheduled from Puerto Vallarta to cross the Pacific in the Puddle Jump, a rally organized by the sailing magazine *Latitude 38*. We were going to catch up the next day, but I got sick with the flu, which delayed our departure almost a week. The day of our departure, March 30, 2006, as we left the protective harbor and headed out alone across the vast Pacific Ocean, would be the most exciting day of my entire forty-three years of marriage and sixty-nine years of mortality. Judy reminded me, "except of course for our wedding day and the birth of our children." She was maybe not quite as excited.

These stories are an attempt to capture some of the more memorable moments and events on board the *Nereid*. We start with a crash leaving Port Townsend and, six years and 20,000 miles later, end at the Boat Lagoon Marina in Phuket, Thailand. Phuket is about halfway home, but Judy and I are in no hurry. Our trip has taken much longer than expected, partly because of our proximity to many new and exciting places. We have taken many side trips, and once a year we fly home to "normalize" ourselves with family and friends in the USA. Highlights of these trips are part of "La Grande Adventure."

The stories are grouped geographically, and each is an independent experience to be read in any order and hopefully inspire you to build a dream.

Part 1

Pacific Ocean

Chapter 1

Passage to Marquesas Islands

S/V *Nereid* Log

Day 1: The Adventure Begins: March 30, 2006

Well, it looks like the weather has finally cooperated and given us a window of opportunity to get out of Dodge. We have been in Puerto Vallarta for three months and it's time to be moving on. Our progress in this adventure can be tracked on the Internet along with that of other vessels at sea by going to Google search and entering Pangolin, Yotreps; from there, you can find a list of vessels at sea. They are listed by boat name and call sign. We are on the *Nereid* and our call sign is KD7ZUD.

You can also see Ross and Laura's progress in *New Dawn,* which is out about 1,100 miles, as they have been at sea eight days. The entire passage is approximately 2,800 miles to our first landfall in the Marquesas Islands and usually takes seventeen to twenty-eight days, depending on a variety of factors such as weather, equipment failure, etc. Whatever happens, this

April is going to be a very exciting month. We can be reached with short messages at sea by email to KD7ZUD@winlink.org or when in port at rayjudye@gmail.com.

We had a successful first night and, after an uncomfortable adjustment to her new seasick meds, Judy is doing much better. The seas are a bit rolling, but there is enough wind to do 5 to 5.5 knots. The 0.5 translates to a significant distance over the length of this voyage—as much as 300 miles. Not going to get much email out this day, as too many things to check out. Our wind generator is producing for the first time and will reduce the need to run the engine to charge the batteries. After last night with the auto pilot, radar and frig all demanding their shares of the pie, there is going to be some greater expectation from "windy." It looks like he will perform. The first twenty-four hours always produce the greatest anxiety level with so many systems coming into play after a long rest in port. Typing on the computer is going to be a bit more challenging in this rock-and-roll scenario.

Day 2: Mexican Navy

The trade winds are going to make for a pleasant voyage, with only one sail set for this first leg of about 1,800 miles. Sailed with just the massive headsail, the genoa, through the night and averaged 6 knots. Not much of a swell, making for "swell" sailing. Late night picked up a rather large boat on our radar that seemed to be waiting for us. I stayed on course until I could see; it was a fishing boat with several men working the back deck. We had plenty of room to pass, but a last-minute course change by the fishing boat put it coming across our bow. I was forced to turn off to port with a ninety-degree course correction. He either didn't see me or decided a sailboat was infringing on his domain. Judy contends the first possibility and I hold to the less excusable option.

Shortly after that, we heard on the VHF radio, "Sailboat, sailboat, this is Mexican Navy."

I answered.

"Are you okay?" asked someone very polite and with excellent English.

"We are okay," I replied, "but just avoided a fishing boat."

"Where are you coming from and where are you going?" he asked.

"We are coming from PV," I said, "and headed to the Marquesas."

With that he wished us a safe and pleasant journey. The surprise was really the voice of the Mexican Navy and their concern. There was a small blip on the radar about twelve miles off that may have been them. Anyway, let it be known that the Mexican Navy is out here and if needed they are ready to assist. Since the Mexican Navy can't be everywhere, I will take avoidance action much sooner next time.

Day 3: Smooth as Silk

We are out about 350 miles and have not had much luck contacting anyone on the radio—either too late, not enough signal or too much interference, or all of the above. Wind generator is now called "Top Job" after the 007 character, since it almost took my hand off as I was trying to stop it. Actually it didn't seem to be going that fast, but slight miscue on that. Anyway, after only a warning shot as an apology, he is putting out eight amps. Solar panels are putting out eight to ten amps now that the boom is out of the way. I thought they were on their last legs, but evidently they want to be on the team. Cruised the last twenty-four hours with the genoa and double-reefed main. Our speed ranged from 6.5 to 7.5 knots. Wind is variable to 25 knots from the less variable NE. The trades are an amazing way to travel; I have been getting the grib files each day for the weather, and it looks like more of the same.

One persistent impression under these conditions is the smoothness of the ride. It is like we are traveling on air with almost no sound of the boat interfacing with the water. The best description is indeed that we are gliding along, smooth as silk. Beth Leonard, author of many excellent cruising articles, named her boat *Silk,* and now I understand. I have a special appreciation for Robert Perry, the Valiant yacht designer, for such a safe and smooth traveling conveyance. There will be days ahead when the silkiness concept is tested more rigorously.

Day 4: Motoring the Trades

After a delightful sail yesterday and talking up the greatness of sailing the trades, they are gone today and we find ourselves motoring along at 5 knots. Actually, make that motor sailing, as the double-reefed main and staysail are making the most of the light, variable winds. Motored through most of the night, then the wind picked up this a.m. with enough consistency to operate the Monitor windvane. Ah yes, another piece of equipment not fully tested or operational before this passage, along with the navigational program, wind generator, reacher-drifter, whisker pole, and anchor placement. While the learning curve may be sharp in our case, sailing affords an unusual amount of time to get familiar with your stuff, as the distractions are few and the time is all yours to learn and share with your mate.

Our Monitor windvane is an ingenious piece of equipment. It requires no withdrawal from the battery bank. We are now sailing silently with the Monitor,

"Monty," doing all the steering. The Alpha autopilot is a good unit but tends to oversteer; at least the wheel and rudder work very hard. Enter Monty, and the wheel makes only the slightest correction, and we both stay on course and eliminate much of the wear and tear on the steering system.

No other boats in sight. It's kind of a big place out here not to see anybody. Judy reminded me that it is still not too late to turn around.

Day 5: Trades, Where Are You?

After coasting along at 6 knots, we hit an area with not enough wind to keep the canvas flexed but just enough to slap it around until we are forced to make some changes. Traded the genoa for the staysail and turned on the motor and realized the windvane does not communicate with this noisy beast. I disengaged the Monitor at the wheel but forgot to pull up the Monitor rudder, and this made for some sluggish hand steering. After too long I realized there were one too many rudders giving directions to the boat. At least I didn't engage the Alpha system for a third factor. We have a tired crew this p.m., but sailing conditions have improved. The Monitor is running things again, and at the moment we are clipping along again at 6 knots. We are on a heading of 240T, the maximum extent of the broad reach but 15 degrees short of our desired heading of 225T. We will have to make up these 15 degrees and more if we are to make our planned crossing of the equator at 130W. When I checked in on the Seafarers' Net, I was asked if I was going to Russia.

"Having some wind issues," I replied.

Lunch was the highlight of the day, with nachos and all the trimmings—another amazing surprise to appear at the companionway from an amazing lady.

Day 6: Communications

We have a radio check-in each day to keep tabs on our position and monitor any emergency traffic, which is good, especially for some of us old guys. I am using the ham network, and they are not as schedule oriented as the Sail Mail service some other cruisers are using. The only advantage to me is that it is a free service, since I have my ham radio license.

Judy has decided to write some things on the computer and send her first emails. What prompted this was my memory lapse of significant events that have taken place on our journey to date. She has an excellent memory for details, so I persuaded her to journal her thoughts as she realized I would have no recollection of this entire trip in a few years. Besides—the underlying message in the movie *Door in the Floor*—the secret to good writing is details, details. She suggested that I should send an email ahead of hers so that those in long expectation of this event can prepare themselves. In some cases a CPR unit should be standing by.

Day 7: All Alone and Just Fine

We made a significant course change this a.m. that will put us back on a more southerly heading. We are at 13:55N, 118:11W. Our new heading is 208T. It was a wild night, with ten-foot seas and gusts to 30 knots. We reefed down to a third reef on the main and staysail but are still moving along at 6 knots. Sometimes we need a reality check, as it seems like a dream, and so far a very good one. I look at Judy in action and can't believe how quickly this grandmother, retired dental hygienist and beautiful babe has become a solid sailing companion.

Basically, we are alone out here and we are going to be just fine. I am a very lucky man!

Day 8: Are We on the Same Boat?

Winds are highly variable in direction and speed, on top of a rolling sea of eight to ten feet. Some swells crossing in different directions, slamming against the boat, sounding like rifle shots. It is not a restful state for body or mind. Sleep comes more easily in the cockpit, as the sound reverberates in the interior of the boat like a giant speaker box. The amplitude of this speaker box turned up a notch as we entered a dark overhead shadow that blacked out the moon and our faithful following stars, signifying we were proceeding through a squall or undecided atmospheric condition. After a sleepless night for both of us, I was greeted with a smile and a plate of fresh fruit from my mate and by her upbeat presence.

"Have we been on the same boat through the night?" I asked.

"Yes," she said. "I decided the only thing I have any control over is my attitude, so good morning, my darling, and have some fruit."

Day 9: Surfing the Swells

Healthy following seas, or rather, swells ten feet, moving fast and coming up behind us like some monster about to swallow us up—but our beautiful boat always rises to the occasion, leaving the monster swell under us. Then we go boat/body surfing down its backside on our twelve-ton board, thank you very much. I have a much greater appreciation now when people wish us "fair winds and following seas." Indeed, these following swells are a boost to everyone and everything. We just broke the thousand-mile mark.

Day 10: Trouble on the Way to Paradise

Good idea from Ross to walk the deck once a day and look for stuff aside from squid and flying fish. Walked the deck this a.m. and found a familiar Allen screw that had come off the staysail profurler. I was able to get it back in place and will keep an eye on both profurlers. Could this be only an early warning of trouble to come?

Top Job, our wind generator, had performed magnificently but suddenly, without warning, lost his job. I had just settled down for an afternoon nap.

"Come here quickly," Judy shouted. "Something is wrong!"

The stainless-steel wind generator support had come loose at the base of the frame. The frame supporting the wind generator extends about fifteen feet overhead and, with the heavy generator whirling at high speed, had become a creature of potential mass destruction. We got the blades stopped and secured the frame with numerous ropes at various angles and tensions, but we could not stop the whipping action from the heavy generator on top. The weld that secured the frame to the stanchion was slowly separating from the rail. The unit was going to come down, one way or another.

One thought was to let the whole thing fall back into the water and donate it to the environment. It could likely take out the Monitor on the way and end up wrapped around the rudder and prop. To bring the system forward meant the risk of hitting the backstay. Like in slow motion, along with our thinking process, the weld continued to release, just like in the movies.

Oh, how I wished this was just a movie. I had about five minutes before the decision would be taken away from me. To keep our options open, we removed the cockpit sunshade and supporting frame, all the time watching the weld continue to separate. We moved the boom out of the way. When the weld finally broke, I was able to stabilize the unit and at that moment decided the best way to go was to walk it forward into the cockpit. All the pieces were recovered. Still, it was a sad moment; much time and expense had been put into getting it operational, and it had been performing magnificently.

Anyway, we were lucky that no serious damage was done. We huddled for a moment and gave thanks to our other crewmember who had been with us throughout this adventure. We looked forward to another day at sea, but with Top Job taking a nap.

Day 11: "No Soup for You"

No wind today. I hope it wasn't something I said. I can see why sailors get superstitious awaiting a weather change. Today has not been a good day for making any headway, only about twenty-five miles in the last twenty-four hours. Winds are light and highly variable in direction. There are no good sail set solutions, at least none that I can find. Last two days have totaled only about sixty miles. It has become very frustrating trying to work the sails in these light winds. We spent the evening hours motoring and, after a nice meal and a cockpit shower, we shut everything down. With Watchman, our radar, set to detect any vessels or unusual objects in the water, we just drifted along and watched *Seinfeld*.

Day 12: No Wind

We have been at sea for twelve days and have covered only about one third of the way to the Marquesas Islands, which are now approximately 1,500 miles away. It appears this crossing could take a month or more. Sent a note to my brother, who has a fear of being out of sight of land. I assured him that it's not that scary because the cloud cover comes down all around us and looks like landfall, or like land is just behind the clouds.

No wind the last three days and so we have been taking it easy, just bobbing and weaving with the swells. Hit a rainstorm that dumped tons in an hour. Good time to take a shower with our clothes on—just squeeze out the clothes, let them dry, and we have washed our bodies and our clothes all in one efficient step. The temperature is always warm, day or night, so the rain is a welcome cool off.

Day 13: Still No Wind

It was another frustrating day of only twenty-five miles, which included two hours of motoring. Monitor windvane is not good in these light, variable winds, and the sails take a flogging. Drifted in the night with our radar, Watchman, on duty and settled in with an episode of *The Sopranos*. I couldn't hear well on the Puddle Jumpers Net so didn't check in. Anyway, hope that wasn't too disconcerting. Also couldn't get through on the Seafarers' Net. We are only at 8:27N and 121:41W. I didn't expect to hit the becalmed area this early.

Day 14: Pole to the Rescue

Same conditions as yesterday but slightly more wind. Winds are less than 10 knots and change direction by the minute. Very frustrating. Took this opportunity to get acquainted with the whisker pole and got it positioned and extended to control some of the movement of the genoa. This maneuver, along with relying on the Alpha autopilot, has solved some of the light-variable-wind problems of the previous three days, and we are maintaining a speed of 5 knots in a SW direction. Four more days of this and we will be at the equatorial zonal crossing.

It is very comforting to be moving along at this speed and not have the sails slapping around. We have poled out the genoa to a broad reach/running position and a double-reefed main that is at a close reach position so as not to block the genoa. We went with this setup through the night and had a hundred-mile day.

Day 15: More of the Same with Big Savings

Continued with the same sail set as yesterday, and with minimal attention to sails we had a 120-mile day. Winds are again variable and light, usually less than 10 knots. It's been fifteen days at sea and we haven't spent a dime. This will be the most cost-effective month of my life. Spent some quality time talking about what our kids and grandkids have been doing and things they have said. We had a talk yesterday on what we would do when we arrive in the islands. In fact, we have had many talks out here—it is quite fun.

The sunrises and sunsets are absolutely breathtaking. The seas are calm with very little wind, just enough to keep us going 5 knots. The only sound is from the water passing against the side of the boat. Wish there were some way others could enjoy this with us.

Ross and Laura should be at the island today; we are another ten days out with about a thousand miles to go. We can't believe we have already come 1,400 miles and will be starting our sixteenth day at sea and have not seen another boat since our second day.

Day 16: Squall from Nowhere

As we were having another easy sail, I was below at the nav station surrounded by my instruments, which assured me everything was all right. Judy was on watch in the cockpit when, suddenly, she screamed.

I sprang from my chair to see what was the matter, when out in the cockpit I faced buckets of rain pelting down from an enormous, ominous, dark cloud overhead. We threw everything we could move into dryer, more protected areas.

"Where did that cloud come from, my darling?" I yelled above the noise.

"I must have been into my book. I have no idea!" she shouted back.

Suddenly, the winds were gusting to 40 knots. What an oiled team we have become. We doused the genie and, as the winds dropped into the high 20s, we put out the staysail and cruised along at 7 knots. The genoa furled nicely off the pole, as it had been capturing the unidirectional fractional winds of less than 10 knots prior to this excitement.

Day 17: South Winds on the North Side

Had to check the compass several times as strong winds were coming—sure enough—from the south at 25 knots, and we are 04N and 126W. This wasn't supposed to happen until we crossed the equator. Furled up the genie and weathered the stronger stuff with staysail and mainsail still on a third reef from the night run. With pole in place, I decided to try the genie at 15 knots, but this proved too much. Seas were four feet, also coming from the south. What's with this southern wind system crossing over the line before I am ready?

Contacted on our VHF another sailboat, *Sandpiper*, near us but not visible, and they reported the same conditions, so I wasn't losing it after all. This is evidently a common occurrence and a sample of events to come.

Day 18: Record Day

Two records this day. First and foremost, we made our left-hand turn to cross the Intertropical Convergence Zone (ITCZ), and in so doing picked up a steady easterly wind that gave us a smooth ride for a record 130 miles on the twenty-four-hour clock. We furled the genoa and double reefed the main, which was an insurance policy in case the tricky and intense winds and waves of the zone were to catch us off guard.

No such disruption. It was a smooth sail all through the night and the next day. Our second record of the day was crossing the hemispheric divide at 0510 UTC (10:00 a.m.) at 129:04W. Beautiful morning, and we had a special moment to gives thanks to the man of the hour, his majesty himself, the one and only, purveyor and ruler of the seas, King Neptune. A bottle of our finest sparkling blueberry juice, selected from the shelf of Trader Joe's, was opened for just this occasion. With 1,900 miles under our keel and a mere 700 to go, we feel pretty good about our boat and ourselves.

Day 19: New Record across the Zone

We had an exceptional passage across the ITCZ over the last two days, with steady winds from the SE at 20 knots. We did reef down the main but let the genoa hang out all night for a record 142 miles. The thinking at the time was that in the event of suspected ITCZ activity we would set the staysail and furl the genoa, the only gamble being the double-reefed main, which more conservatively could have been triple reefed, but the seas never indicated anything of concern was on the way. We are also getting anxious to make landfall. Each day we hear of more and more boats arriving, and we're starting to feel left out of something. Anyway, our crossing of the terrible ITCZ turned out to be some of the best sailing we have had yet.

As Ross sometimes says, "Dad always gets lucky."

Day 20: "Our Zone"

We only thought we were through or had escaped the zone. On this day at 02:28S and 129:50W, we hit what we are calling "our zone." We had winds from the SE to 30 knots with sustained gusts to 40 knots. No rain or warning of the weather. However, the sea state continued to become more confused, with swells of fifteen feet and an occasional twenty footer trying to share the cockpit with us. The main was on a double reef and the staysail was double reefed, and we still sustained a boat speed of 7 knots. Swells were the most contentious, as our heading put us nearly abeam of the SE sea state.

Rough night with swells hitting the side of the boat to make it sound like the *Nereid* was breaking up. Headsails can start a ferocious vibration at these wind speeds, but we eliminated that with enough tightening of the sheets. Good news is we made 140 miles under these double-reefed conditions.

Day 21: Rough Day

At 04:07S and 131:18W, we were still in our zone, with winds similar to Day 20 and another rough night dealing with the sea state. We cleared our zone by the next day and could see open sky ahead on our heading of 230T. Surveyed the deck. The only casualties were a dozen small fish lodged in the scuppers. This was another record-setting day of 148 miles, our best yet.

Day 22: Only 300 Miles to Go

At this point, more and more of our conversation and thoughts are on the landfall ahead. Starting out on this journey, we had no idea of what it would be like to be at sea for twenty-five days. We did think there would be more time to read and generally relax and enjoy the scene. This has not been the case, as there is always work to do and it takes more effort to get the work done, and we can never completely relax. It's kind of like hunting in Alaska. At one moment you are enjoying the scenic wonders, and the next minute you are about to lose your life.

Our day-to-day existence at this point has become more focused on the basics of eating, drinking water and sleeping. Along with this, our bodies are always at some level of perspiration or stickiness. The boat has become a biome of life in a gumdrop—always at some level of discomfort but also very, very sweet.

Day 23: Motor Time

We had been very lucky up until now in not having to motor, but this close to our objective and needing some R and R, we motored most of the day and were able to get in a good hundred miles plus. We had motored our first few days but since then had only motored to keep the batteries charged, and that was only during the last half of the voyage after losing the assistance of our wind generator. Our total motoring time to date is eighteen hours. Some of the fast arrivals on this passage have been so at the expense of their gas tanks, which is okay but needs to be factored into any record-breaking performances.

Day 24: Land Ho

Didn't record the time and wasn't looking for land particularly. I just looked up and there it was—the outline of a landmass on the horizon. We felt like explorers who had discovered a new world, and actually that was true. We motored a few more hours to within twenty miles of the island and then shut down, as we were too far out to reach port before nightfall—we hove-to and drifted about ten miles. The island profile was visible all through the night, and the eerie thing was there was not a single light or any sign of habitation.

Day 25: Port at Last

After 2,800 miles and twenty-five days at sea, we arrived at Hiva Oa about 10:00 a.m., but heavy fog and rain prevented immediate entry. Entered Baie Tahuku on Hiva Oa about 12:00 noon. We received a nice welcome from the cruisers, including Alison and Paddy on *Zafarse*, Robert, Nike and boys on *Lawur*, Ross on *Kabuki* and our own Ross and Laura on *New Dawn*. Ross guided us in with his dinghy to an anchorage spot, as it was very crowded with boats, all carefully aligned with bow and stern anchors. It was nice to finally rest at anchor.

That evening when we stepped off the boat onto land, it was like we were in an earthquake. It felt like the ground was moving to the point of having to hang onto someone or something. It took us several days to completely regain our land legs. Ross and Laura arranged dinner at a hotel, there were many other cruisers in attendance. Evidently, we were a mild curiosity, everyone congratulated us and were proud that we had done this thing alone, just the two of us—but I think our age added a touch of enthusiasm to the accolades.

Judy's Observations

Twenty-five days at sea…it changes a person. Physically, the changes are everywhere to be seen. Weeks without tweezing, shaving, filing, cuticle crème, lotion or night crème leave the body with a whole new look. I accidentally saw myself in the bathroom mirror and wondered, *who is this person?* Thank goodness we don't have a full-length mirror!

I'm not sure I've ever seen my real eyebrows before. The best word to describe them is *huge*, or maybe *very black*, or *wild*. Glancing at my legs in the sunny cockpit was shocking. It's that very black, wild hair again. I have to touch them to make sure they are my legs and not Ray's. They're mine all right! But they look more like a movie prop, maybe for *The Return of the Werewolf*. Hair on my toes…yes, and from ankle to knee. In among the inch-long, slightly curly black hairs are fuzzy white hairs. Kind of like Mary's little lamb.

My eyes go back to my feet, and for a moment, I think I must have leprosy. The skin on my feet is peeling off in layers, mostly the soles and in between my toes. Something must be done, so I take my second cockpit shower of the day. This time I really scrub. But there is no end to the shedding skin. I finally give up for today. Our feet are wet a lot.

By now Ray's feet are ultra clean, to the point that they look like he's had a French manicure…the kind with very white tips. His beard is much longer and fuller, looks a lot like Hemmingway's. Back to me…do I just go au naturel, the real Judy, or do I wait for that anchor to drop and get out my tools and go to work? Hmmmm.

Part 2

South Pacific Islands

Chapter 2

Marquesas

Headin' South

We came from Alaska, layered with clothing. In Alaska, multiple layers are essential for every body part except your breathing area. The breathing area is temperature-controlled by an extension of your parka hood, which creates a warm tunnel for air exchange and vision. The tropical climate has brought a drastic change; we are now more concerned with keeping the body cool.

It eventually became apparent that the layering concept did not apply, and we cautiously shed and stowed most of our wardrobe. In fact, clothing has become optional, depending on the exposure and activity level. This is evidenced by our tanned skin, making my skinny legs look good and our bodies have a more youthful look. Much to the horror of the dermatologists that have their offices in the basement and cover their bodies carefully to avoid the solar rays, we have become sun worshipers. The tropics have had an ongoing moisturizing effect on this aging dermis.

A side benefit of this new freedom of exposure is the amount of time saved in the process of getting dressed in the morning or changing clothes to go to work or out to dinner. Getting dressed or changing clothes amounts to slipping on a pair of shorts. Shoes are always optional. There are shorts for dressing up and shorts that have been in the engine room and shorts that have not yet been in the engine room. That's it, ready to go in less than a minute.

Significant amounts of time and energy are saved by not shopping or shopping only for a new pair of shorts. Shoes in the traditional sense are nonsense in the tropics, and what used to be our shower shoes are now acceptable for everyday and dressing up. The time saved in dressing and shopping is one of the reasons the island natives have so much leisure and require less cash flow. Their more relaxed lifestyle with less stress is due in part to not worrying about what to wear or being concerned with fashion trends. They don't need to work long hours to keep their families fully clothed or keep up with the neighbors.

When we head south to New Zealand, we will feel a temperature change. We will be getting back into the layering concept and spending more time and money on clothing and thinking about what to wear. I hope we can retain our indifference to what is the trendy thing. Oh oh! There it is already, some wasted mental energy on what to wear in Kiwi land!

Checking the Anchor

Experience has proven it a good idea to check the set of the anchor to get an idea of the holding capacity and how it can best be retrieved. We usually anchor in about thirty feet of water. This makes for a nice snorkeling exercise for at least a touch-and-go on the bottom, and with some additional conditioning, I expect to stay down longer. Except for the exercise, there is really no need to dive down to see the anchor. The water in the tropics is so crystal clear you can see everything when just hovering on the surface.

I expected when we arrived at the islands there would be visitors, and as we entered the protected waters of the reef, we were greeted by several nurse sharks, four to five footers. These guys qualify as sharks but look like they could use more exercise. I decided to check the anchor the next day.

Backing down the ladder, I eased into the water and looked around. No visitors, so I started my swim to the bow of the boat to follow the anchor chain. I had been in the water about three minutes when I noticed my guests, several blacktip reef sharks, keeping their distance, about twenty feet away. I continued my survey. In another three minutes, the number of curious visitors had doubled. I processed this increase and decided they were all too small to take on this tough old bird. Another three minutes and more visitors at all depths forced my decision to terminate the survey, so I headed back to the boat ladder.

I did not feel I was in any real danger, as these guests were only in the four to five-foot range, probably just big kids. It became obvious to me that the blacktip shark was the quintessential shark, with all the right proportions and attitude. They look you over with their big eyes and circle slowly at a distance, obviously considering a person more as a meal than a threat. I guess my balance of courage was tipped when I began to consider the parents of these kids, who had not yet arrived. I decided the anchor was just fine and it was time to get out of their backyard.

Ten Minute Rule: Do not swim for longer than ten minutes at a time. If possible, someone should also be on watch for any uninvited guests.

Water on the Islands

We have to be careful with our freshwater supply. Our boat holds 120 gallons, but the available freshwater on the islands is limited. We have been catching some rainwater from a makeshift watershed across the stern, but this water is used for washing and not drinking. We presently have about forty gallons and are several days away from any additional sources. Our water maker produces about eight gallons per hour but needs a new high-pressure hose and is going to be out of service until we can get to Tahiti.

In the meantime, water conservation measures are in place, and it's surprising how much water we use or think we need on a daily basis. Showers are now limited to whenever you can't raise your arms anymore, not from any hygienic issue but when body parts begin to stick together.

Showers are taken in the cockpit, and we use my grandmother's method for camping trips. Her face would get red and she would not be able to stop laughing when she would explain. It goes as follows: take a wet washrag and wash down as far as possible, ring out, wet again and wash up as far as possible. Repeat the process one more time and then wash "possible."

While her method may not be the most thorough washing, it does remove the stickiness factor, which is simply an exfoliation problem. It is surprising to see the amount of residue that has settled out of the water column from the washrag rinse. This fine flocculent deposit is the old skin cells that we shed unknowingly in a normal, hygienic life.

Now the final deduction on body stickiness, and yes, it is all related. The sloughing epidermal cells become sticky glue when mixed with your body sweat, thus putting the bind on your body parts. With our keen insight into the mechanism of our bodily functions and bathing needs, we will be able to plan an even more efficient use of the water supply if needed.

Disclaimer: Please note that Judy strictly forbade the issuance of this "gross" email and wishes to stand apart from any credits or further inquiries. If her assessment is correct, please accept my apologies.

Rite of Passage

After the 2,800-mile sail from Mexico to the Marquesas Islands, to acknowledge such feats, sailors for centuries have acquired tattoos. It is part of the rite of passage upon rounding Cape Horn that you wear an earring in the ear closest to the Horn.

Having reached age sixty-nine and upon completion of this leg of our voyage, both awesome feats, I followed tradition with a tattoo in Nuca Hiva of a Marquesan turtle on my left shoulder. To the Marquesan, the turtle represents the many pathways we explore from childhood on our way to becoming an adult. So, for $50, I found myself sitting down in a native artist's backyard patio, waiting while he prepared his equipment. My only concern was not whether I should do this but whether my old, dried-up skin would burst into flames.

It has been almost two months of displaying my new body art at various informal social occasions, and I am happy to report the responses have ranged from silent nods to approving smiles, raised brows and—a highlight—four ladies overcome with excitement upon being given permission to touch it. I can now understand why more extensive coverage could be desirable.

In several cases, a person has come up to me and said, "Where did you get your tattoo? I got mine…" And up comes a sleeve or pant leg to reveal their signature piece. So with the decision came some new friends.

How do I personally feel about desecrating the body with this art form? I can only say that this was the time and the place for me, which was really low risk, as I am not up for a job interview or planning a new career. And finally, there is some mystique that comes with a tattoo that gives you a little more self-confidence, a little more unpredictability which isn't easy to achieve in these latter years and overall a temporary offset to the inevitable march of time that paces us all.

It is not important to wait until you are sixty-nine years old or for a rite of passage, but in my case these were factors, and besides, Judy thinks it looks great.

So the next time you see a turtle, let it remind you that whatever you're experiencing now is just a phase you're in and the possibilities are endless.

Judy and the Pirates

As we navigate our way across the South Pacific and contemplate the possible next step of continuing around the world, the conversation with other cruisers will often lead to the subject of pirates. Accounts of run-ins with pirates range from shootouts (the Alaska Alternative) to letting them take what they want (the California Alternative). The Alaska Alternative seems to be losing ground, which is good, since we are now Alaskans without guns.

Those of you who haven't been on the *Nereid* or visited our home in Alaska may not know we already had a contingency plan in place for those "takers of other people's things." We have been giving our things away all along!

If we have something you like or comment on in the presence of my darling, say no more, it is yours. In the event of a visit to our home, if you had not found anything to your liking by the time you were ready to leave, she would present you with several items that may have interested you. It was just the nature of things at our house. It is the same in our new home on the water, although there are fewer items available for dispersement. However, not to worry, even mementos of our travels, which were selected with great care, are candidates for relocation, depending on the recipient or special event.

In the earlier days of our relationship, I was very protective of my stuff, as I am a "saver" and I married a "giver." While I spend my time thinking about what I would like, she is always trying to find something you would like. My darling is happiest when she has found the perfect gift from our belongings. Back at home, there were times when I would come home from work and know something was missing—usually something I was saving in the garage for later use. Now I know in the long term, especially if you go cruising, it all ends up with some stranger at a yard sale, so best to relocate it to someone you know.

I have been trying to change. I know there is true joy in the art of giving. I think I am making progress, but just yesterday when a charming couple from Australia stopped by our boat and Judy was bringing out all the treats, I said, "No, they can't have those cookies, they're my favorites." Our guests, of course, thought I was kidding.

I think in these later years I have eased up some and experienced a taste of the joy of giving. So, to all the pirates out there that we may come in contact with, we look forward to our brief time together. We hope you will find the things you need and that are important to you. In the event that you are disappointed, I know my wife will have constructive suggestions that will help you find something by which to remember us.

Warning: "Saver" is not to be substituted with "cheap" without the written consent of the author.

Mexican and Marquesan Cultures

As to be expected, there are some nuances or differences between the two cultures that may be of interest. To start, there's no hustle here on the islands. For example, when we brought our dinghy to shore in Mexico, there were three or four young boys ready to help us pull it up the beach. Of course we were expected to pay a few pesos for these services, but at least in my case, their help was appreciated.

The Marquesan does not offer assistance, but would not expect or accept any payment if services were rendered. The boat ramp in Atuona is a rough, irregular surface of large rocks, making it difficult to pull a dinghy out of the water. Our struggle went apparently unnoticed by the Marquesan teen washing his truck on the ramp.

The ideal vehicle here is the four-door compact pickup, as there is always something to haul, and that something could be me if I am hitchhiking the two miles to town. Marquesans are happy to share their pickup beds. It was a first to see my darling walking ahead of me with her thumb raised. Laura is a bit more aggressive, making eye contact with her thumb out, which has improved our chances of a ride probably 75% over the more passive walking with a casual thumb to the side.

More dogs and fewer cats here compared to Puerto Vallarta. Dogs on the island are very submissive, so maybe aggressive and independent pets have been selected out by the Marquesans.

We had our laundry done by a local lady, came to $45 for three loads, which were slightly damp. Laundry in PV was $4.50 per load and always came back spotlessly clean and totally dry. More competition may be the answer for the laundry service in this island paradise.

Both cultures enjoy a good holiday, and so far every other Monday has been one. Work hours are the same, as the heat dictates a break in the workday, so from 11:00 to 2:00 there is "no soup for you."

Chickens are abundant in both cultures; however; in Mexico, they are found mostly on supermarket rotisseries or neighborhood barbecues. Chickens on these islands are alive and well and roaming freely, with no apparent rotisserie concerns.

Tattoos are common on the islands, tastefully done, and have been handed down over many generations.

There is no public transportation on the islands, whereas every other vehicle in Mexico is either a bus or a taxi available for your traveling convenience. That's okay; if we really need to get somewhere, I will just go get Laura.

Marquesan Heart

We visited the open-air market in Taiohae Bay, Nuka Hiva, which gets started very early—like, 4:30 in the morning—and if you are late you miss the good stuff. This required traveling by dinghy to the very crowded dock landing, which is always a challenge even in daylight, let alone in the dark. In spite of the early hour and docking challenge, there were five of us, sleepily crowded into the dinghy and headed to the market.

The local farmers had their goods spread out in the backs of their pickup trucks. The fishermen were at special tables, carving up their catches of every description. A pastry/coffee truck was a very popular place to start for those who needed to wake up or wanted their favorite French pastries. Aside from the local fruits that are always in abundance, like mangos, papaya and bananas, there were tomatoes, cabbages, carrots, lettuce, peppers and magnificent giant grapefruit or *pamphamouse*. There were huge white radishes, which could have been imported from Alaska, and corn on the cob, some of which Judy quickly selected.

Except for the early hour and mode of transportation to and from, this market was like any other farmers' market, with the exception of one detail that is an integral part of the Marquises culture—the need or desire to give something extra. Also in the villages we have visited there has been a giving or desire to share some of their abundance. Not an easy concept for this seasoned capitalist.

Now at this early-morning market, one might expect the vendors to be more profit oriented, but not so. With every purchase, the vendors added something. Every business transaction was conducted with the same spirit of giving, concluded with a handshake and a feeling of goodwill expressed in their smiling eyes. They are a beautiful people with huge hearts, still in touch with their traditional values.

Chapter 3

Tuamotus

Passage to Tuamotus

We are off for the Tuamotus. Our first atoll of the many choices will be Raroia, which has an easy entrance and a small village. It is famed for being where the Norwegian explorer Thor Heyerdahl crashed and sank his reed raft the *Kon-Tiki*. We hope to do better than Thor. Anyway, leaving the Marquesans behind, with many fond memories and a tattoo, we were ready to move on. Ross also has come away with body art, also of the turtle but much more intricate and complex, as I am sure his life will continue to be.

We left Ua Pou yesterday about 2:30 p.m. and are out about 133 miles after twenty-four hours. *New Dawn* is about fifteen miles ahead of us, having traveled with more canvas during the night. This puts us with about 288 miles to go in what are presently quartering seas that can make the passage wet at times. A single rouge wave made it into the cockpit last night, but no damage.

The bananas, about seventy-five on the stalk, swinging in the cockpit, are taking the brunt of the heavy seas. We are a fruit wagon of pineapples, mangos, grapefruit, star fruit and something the locals call *pome*. We also have six papayas, the size of small watermelons, which are quite delicious with lime juice. Listen to this old meat eater going on about the fruits.

Fish is the meat of choice. We have had an abundance of yellow fin tuna, which Judy has learned to prepare to perfection. We almost entered the dietary kingdom of the wahoo; Ross hooked one for a few minutes, but after an acrobatic display, it broke his eighty-pound test line. I call that "catch and release." Anyway, there are some really big fish out here.

Treasures of Cruising

To buy a sailboat and sail around the world brings with it the obvious benefits of meeting other people, both fellow cruisers and the new friends you make visiting other cultures. There is also the added attraction of seeing firsthand more of God's handiwork, the sunsets, the rolling seas, coral reefs and minions of species seen only in picture books or on TV. What has become an added benefit, to some surprise, is the free time we now have to read and write in the absence of TV.

My reading time has increased, and I have gone from instruction manuals for the boat's operating systems to most recently *The Children of Henry the Eighth, Sherman's Civil War* and now *Franklin and Winston: An Intimate Portrait of an Epic Friendship*. Let me just say that Elizabeth saved England and Churchill saved the world.

Since we have no TV, there is this block of available time in which to read. I would propose, if elected when I return, to only have TV every other year—any shorter period, people would just wait it out and not pick up a book. As for writing, Elizabeth, Churchill, Sherman, anyone of note wrote several lengthy letters every day, and they were crafted with a command of the language we only read if the TV is off.

We have a TV on board with VHS and DVD but have limited our viewing pleasure to one episode of a series or movie once or twice a week. In the event of a serious weather situation, it now could serve as a sea anchor or drogue. Anyway, if you should decide to go cruising someday, make yourself a book list and load up on the printed works—it's one of the real treasures of cruising.

Some books read by Judy Emerson while at sea:

Albatross
Red Sky in the Morning
I Wish I Had a Red Dress
Narrative of the Life of Frederick Douglas, an American Slave
The Keeper of Lime Rock
Easy as She Goes
Fanny Mae and the Miracle Man
Welcome to the World, Baby Girl!
A Chance to Forgive
Ethics for a New Millennium
The Book of Secrets
Chairman of the Bored
Horse Heaven
One Thousand Acers
Good Faith
The Five Love Languages
Turn Me into Zeus' Daughter
Trace
Three to Get Deadly
The Street Lawyer
Snow Flower and the Secret Fan
Woman an Intimate Portrait

The Kennedy Women
Angels Flight
Mr. Perfect
She Comes Undone
God and Mr. Gomez
Maiden Voyage
The Doorbell Rang
Shadow of the Wind
The Secret Life of Bees
The Curious Incident of the Dog in the Night-Time
Lobster Chronicles
A Time to Kill
Plain and Simple
Jesus Came to Harvard
A Message from Forever
Ethics: Inaction in Action
Three Christmas Stories
A Return to Love
People You Meet in Heaven
Lance Armstrong/Not the Bike
The President's Daughter
Three Bedrooms, One Corpse

The Intruder

We were weathered in at the south end of the Tahanea Lagoon in the Tuamotu Islands, anchored in thirty feet of crystal-clear turquoise water with the wind gusting to 40 knots. It was after dinner and we were feeling cozy, reading and enjoying the protective security of our boat as it met the howling wind with relative ease.

After a time, Judy got up and went to the galley for a glass of water. Returning with the glass in hand, she shrieked suddenly, slapping a hand over her mouth. Water spewed from behind her hand as she pointed at me with her other hand. She had my best undivided attention, but I had no idea what the problem was. "Talk to me, Judy!" I cried. "What is it?"

"It's right beside you on the table!" she shouted. "Get it!"

With these coordinates, I turned and spotted the intruder. It was at least three inches long, fully equipped with wings and antennae, glistening golden brown in the light as if from a fresh bronze casting. It was the largest cockroach I had ever seen.

How could this be? We had taken every precaution. If we found cockroach eggs in any cardboard packaging, we disposed of them immediately. Cardboard was not even allowed on the boat, since the eggs could be within the glued layers and not readily visible. So how in the world did this big boy get on board? He had to be fully grown; maybe he had even skipped his juvenile stages and gone right to this oversized adult.

My immediate response was to kill the beast. I glanced around. Closest to hand was a copy of *Cruising World Magazine,* and I rolled it up to start the termination process with repeated blows. Meanwhile, Judy, having recovered her speech, shouted, "No, not that way! The eggs will go all over and we will never find all of them!"

She was right. I hesitated, with the magazine poised in midair. Judy handed me her empty drinking glass to trap it alive, but we were too slow. The intruder, being more decisive than us, was on the move and disappeared under the table and into a maze of potential hiding places.

Our restful evening now officially interrupted, we began to remove items one by one, carefully turning them over and inspecting the exposed spaces with our flashlights. No sight of him. Judy started to worry that he had brought some of his friends.

And then, just as suddenly as he had appeared before, there he was, on the table again, behind the globe, appearing to enjoy our dismay as he watched us disassemble the stuff under the table. It was then, when we made eye contact, he seemed to know it was time to go. Again, before I could make a move, he was gone. We had missed our second opportunity.

That night we had a restless sleep with flashlights near our pillows. There were at least three of us on the boat now, and all we could hope for was to get back to a more comfortable twosome soon.

Early the next morning, at 0140 hours, while resting in the banyos, in the dim light I happened to notice a discoloration of some sort on the floor in front of me. I couldn't believe it. There he was, in all his splendor, and he was in range. He was so huge I flashed for a moment that he was able to catch my blow and push me away.

My choice of weapons was extremely limited. My hands were shaking as I slowly pulled the hand towel off the rack beside me. I knew I had to act quickly; indecision had foiled my previous attempts. I decided that even a direct hit from the towel would only stun him and he could escape again, this time into the crowded v-berth, an area of no return. I would have to make a very definitive move.

Wrapping the towel around my hand, I made my approach. The intruder appeared to hold his ground as I slammed my towel-covered hand down on him with such force I felt my shoulder almost separate. Worse yet, I could have created another through-hull in the *Nereid*.

In the dim light I could not tell for certain that I had him, so I twisted and ground the towel into the floor to prevent any escape. Then, carefully, cautiously, I unwrapped the towel. Let me just say that the invader had been successfully neutralized.

Based on the latest French weather forecast, we would be weathered in for at least three more days, with winds picking up to gusts of 50 knots, but no worries. It was just the two of us—at least for now.

Ross and the Walkers

In Makemo we did some casual shell collecting, but after a week, our shell jar held only a few specimens. It was apparent that a more concerted effort was needed if we were going to add significantly to our collection. While shells of every description are found in the *magasins,* or shops, and in various artisans' homes, they are not that plentiful on the surrounding beaches.

While waiting for a world-famous black pearl artist, we went for a stroll along the beach and did some collecting. We collected for about an hour and came away with some nice shells. Many of the shells we picked up were occupied by hermit crabs, and we did not keep those. We gathered our finds together and laid them out on a large rock, some cowries, cone shells, many gastropod shells and a few bivalves.

After a few minutes, several of the gastropod shells began moving across the rock. We dubbed them "walkers"; Ross volunteered to return them to their habitat, which was some distance away. Upon his return, we had discovered another three or four walkers, and he turned around and headed back out to return them. This left us with about half of the shells we had originally collected.

Back at the boat, which was anchored a good distance off shore, we discovered that about half of our remaining shells were also walkers. Next, we got a call on the VHF radio. It was Ross saying that about half of his remaining shells had turned out to be walkers and he was going to take them back. I had planned simply to drop my walkers over the side at this point and wish them good luck. I told Ross of my plan, but he said he would stop by and pick them up. These lucky walkers were going home.

We were now left with four gastropod shells and six cowries. Next morning, the four gastropod shells had moved, one to the bow of the boat, about a thirty-five-foot haul. Again there came a call on the radio; it was Ross. He also had found that his remaining gastropods shells were occupied, and he was going to take them back. Again he stopped by and motored off to return the lucky walkers. We had no idea there was such a housing shortage and decided to defer further collecting efforts in these areas.

Ross has always been a kind and gentle spirit. His mother recalls a visit to his school in second grade where she saw him in the schoolyard with his back against the wall fighting off two bigger boys who each had a shoe off and were trying to hit something behind him. He said, not looking at her, "Teacher, teacher, these boys are trying to kill a good bug."

It was a walking stick, and it was slowly making its way up the wall. Thanks again, Ross, for showing us the right thing to do.

Church in Makemo

Makemo has a centrally located church, of grand proportions for a village of only about two hundred people. Services started at 8:00 a.m. Sunday morning, and it was a major effort to get from the boat to the church on time.

We had looked in on the chapel earlier and noted the choir loft at the back and the large number of wood benches—too many for this small village, I thought at the time. We arrived ten minutes early and were surprised to find the church grounds overflowing with people. When we made our way inside, it was packed; the only open seating was along the wall on narrow ledges. Within a few minutes, two young men, about high school age, got up and offered us their seats. There was no dissuading them, so we graciously exchanged seats. Every person on the island must have come to church. Not only was the church filled with people, but the congregation was perfectly quiet. The talkative group that had been outside on the lawn now sat inside with hands folded in reverent anticipation.

The service was conducted in a combination of French and the local language, but the singing of the "Hallelujah" chorus accompanied by an electronic organ needed no translation. The inspired singing projected from smiling faces, and the incredible acoustics of the chapel made for a humbling moment of reflection and assessment of purpose.

At the end of the service, everyone was getting ready to file out when my eye caught this very large native man several rows ahead of me. He stopped and, with a big smile, extended his hand across the rows to me. I reached around several folks and was just able to touch his huge hand, upon which we both gave a smile in recognition of our long-range contact. All in all, it was a great experience, and to think we almost didn't go.

The memorable moments or gems of the South Pacific are not always where you would expect to find them.

No Mechanic in Makemo

Our dinghy outboard motor has been an ongoing problem, with the loss of our motor hoist, a leaking gas tank and the motor not starting. The hoist and gas tank had been compensated for, but the outboard refusing to start was the most frustrating and required technical assistance outside the immediate expertise onboard the *Nereid* or *New Dawn*.

Makemo, with only a population of about two hundred people, did not hold much promise for any local talent to come to the rescue. While wandering around the village, I would tag onto conversations an inquiry of whether there was a mechanic in Makemo. The answer was always the same, "No mechanic in Makemo." I even had it on good authority from the chief of the village that there was no mechanic in Makemo who worked on outboard engines. I had resigned myself to not getting any help for several more weeks until we arrived at Tahiti, where there are good mechanics but they are said to be very expensive.

I continued to inquire about a mechanic almost as an afterthought and was totally surprised when in the small *magasin*, or general store, the owner said he knew someone who could fix my motor. We made an appointment to meet at the dockside the following day at 1 p.m. Much to our surprise and right on time, there was the store owner with his two-year-old daughter and a young native friend who confirmed he could fix the motor.

Our dingy was tied out at the end of the pier. The friend grabbed a well-used toolbox from the back of his truck, and we all headed out to the boat. With the sun at midday beating down on all life forms, Ross suggested we drift the boat under the pier and work in the shade. The store owner took this opportunity to play with his daughter in the crystal-clear water beside the dingy under the pier as his friend went to work. This was a first for me, engine repairs under a boat dock and parents playing with their kids in the water under the dock with us.

I could tell by the contents of his toolbox and his approach that he knew what he was doing. First, he checked the spark while cranking the engine; then, he checked the fuel flow and disassembled and cleaned out the carburetor. After about forty-five minutes, he had reassembled the engine, and with one pull of the starter rope, the engine was running.

When making inquiries on the islands, ask more than one person, be patient and always keep a positive attitude. You are on island time, and it may take some getting used to seeing you before assistance is offered. Oh yes, what to charge for services rendered was evidently the hardest thing for them to determine. The store owner and his friend, after private conversation, eventually settled on 300 francs, which is about thirty dollars. Trying to pay more is not appropriate, but throwing in a can of salted nuts or some such treat is greatly appreciated.

No mechanic in Makemo—don't you believe it.

Our Friend the Grouper

We are anchored on the atoll of Toau in the Tuamotus. A local family took a group of us to see their pearl-culturing farm, located on one of the *motus,* or small islands, within the lagoon. We were transported by powerboat with a 150-hp outboard motor, which is a lot of horses and commotion. The tropical paradise offered the usual activities of snorkeling and bird watching, including nesting boobies. There were at least fifty overhead nests, each containing just a single gangly chick, covered in fluffy white feathers, watching us.

The star attraction was a large camouflaged grouper, estimated at ten pounds. We had hunted groupers before, but those were much smaller. Our hosts had promised our group the fish would appear, claiming he would hear the motor and move near, into a small cove at the anchoring site, and await the arrival of his friends. As Charles Burkowski, poet of *Barfly* fame with Mickey Rourke and Faye Dunaway, would say, "Hello to all my friends." As we waded ashore, there he was, bumping his head against our feet and ankles in greeting.

The local family began feeding him five years ago, and the grouper is now conditioned to the sound of the motor for the arrival of food. We all took turns touching him as he swam in the clear water. Ross caught a good-sized *Pachygrapsus*, or lined shore crab, for a proper snack. The crab was about four inches across the carapace, and when Ross held it in offering under the water, our friend ate it in one fast and clean gulp. Your fingers were in danger if you had slow reflexes.

We shared our picnic lunch with the grouper. He enjoyed our sandwich scraps, a chunk of mango and some potato chips. This fish charmed us all and changed our thinking about his species. When we went out spearfishing the next week, we didn't go after any groupers and harvested only parrotfish and trevally.

Is it possible to form a relationship with a fish? Maybe we have not been giving them enough credit. I can't help but feel there was more to his motivation than just the possibility of food. The common goldfish, *Carassius auratus auratus,* rises to the top of the tank at feeding time, but unlike the goldfish, our friend the grouper has options. The open sea is his home and food is plentiful, but he remembers the sound of the powerboat and comes out to say "Hello to all my friends."

Diving with the Young Men

While weathered in at Tahanea, we had the good fortune to have the motor yacht *Senses* join us. *Senses,* which comes fully equipped with six auxiliary boats including a sailboat, Hobie Cat, inboard all-weather motor launch and several inflatables, is fully equipped and even includes a helicopter. It was no light assumption that they would have facilities to fill our air tanks. While discussing this over the VHF with *New Dawn* and *Kabuki,* the skipper of *Senses* broke in and offered to fill our tanks. We took him up on his gracious offer and then headed out for a dive with fresh tanks topped up to 3,200 pounds of air.

The dingy was packed with gear for the three of us, and we anchored over a nice coral reef that looked very promising for its diversity of marine life. I was with two other boat owners, my son Ross and his friend, also from Alaska and also a Ross—so it was two Ross's and a Ray. This Ray was thrilled to be going diving but knew his son would be watching for any sign or incontinuity that suggested Dad may be getting too old for this stuff. He could be right, but with many hours of diving experience to draw upon, I had been holding my own with these two excellent young divers.

We had anchored on the reef, and friend Ross was geared up and over the side in minutes. Son Ross was waiting for Dad to get suited up and into the water. I was pulling on my lightweight unisuit/wetsuit, which always seems to be a size too small, but with one leg in the suit, my other leg was presenting more resistance than usual. It took a major effort, but I finally got my other leg into the suit. As I groped for the sleeves for the final folding of my body into the suit, it became apparent that something was drastically wrong. I stood up to straighten things out and I saw the problem. I had put my leg into the sleeve of the wet suit. Now hanging down between my legs was the unoccupied wetsuit leg, waiting as if for some incredible endowment which I did not have, nor any Tiki for that matter.

In my younger days of diving, this would have been a hilarious moment, but now it was more an indicator of whether or not Dad should have sold the house, bought a sailboat and gone sailing around the world. Son Ross was very kind and helped me into the right sleeves and legs, but I had to wonder—maybe there was some mental slippage going on. Anyway, the important thing was we got into the suit correctly before friend Ross returned. We had a wonderful dive and even found some serpulid polychaete worms of my graduate school days. I am okay and I hope Ross thinks so too, but one thing is for sure, I will be paying more attention on the next suit-up. Life is good!

Good Naked and Bad Naked

One trend of note in our travels has been the need for less and less clothing. Our conditioning years in Alaska taught us that you can never have too many clothes. Layering was the answer, and as you warmed up, you removed a layer. In this tropical climate, "layering" usually involves one at most and, more often than not, no layer at all.

We have several plastic bins stored in the v-birth area with a variety of clothing that has not yet made an appearance and, with the present trend, never will. In a few short months, the *Nereid* has become a clothing-optional vessel, with no questions asked or eyebrows raised. This goes for outside in the cockpit, but we are still not about to reveal everything at anchorage in the vicinity of fellow cruisers. It's not that we have anything to be ashamed of; it has more to do with the presentation. Quoting one of our favorite modern-day behaviorists, Seinfeld, "There is good naked and bad naked," and this morning as we lay at anchor in Toau, we saw examples of both.

One boat of avid sports fishermen features a Canadian chap who removes his clothing and, buck naked off the stern, does a few casts for some reason. This fellow is an example of bad naked, with front overhang that keeps his relatively small member out of his own view and out of the sun. Contrast this with the boat off our port stern, where there is an Australian fellow that

does a morning swim and then walks around the boat to
dry off, only in this case we have more of a
Michelangelo's *David,* a well-proportioned fellow in every
department.

  As we travel, I am sure there will be other
countries represented to fill the wide range between
Canada and Australia. I may even reach a confidence level
where I can represent my own country in this survey. In
any case, I look forward to establishing some trends,
especially with the ladies, and if someday Judy should
decide to be counted, I will know we have been out here
too long.

Please Note: Future observations in this survey will
continue to be based on a random plethora of "in-your-
face sightings of opportunity," and no effort will be made
to seek out or actively acquire additional data.

Chapter 4

Tahiti

Sunday in Tahiti

We had talked about going to church but had not made the effort to locate a time and place to attend a service. However, this Sunday found us down at the marketplace along the beachfront in Papeete, Tahiti. As we were threatening to buy some stuff, church bells began ringing.

"Do you want to go and find the church that is presently calling us?" our Australian friends asked.

"Let's do it," we said.

We were off. With the help of the bells ringing and the sight of the steeple in the distance, it was easy to find our destination, and we arrived on time.

We sat in the balcony, out of view of the main congregation, as we only had on our cruisers' best, which was a bite casual. We had an excellent view of the beautiful scene below us. The church was filled, with the ladies all sitting together in white dresses and white hats. The men, in dark suits, all sat together. There were eight sections, four with men and four with the ladies. The singing was in the native language, like our church experience in Makemo, only this time there was more of a harmonious exchange between the men and women and the different sections.

My only regret was that they did not have a CD for sale of this musical exchange. The service was in French with a few key words of universal meaning, but the singing was exceptional and inspired us to stay to catch the last chorus. We came away with a good feeling and, instead of resuming our shopping, we sat on the beach and just enjoyed the moment.

Upon returning to our boat, I felt the need for more music and so perused our limited CD collection and selected the sound track of the movie *Mission*. There was some connection that I cannot explain, maybe something to do with the contrasting violence and peacefulness of the human condition. What I do know is that the Polynesians have a special place in the grand scheme of things, and rightfully so.

A Time to Dance

We happened to find ourselves in the cultural hall in Papeete, Tahiti. We arrived late and came in through the wrong door, but we were just in time to catch the young native dancers behind the stage changing from their street clothes into costume. They were stepping out of their everyday lives into the past for a few brief moments. The stage was already set, native drummers in attendance with a wide variety of sizes and shapes of drum. There were four empty seats in the front row and, since there were four of us, we boldly took them.

The drummers began slowly as the dancers came onto the stage. There were about forty dancers in alternating rows of males and females, all moving together to the beat of the drums. The drummers picked up the tempo and the dancers came alive. The natives we barely noticed on the street, now in costume, had changed into an exciting, primal moving force. I could practically feel the potential violence as well as the softness of these people. They had all stopped what they were doing and come together to produce a spellbinding effect on their audience.

My spell was broken as a young native dancer stepped down from the stage. "Time to dance," she said to me with a wide smile.

I checked my pacemaker and she took my hand and we headed for the action. Other native dancers chose several more from the audience, and we all found ourselves on the stage, moving to the beat of the drums. Her movements were doable even for this over-the-hill contender, all except for the squat twists.

"No way, Jack!" my knees said.

I had to go to a one-knee stance and a careful 180-degree twist to the other knee. What was not doable was to maintain eye contact with my partner and effortlessly return her seductive smile. My lovely dance partner was still smiling as they carried me from the stage. No, just kidding, I made it under my own power. She led me back to my seat, where we thanked each other and said goodbye.

The young native girls of Tahiti are fascinating, with a soft politeness and a hint of wildness in their eyes that in combination with everything else would make any sailor—now or of olden days—think they were in paradise. I know this old sailor was so moved. Then it was over. The drums were silent and the dancers changed back into their street clothes and merged back into the crowded streets of everyday life.

It had been, indeed, a time to dance.

Getting to Know You

We contracted a guide service to take us into the interior of Tahiti.

This was a one-day adventure from the back of a Land Rover with the canvas top rolled away to open up the viewing angles. The scenery was impressive even for us Alaskans, who have seen plenty of mountainous areas.

The jungle holds a combination of indigenous and introduced species, which in some cases are displacing the native flora and fauna. According to our guide, even the innocent-looking doves, introduced a long time ago, have driven out many of the island bird populations.

There were seven of us bouncing along the back road: Judy and I, our son and his wife, our husband-and-wife friends from Australia and a medical student from the Netherlands. After about an hour of driving deeper into the hot and dense jungle interior, the guide pulled over to the side of the road.

"There are several places to go swimming in the river, but the swimming hole just ahead offers the most privacy, and you will probably have it to yourselves," our guide informed us.

"I forgot my swimsuit," the med student announced when we reached our spot.

We had all been told to bring one.

The guide didn't say anything except to point out that the spot has an unusual rock the natives had identified as looking like a male body part. The rock did have a certain resemblance, but evidently not enough for missionaries to have had it removed.

We were starting to get our swim gear together when our Netherlander friend headed for the water in only his tan lines. It was a startling moment as our son and daughter-in-law decided to do the same, followed by our Australian friends, who were closer to our age. Oh well—being the oldest and wisest, I suggested to Judy that we do the same.

"Why not?" she said to my surprise.

I couldn't think of a reason, and there we were, all seven of us in the water and keeping our swimsuits dry. It was a great moment and definitely the highlight of the day.

I would do it again, but it is more of an impulsive thing that would be hard to plan. In this setting and group of people, it seemed an entirely natural thing to do. I would actually like to do it again because I forgot to look.

Drums and Hips

While in Tahiti, we attended a competition of dance teams representing Tahiti and the other communities in the Society Islands. This is a tradition that goes back 124 years. There are two weeks of competition. According to the program, in the last few years the presentations have gotten away from the traditional dance forms, and this year the emphasis was to be on a return to past years. Let me just say the past is definitely worth reviving.

Each dance team had their own accompaniment consisting of drummers for ten large, free-stranding bass drums, ten marimba types and ten smaller drums. These drum combinations created an atmosphere that built and carried off our conditioning in search of some primal essence. The dance teams consisted of fifty to eighty dancers. Usually the men came on stage first, in low, crouching moves as if hunting or scouting the area. Their buffed, brown bodies glistened with an intensity of purpose—Judy's observation. Their vitality was emphasized with intricate dance steps, some of which shifted their weight to alternating full knee bends, their other legs extended to the side.

Then came the ladies. Oh, my goodness, the ladies—they moved effortlessly across the stage. Their hands and upper bodies were still and only their hips were moving to the beat of the drums. When the drums picked up, their hips stayed with the beat. They were always smiling with confidence, knowing the audience was watching and captured. Let me try to describe this one more time. The ladies are smiling, their arms and upper bodies still but their hips moving rapidly and effortlessly as they seem to float across the stage.

When viewing the performance of an individual or trying to take in the entire spectacle, my visual senses were overloaded, and I found myself sampling the moment here and there. With two weeks of this dancing competition ahead, we planned to attend at least one more performance. It was an overwhelming experience that really came down to drum beats and hip movement. So there it is—what happened here in Tahiti on a warm evening in July.

Wish you could have been here. We even had an extra ticket.

Note: In the early 1800s, the missionaries banned dance, songs and games. It wasn't until 1846 that a French governor, Armand Bruat, short on popularity, authorized the return of native dance and song. He became very popular indeed. *Viva la France!*

Making Things Happen

We have been sitting around the dock in Papeete, Tahiti, for almost two weeks, enjoying the conveniences of dock life and getting ready for the next passage. There have been a few breakdowns and equipment upgrades as part of the cruising life. Stuff that has lost its usefulness or was never used just accumulates.

Someone would say, time and again, "What we need is a dockside swap."

Nobody ever took the initiative to organize such a happening. Questions would come up: do we need to get permission from the harbormaster, would anybody be interested, what would be a good time and place?

Two days ago, Judy said, "I am going to have a swap meet on the dock." She didn't ask anyone's permission, she just picked up the VHF microphone and said, "Attention the fleet at Marina Taina. Tomorrow at ten o'clock in front of the two Alaska boats at the head of the last dinghy dock, there will be a swap meet. Dig out those treasures of the bilge you're not using anymore and even that old captain for an exchange."

Now, to put this in a proper context, Judy is someone who does not like to talk on the VHF radio or take the lead on a project, but she was now speaking with this transformed voice and complete confidence. In a few seconds the message was out there, and things began to happen. Boaters were calling in for confirmation on the time and place, some announcing what they had for sale, and one even wanted me. The ball was rolling. No more wondering if it was okay, or when and where.

The swap meet was a big success. Almost all of the items for sale or exchange found a new home, including some big-ticket items like outboards, stainless-steel anchor chains, a kayak, a SSB radio and roller-furling head sails.

Yes, there was a great spirit of exchange and bartering taking place, but the overriding benefit was the social exchange and meeting some new people. What was to last an hour turned into a three-hour event of high-spirited conversation.

The obvious message here is, when nobody takes the lead on something that should be done, don't wait for someone else, just do it yourself—make something happen. Oh, yes, I guess someone was just kidding, as I didn't get traded out. Which was good. I need time to discover more about this amazing person I have been married to for forty-four years.

The French Connection

We have been in French Polynesia for almost three months, and it has been a most enlightening experience. Being from the United States, we were somewhat apprehensive about our reception. We came with stories of the French not liking Americans. If we can't speak their language, they will give us a bad time and their attitude will be haughty and superior, especially if we profess to like our roast beef well done.

I am happy to report that none of the above has proven true. From the Gendarme official at check-in to the French person on the street or in the supermarket when asking for assistance or a translation to English, they all, without exception, have been most helpful, usually with a smile.

Yesterday, in the supermarket shopping for a spaghetti sauce with meat, I asked the petite French lady beside me, whose little boy in the cart was watching me intently, if she spoke English.

"Yes," she replied with a big smile and then proceeded to translate the contents of our many options. With her recommendation, our choice was made, and she ended with, "I hope you have a lovely dinner."

It was a pleasure to hear the English language treated with her heavy French accent.

I am reading Winston Churchill's book *The Gathering Storm*, an excellent account of the factors leading up to the Second World War and the participation of the French in that unfortunate experience. If the Allies had not pressured France so severely to disarm after the First World War and if Chamberlain had not jumped to the beck and call of Hitler, the German generals would have taken out the crazy man. This book should be required reading when cruising and in all public school systems.

We had intended to follow through on a self-taught French language course but did not discipline ourselves in this endeavor. We picked up only some of the more obvious French phrases and have fallen short on the numbering system. I could never get much beyond the *uh* for one and *duh* for two, which in some conversations, if we answered a waiter's question with *uh* as recognition and *duh* as a hesitation, resulted in him returning with three of whatever he was offering. French is not as easy as Spanish, where one can turn some English into Spanish—like "hamburger and Coke" is *hamburguesa y Coca.*

Actually, we may know more French than we thought. I look over the grocery bill of yesterday's purchase. Evidently carrots, M&M's, Tostitos and Kellogg's Corn Flakes are pronounced the same in French and English. In light of this grocery receipt, now when asked *"Parlez-vous Francais?"*, or "Do you speak French?", instead of my usual "No," I'll be moving up to "A little bit" or *"Un peu."*

Departure Withdrawal

We find ourselves cutting the umbilicus at Papeete, Tahiti, and heading out for Bora Bora, 150 miles to the NW, with a stop off at Moorea. It has been four weeks, three more than expected, but it has been fun. When the boat is at the dock, as opposed to anchoring offshore, we can use as much fresh water and electricity as we want and be out and about as the mood or temperature moves us. It is like having all of the amenities we take for granted when living on land in a house.

We will be missing the friendships we have made here, and that is the primary benefit of staying longer in one place. Along with our fellow cruisers, some of whom we will see down the line, the people at Marina Taina have become good friends as well. Laurent Bernaert, who has been our paperwork handler and general everything, always greets us with a heavy accent that sounds like Andre from *Cheers,* the Frenchman who was always hustling Woody's girlfriend Kelly. It's "Judee, how are you today?" Patrick, whose office is on a forty-four-foot Peterson, fixed a leak in our cooling system. He looks like and has the same German accent as the dentist in *Marathon Man,* but comes with a sense of humor. Laurent was never sure when I was joking and always looked to Judee for guidance.

Another personality that will be missed is Philippe. He guides boats into the harbor, then dives down and sets the bow anchor for the required Mediterranean tie-up. We had some strong winds one day and I had to run another anchor line. Philippe placed the line and, upon his return, asked if I was missing anything.

That is a hard question, but I said, "No."

"Well, I guess this sail bag belongs to another *Nereid,"* he replied.

It is always disturbing to have someone find your stuff floating around underwater.

We will also be missing *Le Truck,* which is the standard mode of public transportation in Papeete. They are privately owned, simply modified flatbed trucks with a wooden bench down each side. Travelers pay for their trip when they get off, which requires more trust. Collecting the fare after the trip would never fly in Los Angeles or San Francisco, for example. They will also give anyone a ride, free of charge, to the nearest *Le Truck* transfer station. Again, in the USA there are liability issues and union regulations against this sort of assistance.

We will miss the play money with the big numbers. I always feel like a big spender handing out 2,000 francs for lunch and 10,000 francs at the market. It has been like playing Monopoly and collecting money from the bank for Boardwalk and Park Place.

Finally, we will be missing the French Polynesian standard greeting, a cheek-to-cheek touch to both sides of the face. I have had the opportunity to participate in several of these rituals. It is a personal yet respectful mode of contact, which makes it special. This close-contact greeting will never catch on in the States. We hold our friends at arm's length, except for the occasional hug.

Friends: think about the facial touching during your next handshake, and there you are, with us, on the islands.

Home Wreckers

Edd of *Claire de Lune*, a fellow Valiant sailor with many years' experience, said to me one day, "Ray, it's not a question of *whether* you'll go aground, it's *when* you will."

I can report that we had a minor misread of the channel markers leaving Papeete, as the French have it "red, right, leaving" instead of the American system of "red, right, returning," and sometimes there is no opposing green marker. That said, and despite this feeble excuse to sooth my ego, we had a minor grounding upon departure.

Luckily, we were moving at only 1-2 knots, so the devastation was limited on both sides. The sound and the sudden slowing of our 22,000 pounds sent a charge of adrenaline surging through my body. My brain went into overload, sorting out the chaos and arriving at the obvious, to shift the boat into reverse and back up, which

I did and we were free. I checked for damage upon arrival in Moorea, and there was nothing but minor scratches midway down the keel.

The crush of some of the coral acted as an absorber of the shockwave but left a few devastated home sites, a minor impact to this extensive community. However, as a student and defender of invertebrates, I feel especially bad that I could have caused this unnecessary loss of life and property damage. Cnidarians lead a simple life and, as polyps or zooids, are resolved to a solitary yet communal existence and work hard to maintain their ancestral homes.

My apologies to the friends and relatives of the decreased, and I can only say that we will be more careful in the future as we proceed across a zone of other relatives and ancestral homes. It is, however, with some relief that we have had our first encounter with a solid substrate and it wasn't so bad. Nonetheless, I have to wonder about my learning curve—was this just a warning of things to come?

Anyway, we are now veterans of grounding, and that experience will make us better sailors and give us another story to tell. I know the damage to the reef and the zooid condo complex is already undergoing reconstruction 24/7, and with an abundance of tenants waiting for home sites, it may be a bittersweet opportunity for these new settlers. However, we do not want to be labeled "home wreckers" and will make every effort not to let this happen again. Please accept our most sincere apology.

Chapter 5

Moorea and Bora Bora

Batten Down the Hatches

Today was a lovely day in Tahiti and we were on our way to Moorea, only a short eleven miles and visible in the distance. The seas were flat and windless as we motored through the pass into the open water. It is always a chore to prepare the boat for any excursion or travel to a new homeport. I had debated the necessity of securing the ports and hatches, strapping down the storage boxes stowed in the v-berth, securing the laptop at the nav station and the dozen other things that we would have to do for a major trip, but we did it anyway.

Let me again emphasize that the wind gauge was indicating zero knots and the sea was so flat we could have skated on it during an ice age. After an hour of motoring, we were out about five miles and conditions had rapidly changed. The seas were now coming at us with breaking white caps, and the wind was gusting to over 30 knots. I started to set the staysail but decided to just keep motoring, as it could get worse. The same thing had happened to us coming from Taoa to Tahiti; during the last six miles, we hit winds gusting over 50 knots, and in the black of night. In both cases we had taken the time to prepare the boat, but it was so tempting on this occasion to just wing it across the short distance and save some time.

Turns out any time saved getting out of Dodge, if all the stuff isn't secured, is spent cleaning up the mess after arrival. It's best not to even entertain the thought of shortcutting the departure procedures, just follow them. I was glad we did. Two other boats, with kids, departed shortly before we did, and they fell for nature's little joke and had terrible trips. One boat had a crashing mixture of eggs and Legos. The other boat had ten gallons of water spread around inside and a smashed laptop.

When I find myself swinging hand over hand through the salon like an ape moving through the jungle and nothing is on the floor, I know I have done the right thing. Upon arrival, when all the books, dishes and cooking stuff are in place, I am only too glad to have taken the time to secure everything. We were only missing some limes, which had been propelled from the galley into the salon as the waves had had their way with us. They made for some darn fine limeade—the fruit all soft and primed to be squeezed.

If one takes the time to batten down the hatches, these little weather surprises can be fun, and I hope we will always be able to make that claim.

Meet the Rays

Today was one of those days that make it into the top ten most memorable. I am trying to compose this after a large intake of spaghetti and with a group in the distance practicing their native drums, which are really moving the night air. When we pulled into Moorea yesterday, we dropped the hook in twenty feet of crystal-clear water. We were close enough to shore to warrant an anchor check, which was done with snorkel and mask, as everything can be seen from the surface in this clarity of water.

Secure in our holding ability, we headed out early the next morning in three dinghies, which included two cruiser friends with kids, one family from Austria (*Lawur*) the other from Los Angeles (*Blue Sky*). Our destination was a sandy shoal about four miles along the inner reef barrier, a famous gathering place for rays. When we arrived the excitement was immediate, as the sandy bottom was alive with huge rays, not of the manta type but the more deadly and feared stingrays. These babies were ranging from four to five feet in diameter and had tails of equal length that cut wide swaths over the sandy bottom. Robert, our Austrian friend, was in the water immediately with food in hand and was soon surrounded. Eventually everyone was brave enough to get in the water with about twenty of these deadly fellows.

The water was only four feet deep. The rays would swim to the surface and put their big undulating arms around us, and their wide bedroom eyes seemed to say, "Welcome to my world. What did you bring me to eat?" We had a variety of foods but they really liked our sardines. There was a trick to feeding them—I would take a pinch of sardine and let it go under a protruding front lip pressed against my chest, the food would disappear. A few fish tried to get into the act and take food from my hand, but the really big show were the rays—makes sense to me. With one hand distributing the goods I could, with my other hand, stroke their velvety-soft dorsal sides. And yes, these were stingrays, verified with protruding sting apparatus in place. Evidently the use of such an impressive defensive weapon is a learned or voluntary response, so for our feeding party there was nothing to fear except fear itself and, thankfully, none of these new friends got upset when the food was gone.

Judy may have saved us all when she noticed some of the rays were settling out on the bottom and beginning to partially cover themselves with sand. They would be easy to step on, which would not be good. It was time to get out of the water.

We had debated about stopping at Moorea for the rays, as these things can be overhyped and the trip may have turned out to be nothing more than feeding some fish, nothing special. Not so today. As I mentioned, this event moved into the top ten life experiences for this cruiser. I would have expected this behavior from the more docile manta rays, but for the deadly stingray? Make that deadly only if a human presents a threat.

I may have been premature in selecting the turtle tattoo for my rite of passage, but then there is nothing on my right shoulder…but that would be putting a ray on Ray—probably not a good idea.

Dead Animals

"What is it in here that smells like dead animals?" was the first comment from a new arrival visiting her boyfriend.

Not to pick on a particular boat—indeed, it was more a question of boys versus girls—the dead animal smell had crept into prominence over a three-month period with two guys on board deferring any serious housekeeping until later. The new arrival or girlfriend having determined the source of the dead animal smell, rather than heading for the airport, like a good complement to any crew methodically began washing and scrubbing and in a short time had brought the interior of this fine cruising boat back to acceptable hygienic standards.

The *Nereid* is indeed fortunate to have a crewmember that has kept all the dead animals in check. Because we have chosen to confine our living space to about the size of a single car garage, the bodily activities or residues that at one time were spread over a 3,200-square-foot home are now more concentrated. The good news is that the area that needs to be cleaned is more confined. It probably helps immensely to have a mate who comes from the health care profession and has a low tolerance for any unwanted life forms. So as part of the *Nereid* way of life, every morning, Judy takes a white plastic bucket filled with warm water and mild detergent and she washes down the good ship on the inside. My only task is to stay off the floor until it dries.

I have also been relieved of dishwashing duties. The "quick wash under the faucet while the stuff is still loose" method—a process that saw me through bachelor days with the Forest Service and National Park Service—is not acceptable. Anyway, I am still alive and come with a well-developed immune system. Before anyone passes judgment, let me say that I have applied repeatedly to be reinstated to galley cleanup duties but can't get past the initial interview.

Today is especially noteworthy in this context as my darling has decided the outside of the boat is "filthy" and needs cleaning, and she is presently in the dinghy cleaning the sides of the boat.

So I can say to all my friends, it is with great pride and continuing assurance that I invite one and all to come visit us any time and any place the *Nereid* is anchored, as there will be no evidence or concerns associated with dead animals.

Bon Appetite at Sea

We have moved from Moorea to Bora Bora, a distance of about 140 miles that amounts to about thirty hours of sailing time. I thought it might be of interest, since we have a full day, to provide a sample of the hardships endured on the *Nereid* in the area of food preparation and consumption. Judy's creative time in the galley on this particular trip was done sometimes with stove swinging on gimbals and butt strap in place to keep her from leaving the galley unintentionally and finding herself at the navigation station.

She has become the consummate sailor's cook and added a new notch of saltiness when she cut the sleeves off her t-shirt to cool down. Here is what we had on this passage for breakfast: scrambled eggs with bacon and onion mixed in, mango juice with a dash of fresh-cut lime and, of course, tea, with extra for later to become iced tea. Now for lunch: tuna on coconut-milk bread rolls with lettuce and tomato, dried mango chips and sliced fresh kiwi. Next, for dinner, was a new experimental dish that was excellent and consisted of turkey chunks mixed with bread dressing, cranberry sauce, carrots and some of Auntie Mikel's famous pickled beets. For dessert, there were brownies baked the night before departure.

Of course, there is that extended time between meals that necessitates some fill-in consumption, and on this day the treats included our single shared Coca Cola with cashews and freshly cut pineapple. The pineapples we found at a little market in Moorea the day before departure.

I know it's hard to believe that we are having this kind of culinary experience on the high seas, and there are some cruising boaters out there who either don't believe this story or have found solace in a simple monastic dietary experience while under sail. Please, in those cases, don't hold this news against me, as the cook will not heed my urging to take an easier route to the sailing table.

The seas do not cut any slack for food preparation, and it is amazing that she can produce such an incredible variety and quality of vittles under some of

the most challenging conditions. So anyway, life on the
Nereid is good, and not to worry—our food needs are
fully accommodated. As the French say when they want a
diner to be ready for a gastronomic treat, and they mean
this with all sincerity—*bon appétit.*

Moment of Truth

"Help me," came the small voice from the man
lying at my feet.

Snow was packed in tightly behind his sunglasses,
pressing against his eyeballs, taking away his visual sense.
He had, as skiers say, caught an edge when he started his
descent about a hundred feet above me, and fallen
headfirst down the steep slope. After body skiing on his
chest, snow churning up in his face, he had come to a
stop at my feet. Only moments earlier he had stood at the
top, looking out over the expanse, dressed in some of the
finest ski apparel available. He was poised and looking
good. What a changeup.

Like skiing, sailing has its moments of truth. One
such came the day Judy and I headed for one of the yacht
club mooring balls in the harbor at Bora Bora. Mooring
balls can be a welcome relief after a long passage, as they
take anchoring out of the equation. There was the
assurance that when we hooked up, we were going to stay
there. This time, however, it was the hookup that became
challenging.

After four passes with Judy at the wheel, I was
still hanging over the bow with the boat hook in my
hands. I had made several successful retrievals of the
mooring line, but once the line is grabbed, it is necessary
to quickly secure it. Take too long and the boat—all
twelve tons, in our case—tends to follow its inertial path.
Dignity was stripped away as I tried each time to hold the
boat a few more seconds to secure the line. I was

stretched to almost being pulled overboard. Finally, after conferring with my helmsperson, we executed a perfect hookup, but in the meantime, we had put on quite a show for some of the other cruisers.

We all have our moments, and the next show was from France, as three Frenchmen attempted to moor their boat at the yacht club to take on water. The bow line of their boat, a forty-foot sloop, was secured to a mooring ball, but the stern line, which needed to be secured to the dock, was giving them problems. No matter what he did, the fellow on the dock could not get the line secured, and he kept losing the line into the water. Words in French were exchanged between the three that sounded of a personal nature.

I couldn't help but watch. The man on the dock tried everything. He gestured to his companions that the cleat was on the wrong side of the dock, but there were cleats on both sides. At last, when he did get the stern line secured, the boat kept motoring and the dock began to creak and bend.

The yacht club manager, normally very calm, ran out to save his dock from being towed away. It was time to get involved. I offered to take the water hose out to their boat with our dinghy, which he readily accepted. After we relayed the hose, we motored off to our boat, satisfied that the job was done. How wrong we were! Looking back, we saw the fellow on the dock losing the stern line *and* the hose into the water. He shouted and waved his arms about—not a pretty sight.

Maybe the best thing to do in a case like this is to simply pretend I don't see the 'moment of truth' and just move on.

Bora Bora

When we informed our daughter via phone that we were moving from Moorea to Bora Bora, she was not impressed. "It is just another island," she said. "They are all about the same."

Judy didn't agree with her assessment, but in this case I think our daughter was right. I have not enjoyed the splendor of this island paradise, as it was marketed to be. In fact, I suspect the name translates to Boring Boring.

When we arrived, our exploratory exploits were seriously curtailed by high winds of 30 to 40 knots and a complex low-pressure system that decided to hang around. Consequently, we stayed in the boat for two days with no intention of going ashore. We are at the Bora Bora Yacht Club on a mooring ball and have enjoyed the amenities of showers, free water and a great restaurant with a top chef who dropped out of the big-resort-hotel pressure for the less-demanding cruising community. There is a washing machine, although the agitator is not working, so I am the agitator facilitator.

We toured a pearl farm and made an acquisition that has Judy signed up for one more year of sailing. We also visited the famed Bloody Mary's, a restaurant where many of the world's foremost have scribed their names. We did do a high-speed tour around the island.

One of our favorite cruising couples had the use of a car for two hours and invited us for a terrestrial circumnavigation of the island. They are a younger, high-energy couple, and being with them is always fun. We had planned a two-hour tour of the island, but once in the car and with everybody talking, there was no time for stopping, and we did the island in about thirty minutes. With an hour and a half left with the car, we could have gone around the island three more times. We did have a map with features to see, but by the time someone read the description of a site, we had gone past it.

We did make one stop, at the Bora Bora Hotel, but only after some discussion was the car turned around for this momentous experience. We will catch this couple at another port and look forward to our time together and to recharging.

On a final note, we were walking down the road looking for a small store to buy some bread and asked a lady standing in her yard if we were headed in the right direction.

"No," she said. "It's the other way, but you just wait here." Whereupon she entered the house and came out with a baguette, then handed it to Judy.

With a lift of her finger, she said, "Ah, you wait here again."

She went back in the house and returned with a quart of cold water and a can of minced meat.

"Now you take these," she insisted.

I tried to pay her. The only thing she would accept was the joy of giving, as shown in her eyes and her smile.

I was mistaken. Bora Bora, you are indeed a beautiful classroom.

Ladies' Rite of Passage

I would like to tell you about three very brave ladies who collectively carried each other to a result probably not attainable individually. Yesterday, it was the ladies who decided upon a remembrance of the journey we have undertaken—Marquesan tattoos tastefully selected and placed for maximum effect. Maximum effect is a personal choice and in this case ranged from hips to ankles to behind the ear. Only two of these lovelies made the long passage.

The third but major catalyst prompting the move and final decision was a fly-in sailor who has since returned home. She had planned on three commemoratives: a flower on the ankle, a dolphin on the hip and a Marquesan cross on one of her significant upper-body developments. She came fortified with a bottle of champagne and plenty of treats to keep courage up and anxiety down. She didn't hesitate when called, and when she returned thirty minutes later, she was most excited, a beautiful dolphin on her hip. She had to settle for one tattoo this time.

The artist said, "No more for you today…too nervous."

This opened the time slot for our other two ladies in waiting, and it came down to words like,

"Are you going to do this?"

"I am, are you?"

"Well, I don't know yet, you go next."

"Let me think about it a bite longer."

Lady Number Two said, "I can do this."

She returned with a tattoo just behind her ear, a very painful area to work. This lady, when she sets her mind to it, can do anything.

The artist took some liberties with his designs and when questioned would close with, "Trust me, I am an artist."

There was a twist of creativity in all three cases, and the results were good.

Lady Number Three, closest to my concerns, had talked about having a Marquesan bird representing freedom and imagination. Judy was not lacking in courage—she never has been—and had the most surprising result of all. This unpredictable lady had a last-minute change of mind. The bird planned for her left ankle was instead a beautiful manta ray. A traditional wedding ring has displayed our commitment to each other for the last forty-four years, but this day it was sealed with a more permanent indicator of affection.

It is indeed great to be a Ray!

Molly

"Are those bifocals?"

"Yes, they are," I said, smiling down at the inquisitive little girl.

She took a long pause for continued study, and then she said, "Those were invented by Benjamin Franklin."

The question had been posed and info about Ben put forth by Molly. She and her parents have been cruising for the last four years, so most of her life she has been at sea.

I had the opportunity to meet Molly at an evening social hour at the Bora Bora Yacht Club. After she finished her observation about my bifocals, she walked away and sat down. My adult son Ross and I went over to her.

"May we join you?" I asked.

She nodded with a slight smile and said, "Hi."

She reminded me of our granddaughter, Colette, who at five years old said, "Mama, I understand the food chain, but what did the first animal eat?" This same little girl asked her mom, "If cigarettes are so bad for us, why are they in the world?"

"I'm Ray," I introduced myself.

"Hello, how are you?" Ross said.

"Fine," she answered and then, after a pause, said, "I think I am the only kid here."

"I think you are," I said. "What did you do today?"

Molly adjusted her position on the wooden bench and carefully folded her hands in her lap. "I memorized part of a Chinese poem," she said simply.

Several heads in the social perimeter turned our way.

"Can you recite it now?" I asked.

Molly nodded and very clearly recited what sounded like about fifteen lines.

"That's all I have memorized today," she said, and she gave us a glancing look with a half-smile.

"Can you tell us what the poem is about?" Ross asked.

"It's about spring. I can only tell you what it means to me. I don't know what it really means."

"Have you been sailing for very long?" Ross asked.

"About four years. My first three years were on a monohull, but I am on a cat now and it's really smooooth."

Ross has cat fever and was now completely in love.

"How many languages do you speak?" I asked our young friend.

"I think it's five," Molly said. "French and English, and also some Spanish and Chinese." As she listed them, she counted them on her fingers. After another pensive pause, she added, "I also know some Mandarin and Cantonese, so I guess that would be six."

"You may be the only kid here this evening," I said, "but I think you know more languages than all of the adults."

Molly shrugged. "I might."

It was a social hour that passed too quickly. We were at anchor in the harbor and we hadn't decided whether to go in again this evening. If I knew for sure that Molly was going to be there, it would make my decision easier. As I have said before, there are some amazing things to see and do when out and about on the high seas, and some of them come in delightfully small packages—nice meeting you, Molly.

Sea Monsters

Cruising is like hunting in Alaska. One minute it's the greatest, and the next it presents a life-threatening situation. I was on the walkway at the Bora Bora Yacht Club on my way to make a phone call, and I happened to look down and notice something unusual. I took a closer look and it was a huge centipede, about eight inches long. It appeared to be dead.

I decided to collect it as a study specimen for the grandkids and returned with a plastic bag. As I knelt down and poked it with a stick to round it up into the bag, it suddenly became very alive. With head and forward quarter raised like a cobra, the creature came charging toward my bare feet. These critters with their bite inject venom into their victims, and it can be fatal. I was able to avoid the full-frontal assault and trap him in the bag. I was lucky, as a bare foot could have been easy pickings for our friend with many legs. I was also lucky to have noticed him in time, as he was right at the phone site, maybe waiting to make a call and not appreciating my crowding ahead.

I couldn't get a consensus on what to do with the captured centipede. Finally, it was decided to feed him to the fish that hang out in the pool that extends under the restaurant. These fish have proven to be voracious eaters when food is dropped into their territory. They came roaring out when our friend hit the water and, only inches away, did a 180 turn back under the restaurant. Evidently they know not to mess with Mr. Centipede.

Our friend, now in the water, began to swim out to sea. All legs moving in synchrony, he was like a miniature war canoe, each leg a native paddler. Where was he going, and what was to become of him? We don't know, but there has been talk that sea monsters began as centipedes on tropical islands.

I am sure he holds no grudges; after all, he should respect my survival instincts. I don't think there is anything to worry about—although, we are starting our 1,200-mile passage tomorrow, alone, with no other boats. Anyway, we don't believe in sea monsters—how silly.

Chapter 6

Beverage Reef and Niue

Atypical Eight Days at Sea

"Let's go, let's go."

After weeks of high, variable wind, the forecast finally gave us a window of good weather that brought *New Dawn* and *Nereid* motoring out of Bora Bora Harbor on a calm, sunny morning.

Our first day was light winds and smooth sailing, but by the second day, the winds had lightened so much we had to fire up the engine, our "iron jenny," to compensate for our diminishing sail power. By day three the wind had returned, and by afternoon it was gusting to 40 knots.

With furled headsails and double-reefed main, we clipped along at 6 knots. Sea state increased and the swells began having their way with us. There was no warning of the weather changeup, and Judy hadn't taken her medication for seasickness. She was not feeling well and wanted to curl up and not move. That was pretty much how she traveled that day. Talked briefly on SSB radio with *New Dawn* and everyone was disgusted with the sudden weather change.

By days four and five, winds were more manageable—in the 20 to 30-knot range—but swells were catching us, with an occasional break into the cockpit. We were reminded of a game we used to play with our kids, only now we were the kids and the swells the adults. These were good-sized adults, ten to fifteen feet, and as they came toward the boat, they were saying, "Going to get you, going to get you." As they came closer, they got bigger, and at the last minute, just when you thought they were going to get us, they pushed us along with a splashing laugh. Unfortunately, a few swells arrived with breaking crests that crashed over the rail into the cockpit for a real "gotcha." The *Nereid* is of solid stock and handled the hammering, taking some swells on the beam, which momentarily covered the side hatches with water and flooded the deck.

On day six, the weather front began to change, and by midafternoon there was no wind and we were motoring again. We had 240 miles to go and not a ship in sight. I went on the VHF. "This is the sailing vessel *Nereid* requesting a radio check, anybody out there?" I rarely do this and expected no response but was surprised to hear, "Hello *Nereid,* this is the Greek tanker *Austine,* what is your position?" We exchanged coordinates and weather info but could not see each other. I told the skipper we planned to sail to the Mediterranean, and he said, "You must come to Greece; the weather there is perfect, much better than the South Pacific." He was excited that a husband and wife about the age of his parents were out here, and in his thickly accented but good English, he repeated his invite to visit his beautiful country. It was a special treat to discover a new friend a few miles away.

Day seven was uneventful until about 7:00 a.m., when I went into the salon and felt water on my feet. The bilge pump was running, but water was coming up through the floorboards—not a good sign. My first thoughts were of the ninety-foot sloop that sank mysteriously in the harbor a week earlier at Bora Bora while the family was ashore at a restaurant. I feared the problem was coming from the engine room, but checked first under the galley sink. Warm water was everywhere, even in the drawers in the sink cabinet. As it turned out, the hot water pipe had come loose at the faucet. Judy shut off the water pump; I jammed a pen into the open pipe to seal it until morning, when I could refit the pipe connection. I could not get a clear reading on the water tank gauges. We had five gallons of water stowed on deck for emergencies, but after breakfast and a deep breath, I rechecked the gauges. The water tanks were half full. Just goes to show—always eat breakfast and take a deep breath before you make any dire projections.

Day eight, with only 120 miles to go to Beverage Reef, our Alpha 2000 autopilot evidently needed a rest and stopped responding to any course changes. We spent the first half of the day burning valuable time trying to diagnose the problem, resetting everything, but any course change sadly resulted in a 360-degree turn. Our Windvane autopilot could not handle the highly variable wind direction and sea state. Our options were to slow down, hove-to (park at sea) or hand steer for about twenty-four hours. We decided to hand steer for a few hours and then see if we could go through the night and next day. Our first goal was to make it hand steering until 11:00 that night, trading off every hour.

As the sun was setting, waves were hitting the sides of the hull with sharp bangs, like gunshots. We slept tethered in the cockpit. The weather deteriorated, making it difficult to hold on to the wheel. Judy, all 115 pounds of her, was especially challenged. She had to position her feet wide apart, wedging herself into the space available while hanging on to the wheel, trying to keep on course. Even wedged in the cockpit, there were times as the swells worked over the boat she felt she might rotate with the wheel.

We concentrated on the glowing green light of the compass. The swells would knock us off course, sometimes by twenty degrees, and as we struggled to bring the boat back on course, the swells would hit from the other side. We settled for an average heading of plus or minus twenty degrees. After ten minutes at the wheel, our hands and arms ached. The rest of the hour would go by quickly, preoccupied as we were with the responsibility of steering and looking for other boats. Our radio contact with the *Austine* had increased our awareness of possible boat traffic.

We had a plastic basket secured on the galley counter containing cheese, sardines, crackers and dehydrated fruit. At the end of a shift, we would head for the basket for a bite to eat and drink some water. As the night wore on we became too tired to eat or remove our foul-weather gear and while still tethered in the cockpit, would drop exhausted on the bench seat and fall asleep in seconds.

When daylight broke, it was like we'd been reborn. We had survived the night shift, but there were still twelve hours of hand steering ahead of us. We traded off every ninety minutes, facing winds which had increased to 30 knots. Through the night, we had run with the engine and triple-reefed main, averaging 5.5 knots. This was too slow to make Beverage Reef before nightfall, and we needed daylight to get into the protected waters of the reef. By midday, the wind direction was consistent enough to add the staysail, and with engine and triple-reefed main we averaged 6.5 knots, which would just get us to the reef before dark.

At 5:00 p.m., I confirmed three waypoint coordinates with Ross. *New Dawn* was already anchored in the lagoon with another friend on *Kabuki*. We could not see the reef due to the swells or hear the surf break due to the wind. We had to trust the three waypoints, which got us to the reef and around to the lee side, but we never at any time saw the reef, which was very disconcerting.

It was almost dark as we rounded the third waypoint. What a relief it was to hear Ross's voice over the radio:

"Just to let you know, I have a visual, I can see you, just keep coming straight ahead, you are on course."

We couldn't see him, and Judy kept yelling into the radio, "I can't see you, I can't see you," which suddenly changed to her screaming, "I can see you! I can see you!"

He and his friend were waiting for us in his dingy at the entrance to the lagoon. They had stayed busy fishing and had caught a small yellow fin tuna. We followed them, and once through the pass, they came alongside and Ross hauled himself on board.

"I'll take it from here, Dad," he said with a big smile.

It was dark at 8:00 p.m., when we finally dropped anchor. We were exhausted but happy. We had not wanted to spend another night hand steering at sea, especially near the phantom reef. Ross delivered hot homemade enchiladas Laura had prepared—the best dinner ever. We slept in the next morning.

I am always amazed at how Judy steps up to the plate when needed. She would not settle for anything but equal time at the wheel. Twenty-four hours at the wheel in those conditions was a long time and no easy task for anyone in any age group. We had kept dry sleeping in our rain gear, had snack foods between each shift, drunk plenty of water and kept a positive attitude.

We thanked each other and then we thanked our guardian angels for working overtime.

Beverage Reef (24 hours)

"*Kabuki, Kabuki,* could you come over and catch this shark that is under our boat?" Over the VHF came the voice of Lineus, the seven-year-old son of a German couple on a large catamaran anchored near us. There are only four boats here in Beverage Reef, and Ross on *Kabuki* said he would be over in a minute. Beverage Reef is just that, no land mass, no trees or motus, only the underwater community of coral holding out against the crashing waves.

The only sign of human activity was a hundred-foot fishing boat aground on the reef since last year. It reportedly got tangled in its own long lines and lost steerage, becoming the reef's only landmark.

Breaking waves encircled us, creating a lagoon four by six miles, noted for its abundance of lobster and its spectacular diving. The wind had let up slightly this morning, enough to prompt a lobster hunt but not enough for the fair-weather crustaceans to venture out, and the hunting party returned empty handed.

Shortly after that, a radio call came in to the *Nereid* with an invite to go fishing. The fishing starts as soon as you get into the dinghy, and away we headed for the reef entrance with three lines in the water, moving along at 5 knots. Outside the reef, Ross (of the *Kabuki*) hooked what we thought to be a huge shark, but fifteen minutes of reeling and leveraging to the surface brought a surprising fifty-pound dogtooth tuna, properly named with rows of large canines but too big to keep. After more struggle, it was released to join all its friends. Out here, the problem is catching fish small enough to handle and consume in a reasonable time. I hooked a yellow fin tuna, about twelve pounds, which was small enough to manage and big enough to share with the other three boats.

The return trip was against the wind, causing waves to spray into the dinghy, and backwash from the churning Yamaha outboard brought more water in over the transom. The hand pump was in continual operation to remove the accumulating water. Upon return to the boat, my body-heat balance tipped to cold, and I immediately hosed off in the cockpit, dried, got into sweatpants and a sweatshirt, closed the hatches and turned on the forced-air heat. Slowly, my body temp normalized, just in time for the potluck that evening on *New Dawn.*

New Dawn was anchored only 200 feet away, but it required suiting up into full foul-weather gear, and we still got wet. It can be exciting just getting in and out of a bobbing dinghy, especially when tied alongside a larger boat that is doing its own dance with the waves. Thus ends our twenty-four-hour sample of activities, or a day in the life at Beverage Reef. Next stop, the island nation of Niue, about 140 miles away.

Note: The following evening, in spite of continuing high winds, Ross (of *New Dawn*) and Ross (of *Kabuki*) did a nighttime lobster hunt and came back with thirteen of our spiny friends. So just maybe the stories about Beverage Reef are true.

Niue Ugas

Crazy Uga Café was the name of the joint, but on the hand-scrolled sign, it looks more like *Crazy Ugly Cafe.* Ugly it is not, as they make one of the best chicken sandwiches, with onions and cheddar cheese melted on top and more onions on that. The onions are not cooked, so they retain their original intended flavor, and the result is well worth the ten New Zealand dollars ($7.90 US).

We are at Niue, one of the smallest self-governing nations in the world and one of the largest atolls in the world, so it's little but big. It is about 300 miles from

Tonga and famed for jungle trails, limestone caves to explore and crystal pools of fresh water for swimming. *Uga* means crab, and on this island are the world's toughest and smartest, the coconut crab. They can live for sixty years, weigh up to nine pounds, open up a coconut and easily take off one's finger. They climb the coconut trees and pinch off the coconuts, which come crashing down, hopefully not on your head.

Ross captured one and put it in a large plastic bucket and brought it to the car for us to see. He had placed the bucket in the back seat, but as he was driving along, he felt something near his neck and looked around to see his new friend halfway out his driver-side window. Evidently he had gotten out of the bucket by doing a headstand and hooking the rim of the bucket with his hind legs.

We decided to free this guy, so he was back in the bucket, this time with a lid. We were driving along to place him back in a jungle home when I peeked in the bucket to see how he was doing, but he was gone.

"Emergency! Emergency!" I shouted, quoting our grandson, who was trained to yell a special warning in time of need.

Ross pulled over and stopped the car, and we got out. We found our friend at the back corner of the passenger seat and on his way for a try at another window.

The owner of a local ice cream store, who makes a great chocolate shake for $3.50 NZ, tells the story of bringing a large coconut crab home and, while deciding what to do with it, putting it in the bathroom for the night. Next morning, when he went to check on it, he couldn't get the bathroom door open. Finally he went around to the bathroom window to see what was blocking the door, and the occupant had positioned himself to keep the door shut. He went back to the door and pushed it open a crack and with a small stick tickled the crab under a leg, causing him to release his hold on the door.

There needs to be a study to determine if coconut crabs are ticklish—applied research which could have appendage-saving applications for the human population. I don't know if this crab was rewarded for its efforts or put in the cooking pot. Anyway, our guy is out there, and we hope the ice-cream man made the same call. At least our crab and his friends are not on the menu at the Crazy Uga Café.

Note: Coconut crabs can live up to sixty years and weigh up to nine pounds. Overharvest has greatly reduced their numbers on Nui but with restraint the numbers will return.

Lost and Found

"Are you sure you didn't give those two books away? I have looked and looked all over this boat, and they are not here."

I had been on the hunt for two books I had recently read. One was about how to be a better writer, and the other was *Tales of the South Pacific,* by Michener. I had done several thorough searches of the few places books could be in the limited living area of the boat. So after these thorough but fruitless quests, the evidence was pointing strongly to the theory that my darling, who likes to move out anything that has lost its usefulness, had passed them on. Fortunately, I am still on board.

It was now time to call it, and I asked, "Who has been on the boat in the last few days?"

Her reply was evasive; instead of answering my question, she said, "Raymond, I will look for them as soon as I'm finished mixing this bread." What was she saying—that the books were still on the boat? No, I had established that they were not; we were now at our next step of determining who might have them. Now, the fact that I had moved from "darling" to "Raymond" was significant in that she was taking this whole matter seriously and I had been put on notice that it would be prudent to wait until she was through with her present activity.

It is doubly important at this point to be sure of one's position, so I made one more search of the books on the bookcase, around the bed, on the table, etc. Nothing. So I was more than ready for her to make her search and get on with the next step in this process, calling our cruiser friends who had recently been on the boat. In fact, I did not wait to contact *New Dawn,* where much of our exchange and trading stuff has gone. I called them, but they denied having either of the books. Now it was time for Judy.

She began her search at the port salon bookshelves, and I watched her confidently from my seat at the nav station as she slowly moved her finger along the row of books. I then saw her finger stop for a moment.

She pulled out a book and said, "Is this one of them?" I was in disbelief. It was the Michener book.

I said yes, but she didn't even look at me and was already continuing along the row. Again she stopped and—yes, that's right—she pulled out the second book.

There was no scolding or accusations of being blind as a bat, or of lesser intelligence. She had only a smile and slight rolling of the eyes, not the heavy roll that can cause her to fall backwards.

I said, "I can't believe you found those books and both on the same shelf. I have been looking for them for the last three days."

She had found them both in about thirty seconds. Oh well, this has happened before, but thirty seconds may have been a new record. But who's keeping track? The important thing was the lost items had been found.

Chapter 7

Tonga

King's Men in Black

"The king is dead, the king is dead" came the report over the VHF radio as we were about to depart Niue for the Kingdom of Tonga.

Just at dawn's early light, after 280 miles of sailing and fifty-six hours, we arrived at the kingdom's northern island group of Vava'u. It had been another rough crossing with high winds and large swells. We followed *New Dawn* into the harbor and were told to raft up to them to clear customs, immigration and the Harbor Master. So, with our yellow quarantine flag flying, we tied up to *New Dawn* and awaited His Majesty's men.

The king was well liked and his country would be in mourning for at least thirty days, symbolized by everyone wearing black. The king's men arrived, three fine, healthy-looking gentlemen in black ties, black shirts and black pants. They were big men and seemed to fill the salon as they sat shoulder to shoulder. So now we have the Men in Black looking very stern and businesslike on one side of the table and two elderly, weary cruisers on the other side, smiling but ready to begin the clearance procedure.

After a few pleasantries, two of them managed a smile, and then there was a long pause. We sat smiling and waiting, our documents ready, but nothing was happening. We held our smiles and even managed to quit talking until their silence was broken.

"Do you have any beer?"

We did not.

"It's very hot, what else do you have to drink?"

We offered Cokes around, and all accepted. Only one opened his. The other two put the Cokes into their sacks—so far so good.

"Do you have any cookies?"

Cookies appeared but were unacceptable.

"Do you have any unopened packages? My son likes cookies."

Unopened packages of cookies appeared and went into their sacks.

"Do you have any action videos?"

This was a harder question, as we were unclear as to their definition of "action." After some discussion, one of them asked to see the videos. He got up and went over to our meager collection and began thumbing through them. Evidently no action there, as he returned to his seat with nothing for the sack.

Candy was on the table, and they asked, "Can we take some candy home to our kids? It is hard to find candy in Tonga."

Since we had not gotten into town yet and were still hoping to, I readily agreed, and Judy prepared a bag of candy for the kids.

One of them picked up my sailing knife and said, "I had a knife just like this and broke it. Can I have this one?"

I said, "No, sorry, I need it."

Another one then asked, "Can I check the refrigerator?"

I said, "Okay." The refrigerator yielded nothing for their sacks, and shortly after that, we signed the paperwork.

As they filed out, a fourth man in black arrived and apologized for being late. He was either new to the force or felt the power had shifted to the old guy on the boat—in this case, me, and I was not smiling. He and I sat in the cockpit in silence, just looking at each other, until his cell phone rang and he had to go. Thank goodness for the cell phone, as we could still be sitting there.

Ross on *New Dawn* had a similar extortion hearing and was asked if he had any alcohol on board. He produced a bottle of brandy, and one of them set it down by his notebook.

Ross asked, "Are you taking that?"

He said, "It would make a nice gift."

Ross, always the perfect gentleman, agreed and, with a smile, put the bottle back in the cabinet.

Other cruisers had similar experiences, except those with kids. Evidently the Men in Black modify their behavior in the presence of kids. There could be a new business opportunity in Tonga called Rent-a-Kid.

I don't know if the king would have approved of all these shenanigans but, in spite of the Men in Black, the Kingdom of Tonga is magical.

Mammal to Mammal

The Kingdom of Tonga is one of the few places on Planet Earth where the human species is allowed to swim with whales in their habitat. The recently deceased good king outlawed hunting but decreed swimming with them would be okay. It is restricted to only four divers, accompanied by a guide, in the water at one time.

This day, we were looking for whales, and after about four hours, still no luck. It's like fishing; you pay for the trip and hope for the best. If you don't catch any fish, there is no refund at the end of the day. Each of us had invested 160 panga, which translates to about $80 in real money for this opportunity. I could tell by their body language that our guides were starting to worry about our chances. Yesterday, and it's always yesterday, the news was great, as they had found a mother and young calf. The calf had just learned to breach and, upon this discovery, had continued with about eighty consecutive out-of-water displays.

Today was another day and we had not even seen a spout. We had taken our search more offshore into open water when, about 3:00 p.m., someone shouted "There she blows!" and indeed there were two spouts side by side. They were only about a hundred yards away, and we eased the boat closer until we were traveling beside them at about 6 knots. We stayed about fifty feet away to condition them to our presence. We continued on this course, and occasionally one of them would veer off and almost bump the boat, which we were told was either a mating gesture or just them checking us out. Our introduction to each other went on for about fifteen minutes, and then we were told it was time to put on the wetsuits and prepare to get in the water. Both of the humpback whales had slowed almost to a stop, and we eased into the water with minimal movement so as not to spook them.

It is always a thrill in diving when you first put your face down in the water and behold nature's underwater beauty. This time, that first look into the exceptionally clear blue water, seeing these two huge animals suspended and watching us, was a surreal shocker. It was almost a heart stopper. We all floated motionless in the water, and it was mammal to mammal as we studied them and they studied us.

They moved to within twenty feet of us, and then one of them lifted one of his huge flippers, which on humpback whales are about one third of their body length, as if to wave or communicate with us. I slowly waved back, and then after a few more minutes he rolled over on his back to show us his white underside and mating potential. They were both young males, and they stayed close to each other, like two teenagers out cruising, checking things out. You could see their eyes, one had scars on his backside that looked almost like cuts from a street fight with a prop or large shark. Anyway, he had been out and about experiencing his world. They watched us a few minutes longer, and then, as if having talked it over between themselves, decided we weren't all that interesting, both turned and with a flick of their giant flukes headed for the deep blue and out of sight.

It had only been about fifteen minutes for the entire experience, but those fifteen minutes moved into the top ten for this terrestrial mammal. It is hard to make it into my top ten, but today, mammal to mammal, was without question one of those experiences.

Humpback Whale: Family Balaenopteridae
Measurements at Birth: Length, thirteen to fourteen feet; weight, about 1,500 pounds
Maximum Measurements: Length, fifty-two to fifty-six feet; weight, 90,000 pounds
Life Span: Probably at least fifty years
Reference: National Audubon Society Guide to Marine Mammals of the World

Flag Man

Upon arrival in the Kingdom of Tonga, our first contact with a real Tongan was in the Vava'u group port of entry, Neiafu. We were rafted up to *New Dawn* awaiting the customs officials. On the dock was a tall, muscular man with large features and in need of dental work. He wanted to know if we needed a flag for Tonga. I said we had a Tongan flag, but then he wanted to know where we were going. The officials arrived, but he kept trying to get my attention as the official party boarded *New Dawn.*

Even with the boat width of *New Dawn* between us, he persisted in wanting to know if we had a flag for the next country, which would be New Zealand. I told him we did not, and at that, he wanted to sell us a flag. I was too tired for any sales transactions and told him maybe later. He wanted to know when was later, and I had to say more firmly, "Sometime, but not now." All through his disruptive dialogue, he maintained eye contact, sometimes craning his neck to see me across the two boats. The more he persisted, the more I was determined not to buy a flag that day.

We managed to get clearance into the country, and when we emerged from the cabin, he was gone.

We had been anchored in the harbor for about a week when there was a knock on the side of the boat and familiar voice said, "Hello, old friend." I recognized the voice and the hustle and went topside. There in a rowboat was the flag man. He was looking even worse for wear now that we were up close and personal, but his message was the same.

He said, "I am here to sell you your flag for New Zealand."

I told him, "I don't have any money for a flag at this time, but see me later."

A week later, another knock on the boat, this time the day before our departure south, and again it was the flag man.

We agreed to meet in the market at 1:00 p.m. for the momentous flag purchase. He did not show, and it was a relief. While we had been waiting, I asked one of our favorite vendors if he had seen the flag man. He knew immediately who I was talking about and asked one of the other vendors who spoke excellent English to talk with me. This man warned me that I was dealing with a person who spoke with four tongues—a snake. That he was not welcome in the market, as he and another person were selling things from their boats at outrageous prices—things they would buy at the market and resell. I didn't explain to him about Walmart or home delivery costs in our country. I told the vendor this fellow had missed our earlier appointment. He informed me that if he had missed an appointment, it was from too much hooch or because he was doing some public service time to keep out of jail.

Later in the day came a knock on the side of the boat, and it was him. He had the flag and presented it with a smile. He apologized for missing me at the market, something about a broken sewing needle. The flag was for the right country, but it was very poorly constructed, overlapping thread tracks, irregular-shaped stars, thin cotton fabric and no way to secure it to the boat. He had paddled out to our boat the hard way, using one oar while kneeling in the bow. The boat was sizeable, and he had come some distance.

I could not refuse the purchase on the basis of poor quality, and lucky for him I was into a book by Harvey Cox, *When Jesus Came to Harvard*. It is excellent reading, with a chapter on befriending the outcasts and those of poor social standing. The flag man is all of these and maybe more. As he paddled away with my fifty Tongan dollars, I looked at my new flag and felt okay about the whole deal.

I quietly wished him well.

Jenny to Jenny

Our genoa headsail, which we call Jenny, reminds me of a pack mule I had years ago when I was a ranger in Yellowstone Park. Her name, coincidentally, was also Jenny and, like most mules, she was very smart and sensitive, especially to her working conditions. Managing her should have been in my job description, as she always required additional time and special consideration.

As a park ranger, one of my responsibilities was to resupply the snowshoe cabins and to pack out the gear left behind by the smoke jumpers during fire season. In this endeavor, Jenny was invaluable, but if she sensed that her pack was starting to get loose or something was not quite right, she would stop on the trail and not move until it was fixed. She was very impatient, and if I didn't quickly find and correct the problem, she would shake her pack violently until stuff started flying off.

Sometimes, at the end of a long day, for no apparent reason, Jenny would decide not to get in the trailer, which then required some psychology. I would close up the trailer and pretend to drive off, leaving her to the bears and wolves. Then I'd stop and reopen the trailer, and she would almost knock me over getting in.

Just as Jenny was the horsepower over the trail, our Jenny is the horsepower over the water. We have become quite fond of our *Nereid* Jenny. It gets us where we want to go and transports all our gear. A recent sailing trip, only sixteen miles, was hard on the wind. As we struggled to stay on course, I was reminded of my problems with my four-legged Jenny. Sailing to weather means heading into the wind as closely as possible. Get too close to the wind, and Jenny begins to luff or shake. That is my warning that something is wrong, and if we continue to come into the wind, there will be a slapping and popping of the huge headsail and we will stop moving forward.

The similarities of the two Jennies are quite remarkable. Both Jennies give out unmistakable warnings when something needs fixing, whether it's the packsaddle or the sail trim. Both require immediate attention, which means a timeline of less than a minute to fix a problem. Ignore the warning of either Jenny and you are in big trouble. The Jenny of the *Nereid* would flail itself to shreds and bring the boat to a stop; the Jenny of the park service would simply destroy the pack and not move another step.

Do I have a favorite Jenny? I fully respect both girls and appreciate their sensitivities, and with both have always tried to be expedient in meeting their needs. Both are high-maintenance girls, beautifully designed for the jobs they do. But as for my favorite girl, I would have to go with the *Nereid* Jenny. She doesn't require any psychology.

Bugs

We had heard some wild stories about bugs in the tropics, and being from Alaska, we came with plenty of bug experience. Alaska experience includes mosquitoes so thick they are the lifeblood of many migratory birds. On the Arctic tundra, the new hatchlings roll their heads out of their shells and make their first meals on the swarming mosquitoes. The bugs are so thick they are the motivation for the caribou to keep moving. On fishing and hunting trips, any body parts exposed for a few seconds are targets for mosquitoes and no-see-ums. Some more aggressive individuals find their way up loose pant legs or sleeves.

So we armed ourselves with some of the finest Alaskan repellents, like musk oil, and spent considerable time and money on bug proofing the *Nereid* with screens and nettings. The screening materials are still stowed in the v-berth, and the nettings that were custom made in Mexico to cover the hatches and companionway have yet to be used. We are happy to report that we have been overly prepared in the bug department and evidently spent more time and money on this perceived problem than necessary. We have had some no-see-ums that have sought out the tender and tastier tissue of my darling, but she has always been selected before anyone else.

We did have the brief encounter described earlier with the very large invading roach and the incident with the giant centipede, but that is about it. There have been a few flies entering the cabin, but not in any great numbers; in fact, they are so infrequent that we have given them names. For example, the present occupant is named Richie after one of the bad guys in the *Sopranos*. Richie is not your average fly, but he is representative of the few that do drop in for a visit. He is very fast and almost impossible to catch with your hand or to whack with a swatter. Robert Vaughn, the aging gunslinger of *The Magnificent Seven*, would never have been able to catch Richie.

I may go for the spray, which I resorted to with another fast fly, but will need to wait for Judy to go visit someone or go shopping, as I was justly disciplined last time for using such a potent chemical in the confines of our living space.

Anyway, that just about sums up the terrible bugs in the tropics. Gotta go, Richie has just landed and it looks like I might have a shot. Later.

Night Lights

There are three sources of light during a night passage. The two light shows from above, which we are most familiar with, are the moon and the stars. The moon in its mid phases can almost turn the night into day, the stars scattered as a backdrop of constellations and galaxies; the most famous and special to the Southern Hemisphere, the Clouds of Magellan, will become old friends after some time at sea.

There is magic in the moon and the stars as our sailing ship moves quietly through the night air. But even more magical is our third light source, the mysterious bioluminescent friends in the water around us. On most of our passages, the bow wake has its own special light show of sparkling phosphorescence, which continues alongside the boat but lasts for only a few seconds. So what is going on with this in-water show? Well, as you may know, it is the work of a few species of marine organisms called dinoflagellates.

These single-celled animals are easy to identify under a microscope with their unique two flagella, one tailing behind the body providing steering while the other provides spiral propulsion, as if they had someplace to go. We know they are a major food source for the coral reefs and cause the red tides throughout the world. We also know they are converting chemical energy to light via ATP (adenosine triphosphate), the same molecule that provides our bodies with energy; but of more interest at this time is the discharge of phosphorescent light that occurs in our bow wake. What individual or collective significance have these discharges? Are these discharges a once-in-a-lifetime shot, or are these batteries rechargeable? Collectively, the discharges could be of a defensive nature. There is certainly no male-to-female posturing in this single-celled organism, which reproduces asexually, so what is the deal?

The discharge of light from these dinoflagellates is especially captivating, because the patterns and intensity are continually changing in response to the movement of the boat. These specks of bright light are as if the whole population is saying "Welcome, we are putting our lights on for you."

Whatever the reason, we are most appreciative of this display. We will take it as a greeting or communication that all is well in the dino community, and perhaps as an indicator that the marine environment on which all living things depend is doing okay.

Part 3

Down Under

Chapter 8

New Zealand

New Zealand Crossing

The 1,200-mile crossing from Tonga to New Zealand was expected to be the ultimate test of our seamanship. Cruisers study intently for the right weather window to cross this area, which historically has had some of the worst storms generated out of the Tasman Sea. We enlisted the services of a New Zealand weather guru, who found a perfect weather window that allowed us to stop for a day at Minerva Reef in quest of giant lobster.

Lobster-reef dives are a young, manly exercise that requires wearing a face mask and snorkel with a torch or flashlight in one hand while holding on with the other hand as the surf breaks over you. Coral features create a venturi effect, accelerating the rate of water flow, requiring a strong grip on the coral to keep from being dragged out to sea. Ross had arrived earlier, but the weather had forced him to skip Minerva and continue on to NZ. The weather at the reef was rough, and I found only one very large lobster, just out of reach and too big to hold onto with one hand. We decided Minerva lobstering was better left to Ross and his friends.

We departed Minerva Reef with no lobster, but we did have a nice wind of 15 to 20 knots. We were clipping along at 6 or 7 knots when I decided to do some fishing. A lovely scene—fair winds, sails full, fishing rod in its holder tolling a lure about fifty feet back. With the autopilot in charge, we were just beginning to relax when the big Penn reel, set with drag and clicker on, suddenly screamed, "Fish on, fish on," and indeed, the line was streaking out. Time to do many things: reset the drag, slow the boat but keep it sailing, take over steering from the autopilot. Judy did all this while I freed the tangled net. I played the fish up to the boat, a nice yellow fin tuna, about twenty pounds, only to watch him unhook himself and return to his friends. We would be better prepared next time. I reset the gear, and we were back to trolling at 6 knots.

We were just settling in when the reel called again with a scream, this time even faster and higher pitched. I grabbed the pole; line was flying off the reel. I cranked the drag down until I could smell the drag gear burning. I was being spooled, as they say in fishing circles. I was down to the last of my line and in desperation cranked on the drag until the eighty-pound test line, about to run out, snapped. It was either a big tuna, a billfish like a marlin, or a submarine—we will never know—but I did save my line. So keeping with our conservation policy of sustaining the ocean resources, the score was Lobsters and Big Fishes 3 - *Nereid* 0.

We did score big with our weather window and had smooth sailing all the way to New Zealand, where, reportedly, an abundance of protein sources is readily available.

Crossing with the King

About midway in our crossing, the seas became flat, and it was time to start motoring. It is a very spiritual moment to find oneself in warm sunshine on an endless flat sea of blue without movement or sound. One of the conservationists' selling points for preserving the Arctic tundra environment, and rightfully so, is its heavy silence with no sign of any other human presence. While the silence of the arctic is threatened by man's need for energy, the ocean will always be there waiting, if you are lucky enough to find its quiet times.

We took in the silence for a couple of hours, and I was about to break the effect with internal combustion when something said, "It's time for the King." Not the recently departed Tongan king, but another king that changed all of the USA and the world—that's right, Elvis. In our limited music CD collection on board, we have Elvis's thirty number-one hits. I had not yet played this album on our trip, but for some reason, this was the time. The stage was set, the amphitheater totally quiet, the audience in respectful anticipation. We began the concert with his first chart-breaking hit, the RCA single "Heartbreak Hotel." Our Bose speaker system was pushed to the edge of distortion with our old favorites "Return to Sender," "Are You Lonesome Tonight?" "Crying in the Chapel," "Don't be Cruel" and "Love Me Tender."

Elvis was indeed a special talent and followed his feelings in 1969, against his producer's warnings, with "In the Ghetto," an extremely sensitive topic at that time. He is said to have seized upon the song and sang it with passion and belief. Here's to you, Elvis—you may have left the building, but thanks for being with us this day.

After the concert, we reluctantly started our engine and recalled Elvis's words, "Ambition is a dream with a V8 engine." Our Perkins four-cylinder diesel is no V8, but it will do until the winds return.

Opua at Night

We arrived at the Bay of Islands, NZ, about 6:30 p.m. Entering the bay, we could not raise anyone on the VHF and had no indication of where Opua was in this maze of islands. We expected to find channel markers and lights, but there was nothing as darkness settled in. We finally raised someone on the VHF from Opua but received no clear directions; we at last arrived at the harbor about 8:30 p.m. It was too dark to search out the Q, or quarantine dock, and there were still no clear directions, so we pulled into a vacant slip at someplace called the Commercial Moorings Boat Rental.

We planned to start out early the next morning to find the Q dock and check in. During the night, something was slamming against the side of the boat, and I assumed we had picked up something in our evening escapade. The next morning, I located a diver to check under the boat, as the water was too fouled for my gear setup. He found nothing, but the customs people found us, and we were scolded for not finding the Q dock in the night. Anyway, we apologized several times to the customs lady and promised not to do it again. She remained very stern, and we were given a written warning of some consequence that I didn't understand or inquire about. We signed the statement and were then freed to explore this new land of the Kiwis.

Our passage from Tonga to Opua, New Zealand, with an overnight stop at Minerva Reef, took us eight days. The real news is that our son Ross had an appendicitis attack two days after his arrival here and is now recovering in the hospital in Whangarei, about forty-five kilometers south. He is doing well and we are all feeling very thankful this did not occur while he was at sea. Good timing, as there are excellent doctors and facilities here. He told me earlier he planned to lighten his boat, but I had no idea.

We mean to leave our boat here for the season and fly to SF on the sixth of December. NZ is a beautiful place, and except for the customs lady, the people are very hospitable.

Rugby, A Man's Game

"Rugby is real football the way it was meant to be played, without the body armor you Yanks have when you play."

This has been the theme since we entered New Zealand and Australian waters. You almost have to apologize before entering into any discussion of the subject. We have had the opportunity on many occasions to observe and study this spectacle of human sacrifice. On the most recent occasion—when I was, as usual, the only Yank in an appropriate atmosphere of free beer—I reached my limit on condescending and derogatory comments regarding the sissy way Americans play the game. It was a liberating moment for me, and I am surprised it took me so long to step up to the plate. I had tried earlier in our travels to make the comparison between baseball and cricket, but that was never very effective, because I still don't understand what is going on with the cricketers.

Rugby is entertaining, especially if that is the only sporting event on the "tellie," but it's just the opposite to cricket in complexity. Rugby is a bunch of beefy boys pushing each other around and with few interruptions or time for commercial breaks. There is no need to stop play or plan anything. The idea is just to push the other team back until the ball is over their goal line. There is no huddle; the closest analog is the scrum, where both teams assemble all their players and push against each other until at one end or the other the football appears and someone picks it up and starts running with it. The person with the ball runs straight at the opposing player, but the critical point of this game is to hand off the ball to a teammate just before being tackled. He will do the same, and if all goes well, he scores a goal. It doesn't get any more complicated than that, except some fellows like to run into opposing players and, if tackled, just get up and roll the ball on the ground between their legs to a teammate behind them.

There is no such thing as a forward pass, which is a difficult hand-eye-coordinated effort in which the ball is thrown to the outstretched arms of a teammate running full speed; a forward pass can cover the field in one play or be intercepted and cover the field in the other direction. There's nothing this exciting in rugby—just pound it out with handoffs to the guy beside you. There is no need to have a break in the action, because there just aren't that many things you can do. The huddle in rugby would consist of "I am going to run, and just before he tackles me, I will hand off the ball." In a combination run-pass game of American football, you need to have a plan for each play or you'll get creamed.

When the weather is bad—rain and a sloppy field—the "ruggers" wallowing in the mud until it becomes difficult to tell the two teams apart. There are some hard hits in either game. If you wear body armor, not only can you hit harder but you also get hit harder, and that unfortunately is why there are so many permanent injuries in the armored game. In both games the knees are exposed, but they are more vulnerable from the armored hit. Football, like rugby, is a vicious game, played by those who like to hit and can take a hit, kind of like the gladiators in the Coliseum but without the fans casting their votes to determine who gets to play another day. The Aztecs played a serious game of ball; the captain of the losing team lost his head. We are evolving into a less violent people. That's why my discussion last evening ended peacefully.

Return to Kiwi Land

After experiencing the SF Bay Area winter season, we have returned to New Zealand to catch the start of another winter season. Having escaped with our lives, we are glad to be back, although we miss the kids and are still missing some poundage. After Judy's bout with pneumonia, she is down twenty-six pounds to my eight pounds, so we are still regrouping for the adventure ahead. She would like about eighteen more pounds, and we will get this back with the physical exercise which comes with preparing the boat.

Cruising is an activity for gaining weight if you need some and losing it if you have some extra. There should be a standard weight gain/loss table based on length of passage, a more exciting option than programs that leave you sitting around looking at food you can't eat.

We love the New Zealanders' accent and creativity with the English language. They say they love our accent, which I didn't realize we had. You are a "mate'" when they like you and it's "'good on you'" when you do something good and kids are "littlies." Judy's favorite term is "sweet as." I like to apply the Peter Sellers French treatment of "does your dog bite" to some phrases. If there is agreement going on in conversations, you will periodically hear "yeeeah, yeeeah" and sometimes get "yip, yip, yip, yeeah, yeeah." This is really a confirmation that you are on track with their line of thinking. If concluded with a "good on you," there is your day and you did well.

We arrived with only a short list of things to do and see, which included a visit to the 1,500-year-old kauri trees (the size of redwoods), scuba diving the sunken *Rainbow Warrior*, visiting the historic town of Russell, and observing real kiwis in their natural habitat. I am reliving my fly-fishing experiences through Ross and his friends, who are hiking the back trails of the South Island in quest of record size rainbow and brown trout.

Ross and I jump started my seventieth birthday with a dive off the Sky Tower in Auckland, supposedly the highest legal jump in NZ at 192 meters. It wasn't a free-falling bungee jump, as a line controlled us to keep us from wiping off the tower windows on our way down. It was still exciting, especially that first trusting step off the ramp into space. What to do next year to top this is the big question.

Note: Peter Sellers and a French treatment of the New Zealanders' voice may not be a stretch when you realize Kiwis have forever been surrounded by French-speaking islanders.

"On the Hard"

We spent two months in New Zealand living on our boat in Ashby's Boat Yard, or as boaters say, "on the hard."

Life on the hard in a boat yard has some advantages. There is no movement from the tidal flux, changing wind conditions or boat traffic. Instead, you are greeted every morning with the white noise of someone sanding. It's a sound similar to rubbing your hands together, and in the boat yard, it is always going on. It can be a pleasant sound, knowing work is being done somewhere by someone, but it's also a gentle reminder that there is work to do on your own boat.

Access to your boat on the hard is via a ladder secured to the deck rail. Climbing the ladder is good physical conditioning, and placing your feet properly on the ladder is a good coordination exercise. Extra care was required each morning as I descended the ladder to ground level with a bucket of materials collected during the night. It was always my concern that one slip could bring me down, with the bucket's contents meeting me at the end of my fall. I always knew that if I started to fall, my first order of business would be to jettison the bucket as far as possible from the impending crash zone. I am happy to report that this contingency measure was never implemented.

Upon a successful arrival at ground zero, it was always a moment of truth walking with the bucket, a long hundred yards to the designated dump site. I seldom made this trip before the boat yard was active with workers. While I tried to make the most of my journey by greeting others, I knew they were aware of my bucket.

The only other hazard to yard life is the remote possibility of your boat falling off the supporting jack stands. During a record rainfall of seventeen inches in twenty-four hours, there was in the night a loud crashing sound. I sprang from by bed to see what was the matter and noticed nothing, then sprang back into bed with the news to Judy that nothing serious had happened. It wasn't until the next morning that Judy said to me, "Raymond, what is this?" Her addressing me as Raymond and standing in the cockpit with hands on her hips—these are not good signs. I looked out, and wow; the sixty-foot Italian yacht placed diagonally from our boat had fallen over and just missed the *Nereid*. It was now lying on its side like a beached whale. Not a pretty sight. I immediately amended my report.

Life on the hard is not hard if you are careful, watch your step and make accurate observations.

New Zealand: Goodbye

New Zealand was great, and we will miss many things and new friends. We had not planned to do much except work on the boat, but we did accomplish a few select activities. We visited a grove of ancient kauri trees. These majestic forest sentinels, over fifty feet in diameter, have huge upper limbs supporting tangled canopies. They are much like the redwoods, with the same spiritual presence.

We were also lucky enough to observe New Zealand's national bird, the kiwi, in its natural forest habitat. Kiwis are flightless and thus lead a very secretive life. They feed only at night, poking their long beaks into the soft forest duff and, with the keen olfactory sense at the end of their beak, sniffing out the creepy crawlers. It is rare to sight these birds in their natural habitat, and most observers have to settle for sightings at the zoo.

Another goal was to dive the wreck of the *Rainbow Warrior*, which rests in about eighty feet of clear water off the coast of the Bay of Islands. A special French military team sank this hapless warrior to silence its protesting French nuclear testing in the Pacific. Ross and I did this dive with four others and a guide. The ship rests upright on the sea floor and is still protecting the environment, serving as a habitat for the multitude of invertebrates and huge schools of fish moving in tight synchronous formations.

The historic town of Russell was on our list, and we checked it off with our dinghy as an excuse to put some time on our new fifteen-hp Yamaha outboard. Russell is around the corner and across the bay from Opua, about fifteen miles. Judy and I made the trip easily. We spent the afternoon having lunch and visiting the shops and tourist attractions. The waters stayed calm, and we sped home in record time and didn't get a drop on us.

We will miss the delicious meat pies for lunch, honey-cured bacon for breakfast, apple turnovers, raspberry crumbles (Pink Ladies), homemade jellies from the school bazaar, sausage and onion sandwiches and the two-teabag mornings just sitting in the cockpit, planning to do something.

There are many new friends we will probably never see again. Goodbye Axel, David, Shirley, Bruce and Chris, Jackie and Bryan, Sylvia and Doug, Cynthia and Tim, and good luck to Bruce, who is planning to single-hand it across the roaring forties to Peru. Also goodbye Neil, Don and Barb, and many of those we sailed with across the Pacific: Ross and Ed on *Kabuki*, the Lawur family now in Austria, Toya and Steve on *Cheers*, *Ohana Kai*, *Moorea*, *Monkeys Business*, *Kapaz*, *Arctic Fox*, David on *LaVie*, Barry and Karyn on *Sarabi* and Paddy and Alison on *Zafarse*. It was fun.

We will also miss the New Zealand politics. There was a big debate on Veterans Day as to whether the soldiers marching in the parade to honor the vets should carry real or wooden guns. You can easily lose touch with reality down here, and maybe that is good...sometimes. I suppose if they get in another real jam, we are just an ocean away.

An Aussie cruiser was complaining, "It took you long enough to get here last time."

I said, "We kept thinking you could handle it, at least until we cleaned up some more immediate concerns. But then again, if your soldiers only have wooden guns...I understand."

Chapter 9

New Caledonia

Fast Passage to New Caledonia

Finding a weather window to leave NZ was challenging and depended on the sequence of high-pressure systems coming off Australia that move east across the Coral Sea. In the Southern Hemisphere, the highs circulate counterclockwise, so you try to catch the beginning of a new high for its SW winds and get to your destination before the NW component catches you.

The weather can change quickly, and for this reason we enlisted several weather experts to help us plan our departure. These included (1) Bob McDavitt, a local NZ weatherman; (2) Commander, a NY-based worldwide weather service; (3) grib files; (4) Bouyweather, a system of worldwide weather buoys and satellites; and (5) Des, NZ weatherman on Russell Radio. Three of the five sources said to go for it, and two said to hold for another week. We realized we had too many experts for a consensus, so we decided to go and headed out with *New Dawn* and *Cheers*. They were making for Fiji.

Our weather planning to New Zealand had been easy, with only one professional forecaster and the grib files. Now, with five forecasting sources, we got hit hard and ended up doing a record run averaging 145 miles per day, reaching New Caledonia in five days. The 860-mile passage to New Caledonia should take over six days for a forty-foot sailing vessel like the *Nereid*.

There were some exciting moments, sometimes with a triple-reefed main and staysail still doing 7 to 8 knots. Our first day at sea was normal, with winds from the SW at 15 to 20 knots. However, day two the situation began to change, and by midday and the next two days we were skating down the swells at 8 knots with 35- and 40-knot winds. Day four, we went all night under full sail, hoping to arrive at Noumea in the daylight.

The *Nereid* was designed for these higher wind conditions, and we have always felt safe. There were a few rogue waves that spilled over into the cockpit, but nothing serious. In winds like this, it's like the sails are out of a plaster mold; they seem to change from a flexible fabric to a solid state. Sail design and construction is an art, and Carrol Hasse, our Port Townsend sail maker, is an artist.

There was one unusual incident on our third night. The boat moving smoothly, under autopilot and no ships in sight, I settled into the cabin for some much-needed rest.

I was asleep when Judy woke me, saying, "There is something strange going on and you need to check it out."

The wind was blowing hard, but we were not moving.

I started up the companionway, but Judy grabbed my arm and with eyes larger than usual said, "There is something out there. I can hear it breathing."

I slowly poked my head out of the cabin, and sure enough, there was a heavy breathing sound and the boat was not moving. My first thought, I admit, entertained the possibility of sea monsters, but then I noticed the headsail was back winded and the monitor was trying to hold the course for a net gain of zero, or in sailing terms, we were hove-to.

As for the heavy breathing, we still don't have a good answer, but to quote another weatherman, Jerry Seinfeld, "I heard something."

"He Is Coming in Again"

Upon finding the entrance, through the reef, to Nouméa's Port Moselle, New Caledonia, we were very tired but pleased that we had made our passage in record time. After congratulations all around and our usual celebratory Coca-Cola, and with several miles to go inside the reef, we decided to do some housekeeping. Judy went below to put stuff away and I began cleaning up the array of lines strewn about the cockpit from a very busy night of sailing. With Monty, our trusty wind vane, still in charge, I started to sort out the main sheet.

I was totally preoccupied with this exercise when Judy popped her head up out of the companionway and said, "It seems like we have changed direction."

I looked around, and wow! We had taken a ninety-degree turn and were headed for a large sandbar. There was just time to alter course, and I decided to pay more attention to where we should be going.

When we arrived at the marina, I called on the radio and was assigned slip B29, an easy number to remember for a WWII buff. There was a readily accessible visitors' dock, but I wanted to complete this journey to our assigned slip and get some rest. We motored around some but couldn't find B29, so I dropped Judy off on the visitors' dock, whereupon she found the slip and waved me in.

The rest is a little hazy, but I remember entering the slip. Judy securing the bow line. My throw of the stern line to her was short and fell into the water. The wind had picked up to over 20 knots off the port beam, blowing the *Nereid* off the dock and toward another yacht, the *Phoenix*, tied downwind of the slip. I backed up to the crashing sound of the *Nereid* meeting the *Phoenix*. There were several people on the dock, and of course this slip was in full view of the restaurant, which was packed with patrons on a Saturday afternoon. I understand the skipper of the *Phoenix* was shouting obscenities, and poor Judy at his side was apologizing and saying, "We have a new Yamaha 15 for you."

I can't blame it totally on the wind, and I knew my prop walk was also against me. I had a couple of feet still up on the mainsail, which didn't help, and my monitor steering rudder was still in the water, making maneuvering slightly less precise.

It was these next few moments that we would continue to discuss for some time—I decided to try again.

With terror in his voice, the owner of the *Phoenix* yelled, "Oh my God, he is coming in again!"

He was not the only one in shock. One of the other yachties that had come to help ran back to his boat, not wanting any part of this mad skipper from Alaska.

I can still hear Judy's screams and some of the remaining help offered. "Go to the visitors' dock! Go to the visitors' dock!"

Undaunted, I came in again, and once again, the wind moved me off and I had to back out, just clearing the *Phoenix*. No damage this time. I decided to give it up and, after several attempts, with the wind against me, made our landing at the visitors' dock. There were three camps at the dock, those that looked at me circumspectly and curiously, one angry person, and several who were sympathetic. The wife of the *Phoenix*'s skipper handed me not one but two cold, adult beverages.

Damage to the *Phoenix* amounted to a broken outboard engine rail mount and a broken fiberglass man-overboard rod, both replaced for $340.

However, I still wake up in the night, and if Judy is awake I ask, "Did I really go in again after I hit him the first time?"

She gives me the same quiet smile and says, "Yes, you were very tired."

French Desserts and Visual Treats

New Caledonia is very French; it even has the sirens of Inspector Clouseau going somewhere. A baby was crying in the boat next to us, and several boats away, people were laughing. Crying and laughter in French sound just the same as in English. A smile and greeting with a nod of the head is another universal communication. The temperature here is in the high 70s and it rains periodically on everyone, and physiologically our bodies all require the same conditions for comfort and survival. Aside from all this, everyone has similar hopes and dreams, which puts us all in the same boat.

Port Moselle has an excellent market from 5 a.m. to noon located a short walk from the marina. There is a great standup breakfast/lunch bar where David and Jaunine will serve you, always with a smile. We have our favorite vendors, and as return customers, they have begun to give us advice on the better selection of their fruits and vegetables.

Today, our lady selling papayas took Judy's selection out of her hand and chose another, saying, "Ready now—better."

And a little man with a bad eye is our banana expert. Some relationship building is the key to the joy of this cruising adventure, probably what it used to be like in the USA before the big box stores.

We go outside the market, to the Latin Quarter of Nouméa, for our baked goods. The French are masters of dessert making and we have had some fantastic pastries, cookies and candies. They have done wonderful things with raspberries, chocolate, lemon and many new flavors difficult to describe. These gems are not cheap, about five dollars each. The cookies need to be refrigerated and eaten slightly chilled, so timing, as in most things, is important. We have spent most of our restaurant budget on pastries, and last night, after an episode of *Boston Legal*, Judy pulled out of our frig the two desserts we had selected earlier that day. It was an eating experience to end all.

We have done some restauranting, but the French have a run for their money when it comes to the main food dishes found on the *Nereid* table. We have tried some French fast-food versions of crepes. They had a big write-up by Lonely Planet, but fast food still tasted like fast food. And there is the ultimate disappointment, those golden arches, a short walk from the marina. McDonalds is alive and well in New Caledonia, and any evening there are multiple registers going with lines six deep, plus a busy drive-through. The biggest treat is the kids behind the counter who are working on speaking English. Yes, we have been there.

Last but not least, we have noticed a very different sexual culture. Our first clue was, when checking into the marina, we were given one key for a common door to both male and female bathrooms. Good enough, but once inside you can be heading for a sit-down and to your right is a lady combing her hair at the mirror in the ladies' part. Families can be found on either side, showering together.

On our trip to the beach, we were enjoying the sun and the view when the lady beside me took off her top and lay back for some tanning. This exposure to our right was matched a few minutes later on our left.

Judy reminded me, "A brief glance would be more appropriate than a fixed stare."

I now tried to concentrate more on the view offshore. It was to my amazement that the distant swimmer in the bay decided to come ashore, and as she stepped out of the water in front of us, yes, again—no top. I was momentarily surrounded...my goodness.

One can't be too careful in this relaxed sexual world. The other day, at a store, we were shopping for Band-Aids. I found them and called Judy over, as there were too many choices. There were boxes with Superman, Winnie the Pooh, the Gingerbread Man, two dolphins and about ten other colorful choices. Judy, who had the hurt finger, selected the dolphins. When we got back to the boat, to our amazement, the box of dolphins was really a box of twelve neatly packaged items to prevent two dolphins from adding a third. I didn't feel like trying to explain to the clerk, who spoke very little English, why I was returning them.

The box with Superman turned out to be Band-Aids. Go figure.

Chapter 10

Australia

Bird on the Boom

"Oh look, see the bird on the boom, I think he is sleeping; we must be quiet and not wake him."

These were some of the comments upon discovering our passenger perched on the boom. Even though we were traveling at 7 knots, he was able to put his head under his wing and adjust to the shifting movement of the boat. We watched him through the hatch over the galley, and what a fine sight to see. We had been at sea for eight days out of New Caledonia, and he was a welcome addition to our passage. We watched him all through the night as we did our shifts, and at early light he was awake, doing some preening and getting ready for his day. Identification was now possible and it looked like we had a red-footed booby. Poor name for these hell divers that can plunge into the water from straight overhead with such force it should rip their wings off.

Well, it was a short friendship; we said our goodbyes and watched him fly off to begin his day. What a treat—but wait, what is this? Oh my goodness, he had left behind about three pounds of white plaster, painted all over our Mediterranean-blue bimini. It must have been half of his body weight, obviously a big eater, and the smell, oh yes, there is nothing like the remains of digested seafood. We scrubbed and scrubbed with some of the strongest cleaners, but we will always have a sizeable remembrance of our night visitor.

We were just about back into our routine by late afternoon, when who should come circling in for a landing; he was early, and this time he brought a friend. He had obviously touted the great rest he had the night before with the nice people, and his friend wanted some of that action. They were determined to land somewhere on the boat. This time I was ready with shouts and clapping hands, but to no avail. They circled, swooped, made touch-and-go landings on the spreaders, the top of the mast and the bow, and they looked fully loaded from a fine day of fishing. They had plenty in store for us.

The war was on. They were Hitchcock birds, and the challenge was "who controlled this boat." They took to the spreaders, and I released a spinnaker halyard that swept them off. They tried for the top of the mast, and the wind gauge did double duty in keeping them at bay. Next came the dive-bomber sorties to the bow, circling, and to the stern. I decided to arm. I had to arm. Out came the heavy artillery, oh yes—we carry a Wham-O slingshot loaded with popcorn kernels and split peas. I didn't ruffle a single feather, but the message was clear: no parking here tonight. After about thirty minutes of combat, they flew off, and it was over.

Those of you who are thinking I was selfish with our space and should be more accommodating (Donna), please remember these guys can sleep anywhere, including on the water—their normal habitat—and besides, some serious illnesses are associated with their nightly abstract art projects.

Breasts, Thighs and Small Dinghies

We were a thousand miles out of New Caledonia on our way to Darwin, Australia, a trip of about 2,100 miles, when on day ten our starter battery failed (July 2, 2007). It would not hold a charge, and even though I could jumpstart it from the house batteries, it was a routine that did not lend itself to the upcoming maneuvers through the Great Barrier Reef, where power on demand can be essential.

I checked the chart. We had a perfect wind angle for a run to the nearest port of Cairns, Australia, about 200 miles away. The GBR was just getting started at that southerly point, so we could handle that amount of maneuvering in our present condition. After checking in with customs on our satellite phone, they granted us an exception to the required "ninety-six-hour notice of arrival." When we dropped anchor, we faced a four-hour thorough inspection and questioning, complete with a dog sniffing everywhere and everything.

Three different officials said, "I am going to check your chain locker now." Each time, they watched my reaction to their statement closely.

Near the end of the process, I took Judy aside and asked her, "Do I look like Keith Richards?"

As the inspection party disembarked, having found nothing of interest, they seemed disappointed and we felt guilty of something. Maybe we were drug dealers and didn't even know it.

Cairns is a modern city set to handle masses of tourists. At least one Boeing 747 arrives each day and unloads the masses. It is also Australia's Fort Lauderdale and was packed with college kids on a two-week spring break. In the crowded city beach/park, there were some exposed female upper-body parts, a surprising touch of New Caledonia. Also not to be ignored were thousands of noisy lorikeets that filled the trees along the walkway to and from our boat.

These high-energy birds, with a diet of pollen and nectar, sleep only four hours per day. Just the opposite is the koala bear, which eats only low-energy eucalyptus leaves and can stay awake a mere four hours per day. Cairns is also a city of very happy Australians who speak our language. They like to add an "ie" to many words, like "littlies," "sunnies" and "footies," and the lexicon contains plenty of new stuff, like "scroll" for cinnamon roll and "slab" for a case of beer.

The Aboriginal culture has been fine tuned for the tourist. We traveled to the Kuranda National Park via train and returned over the top of the rain forest via skyrail, very impressive. We saw Aboriginal dancers perform and learned to throw a boomerang, and yes, they do come back, and yes, there are both left-handed and right-handed models.

We petted some kangaroos and I played a didgeridoo, which was made from a large eucalyptus limb hollowed out by termites. We did a GBR dive; Judy had a great snorkeling experience, and my dive with tanks was okay. Maybe I was jaded from too many reef dives. We did see a turtle asleep at sixty feet, and a minke whale cruised the dive boat. The dive boats are huge; ours held fifty people, and it was one of the smaller catamarans in the fleet, which traveled 35 knots to and from the outer reef site.

We explored the nightlife with two new Australian cruiser friends, Ian and Wendy. Ian surprised us one evening with a piece of meat to add to our dinner that he referred to as "skippy." It would have been better if sampled before the petting zoo. We also had several

$4.50 lunches at Rusty's Market, followed by a $12 dessert from Beethoven's, a German bakery.

We watched a serious rugby match outside on a large-screen TV. It was like our Super Bowl, only between New South Wales and Queensland, a long-time rivalry. Rugby is a rough contact sport without pads, but what everybody did have were well-developed thighs. There is a preponderance of thigh development in this country.

We spent time in the museum and were especially impressed with the huge saltwater crocodile, Jack the Ripper. The record, presently at eighteen feet and 2,600 pounds, belongs to Sweetie Pie, a name he earned by tipping over small boats which had something good inside to eat. It was not uncommon to see people packed into small dinghies with only a couple of inches of freeboard on their way to boats moored across the channel. I guess they hadn't seen or heard about Jack or Sweetie Pie.

We got our battery replaced and purchased some other items. Cairns provided an overload of sensory input and we became the quintessential tourists. We met some wonderfully colorful people and had a great time, but about all to be remembered will be the breasts, thighs and small dinghies.

Lizard Island

We did a record-setting 150 miles from Cairns to Lizard Island in twenty-four hours, sailing all night with high winds in the restricted inside passage, a feat that required too much energy to repeat. This next 300 miles will take about four days, with a couple of rest stops along the way.

Tomorrow at 2:00 p.m. we will leave Lizard Island, where we have been weathered in for the last seven days by 40-knot winds. Like Captain Cook in 1770, we climbed the highest peak, now named Cook's Look, and observed the breaks in the outer Great Barrier Reef. He, too, was trapped here for some time, and from this mountain he saw his way out of the reef to the open sea. We will follow his route out past the reef but will reenter at Raine Island and pick our way through the reef to Horn and Thursday islands. It's about 750 miles to Darwin from there.

Cook named this island for its large lizards, and today there are eleven species present, including the large sand goannas, the Australian version of the monitor lizard. The largest we saw was about four feet. They don't hunt humans, but they took their time deciding if they wanted to get off the trail to let us pass. When they did walk away, it was a very deliberate movement, like they were muscle bound with an attitude, and with each step out came their tongues, which added another foot in length.

Speaking of muscle, there's an exclusive four-star resort here, and they let the yachties—as we are called— watch the football games on the giant-screen TV at the employees' beach club. We had the good fortune to see the tri-nation championship rugby game between the New Zealand All Blacks and the Australian Wallabies. NZ won, and I think it was primarily because of their pregame warm-up called the haka. It is a Maori tribal dance intended to warn potential enemies to stay away. These well-developed, very large people stomped, yelled and made faces with such synchronized and ferocious energy that I was surprised it didn't trigger a forfeit by the opposing team and a refund to the 30,000 screaming crazies. They have had to tone it down some, so this haka was without the throat-cutting gestures. Primal stuff.

There is also a privately funded marine research laboratory on Lizard Island. Believe it or not, they are still finding new species every year in this coralline biome. We were given a tour that brought back fond memories of our two years at the USC marine laboratory on Catalina Island. The researchers at the Lizard Island facility are very productive, with many scientific papers and graduate degrees forthcoming each year.

We were holed up here with ten other boats, the largest an eighty-five-foot power boat, *Restless M,* on which Claire and Erro hosted a party the evening before our departure. We were the only Yanks; the rest were Kiwis, Aussies and Germans. The host boat was quite a showpiece and came with a baby grand piano that made for a grand party. We will miss all of these new friends and are now thankful the weather sent us to Lizard Island and kept us here so we could get to know each other. It's been great; plus, when we arrived, Judy started a 900-page tome, *This Much I Know Is True*, which she has just finished, and she is now sitting teary eyed. So it's definitely time to go.

One Tree and Two Leaf Blowers

We were quietly relaxing at Morris Island with its solitary palm tree and sandy beach after a grueling seventeen hours of hand steering. Our trusty Monitor autopilot was sideswiped by a minke whale that had been cavorting around the *Nereid.* We were sixty miles out of Lizard Island on our way to Darwin when it happened, so once again it was time to set a new course, this time to repair the Monitor, which brought us back inside the GBR to Morris Island. We had the island to ourselves, and after the repair, both of us were relaxing. I was dozing in the cockpit when I heard a deep rumbling sound like heavy equipment. The silence was broken by what turned out to be the hundred-plus-foot motor yacht *The Huntress* dropping anchor only 200 feet away.

The Huntress is power everything, but with the engines shut down and the anchor chain having rattled through the windlass and anchor set, it should have been quiet now… Not! Next was the sound of a generator, like the hum of the turbines in a hydroelectric plant, accompanied by great activity. The crew began washing down the deck and topsides. When finished, they launched two inflatables, each with fifty-horse outboards that motored around the mother ship to continue the washing. Launching the smaller vessels, each with their own power winch, set off a new noise.

Cleaning was not over until the crew had gone around the deck with what sounded like leaf blowers. I don't know why, maybe to blow dry some components of the ship? Very noisy and definably a leaf blower sound here; the other sounds were harder to describe. Leaf blower I definitely recognized. Two leaf blowers and only one tree on the island should be some kind of record. After about an hour of this, there was just the hum of the generator. Of course, all this noise brought with it great conveniences for them. I imagine if they wanted to clean themselves up after all this boat cleaning, they would just get in a shower and turn on the hot and cold water.

On the *Nereid* we do sacrifice some basic conveniences, so let me run through my shower routine, which I had just completed before the arrival of *The Huntress*. First, since we have a limited freshwater supply, I used our water maker to make my shower water. This requires pulling up a floorboard, opening a seacock, removing companionway steps to access the engine room, turning on the high-pressure and lift pumps, purging the system for fifteen minutes, checking the water quality with a meter and collecting the water in a bucket placed in the galley sink. The water maker produces eight gallons per hour, and I collected four gallons. It all took about forty-five minutes, counting the purge.

While this was going on, I smartly heated some of this water on the stove to add to the new water, which only comes at the temperature of the sea around us. After replacing the steps to the companionway, I carried the bucket of new water from the sink to the cockpit. I won't go into the shutdown procedure for the water maker. Now in the cockpit with the bucket of warm water, I poured half of it into another bucket for rinsing, a very important step.

That's about it in a nutshell, so while *The Huntress* people may have spent less time in the shower-preparation process, they needed that time to wash their boat. There's only so much time in the day, so we can spend it preparing our shower water or cleaning the boat.

Between *The Huntress* and the *Nereid,* there is one major difference—we have a lot more quiet time.

Go Deep! Go Deep!

We were now doing what is called "day hopping" through the Great Barrier Reef, sailing during daylight hours and anchoring at night. We had left Portland Roads and its happy residents after a great party the night before. With two hours of daylight remaining, we were rounding Rodney Island into Shelborne Bay. Judy was at the wheel.

"The depth gauge says three feet before we hit bottom!" she yelled.

"Not to worry," I calmly assured her, "it must be recalibrating."

Then I saw the slurry of resuspended mud behind the boat. This was not a good sign. I said something else, but mostly I remember Judy yelling.

"What should I do? What should I do?"

Instinctively drawing upon my sandlot football experience, I said, "Go deep! Go deep!"

Which she did, and in a short minute, the depth was reading ten feet.

The *Nereid* with her fixed keel, requires six feet of water and with her eleven tons was not to be denied, so we had evidently plowed a three-foot furrow along the ocean floor. It was fortunate the mud was soft, as we were not aware of our plowing at the time. I rechecked the chart and the *Lucas Cruising Guide*. While Shelborne Bay is shallow, there was no indication of the shallowness at the head of the island. There was one sentence in the Lucas book which said, "Move in carefully as the area is poorly surveyed," so I suppose that covered it.

We motored out and then made another approach into the bay. The wind was building and the whole area was deserted. It felt like a bad idea, but it was either head back out to sea and do the GBR channel at night or anchor somewhere. We had passed an anchorage ten miles earlier where some fishing boats were holed up, but we had promised we would meet another boat here, *Trudel*. They were behind us and running out of daylight, so they were probably safely anchored with the fisherman we had passed earlier and eating shrimp.

We dropped the anchor in ten feet of water, and with the wind gusting to 30 knots, we put out 150 feet of chain—we were not going anywhere. We were about a hundred miles from the tip of Australia in Queensland, and in the bay, there were no lights onshore nor any sign of life. Shelborne Bay seemed like a very hostile place when we arrived, but the next morning was a new day. Sun shining, anchor holding nicely, perfect temperature, there was not a sign of another boat or any activity on land and it was oh so quiet, much like the Arctic tundra.

In Alaska, part of my job was to ask the people what they appreciated most about the Arctic. It took a moment for some to identify its unique quality, aside from the endless ice and snow—the solitude and quietness of such a vast area. Shelborne Bay had the same solitude and quietness that morning. We just sat in the cockpit, ever so grateful to be here and enjoying the moment. After a breakfast of eggs, bacon, grits, yogurt and several cups of tea, we headed out again, ever aware the only constant was change and it could go from good to bad rather quickly. But when it was good, it was so very good.

Top of My Game

After leaving New Caledonia and contending with a minke whale, dead batteries, and wide-ranging weather conditions, we finally arrived at Horne Island, which is the northern-most point of Australia, with Darwin about 300 miles farther west. Upon arrival at Horne, we found not a single boat and no designated anchorage, so the choice of where to anchor was mine.

After we anchored, several other boats arrived and assumed we knew what we were doing and anchored near us. Also with this default leadership position came the assumption that we knew everything about the area. In other words, we were now answering questions instead of asking them.

We took this responsibility seriously enough to be the first to launch our dinghy, and with our new outboard we had enough power to take another couple with us across the channel to Thursday Island for check-in with Australian Customs and to purchase supplies. The crossing, about one mile, could be rough as the weather often quickly changed. The only warning to boaters was not to throw food scraps overboard or swim in the waters, which were loaded with saltwater crocs.

After a few days and still basking in my new role as all-knowing cruising captain, we headed out for Darwin. Two other boats departed with us and followed our every move as we navigated through the channel. In the relatively open sea, about sixty miles out, we came upon a large buoy indicating a shoal area, something to be avoided. In brief, I had underestimated the current and distance, and following some wind changeups, the *Nereid* whacked the buoy and shattered the aft port rub rail, a piece of teak along the hull intended to fend off such intrusions. The rail shattered and the buoy was fine, but the worst was yet to come. While I was lucky and the other cruiser boats did not see or hear the incident, it was apparent to my first mate that the captain had screwed up.

We were past the buoy, and after a damage assessment ensuring there were no leaks or cracks in the hull, there came a barrage of absolutes. "You always… You never... Why did you…" All statements that went unanswered or were never intended to be answered. The epaulets I had earned at the top of my game at Horne Island were ripped off and thrown into the sea. Like government service where one was only as good as his last memo, I had gone from magnificent captain to galley slave in minutes.

It would take some time to rebuild confidence and some study to reassess the challenges ahead. We were lucky; it could have been much worse. One thing was for sure: there was a new summit for the top of my game, and as they say here in Oz when everything is under control, "no worries."

Sensory Realignment

Cruising, with all of its obvious pros and cons, has some interesting side effects worth mentioning. These effects are best noted after being at sea for eight or nine days. During a passage, one's senses become refined or realigned. In the open sea, uninterrupted by the activities and intrusions of shore life, there is a quieting of the senses and a chance to refocus.

On our recent passage from New Caledonia to Darwin, there were some quiet times, and we played cards in the cockpit to pass the hours and interact in a somewhat competitive manner.

For the first time, I noticed the faces on our standard Bicycle deck of playing cards. The queens, for example, all had slightly different expressions, suggesting personality differences. In this case, the Queen of Spades had an obviously seductive smile. This insight added a new dimension to the game, as I was now glad to see her when she showed up in my hand and sorry when she was discarded.

This refocus of my senses to a finer level was now set and vulnerable to overload upon arrival in port. We arrived at Fannie Bay and took the dinghy into the yacht club on what happened to be a Friday evening. There is a great restaurant associated with the yacht club that is very popular, and on a Friday night it was packed with all shapes and sizes of people. The food and drink were flowing, and a live quartet was blasting out tunes of the '60s. It was an instant shock, and the tendency was to overindulge ourselves in celebration of our passage and in response to our refocused senses.

Also, while at sea, there was time to refocus our thoughts and read material we might not read otherwise. In previous notes, I have thanked Elizabeth I for saving England and Churchill for saving the world. After reading the book *Sea of Glory*, a naval history of the American Revolution by Nathan Miller, I need to extend another thanks. In 1781, George Washington, commander-in-chief, had all but given up. After years of struggle, he had about resigned himself to a new flag with a Union Jack in the corner instead of the thirteen stars. With no supplies, no money and men deserting his army, it was about over when France arrived with thirty-two ships of the line. The French fleet, commanded by DeGrasse, outmaneuvered the British fleet under Rodney to block Cornwallis and his supply route, forcing Cornwallis to surrender.

I thanked a fellow cruiser from France, Philippe, and after my detailed explanation, he thought for a moment.

"Well, Ray," he said quietly, "you know it wasn't so much that we wanted your independence—we just hated the English."

I guess that is the way with most armed interventions; nothing has changed. What has changed is my new appreciation for the French. Thank you, and *vive la France*.

Darwin Passage (Summary)

It was a wild and crazy ride, but we finally arrived in Darwin. Our original plan was overly ambitious for the 2,100-mile crossing, with only one stop planned at Thursday Island, but it would not have been our longest passage. The longest to date was from Mexico, to the Marquesas, which was 2,800 miles and took twenty-four days. Comparatively, the run from Mexico was uneventful.

We were nine days and 960 miles out of New Caledonia, almost halfway, when our starter battery would not hold a charge. Our first detour put us in Cairns, about 200 miles away. Winds were erratic in direction and speed, but we made Cairns in two days. The Monitor line was badly chafed and about to break but was repaired at sea. We found good services at Cairns, and after playing tourist, we were off again.

After a night of winds gusting to 40 knots, we had to rest and stopped at Watson's Bay, Lizard Island. We had sailed a hard 150 miles in twenty-four hours, only to be weathered in for seven days. Leaving Lizard Island, we were out about sixty miles when a minke whale took a liking to the *Nereid*. One of the swim-byes across the stern touched the Monitor windvane, our only operating autopilot, which broke off the rudder. I had the spare part, but conditions were too risky to attempt a repair at sea, so we headed to Morris Island. Judy and I traded off hand steering for the seventeen hours it took to reach Morris Island.

We departed Morris Island after repairs, stayed inside the reef and stopped at Portland Roads for a steak dinner and crocodile stories.

There was a minor international incident at the dinner table when an old Aussie who lived up in the hills said, "So what are you Yanks doing about your black problem?"

The conversation of about twenty people suddenly stopped. Being the only Yank at the table, I took a moment to think about this and replied, "How are you doing with your Aborigines?"

Several of Australians in the party quickly acknowledged, "Yes, we do have a problem there."

I think he wanted a fight, but our German friends, after another pensive moment, said, "We all have some things in our history we are not proud of."

Everyone quietly finished their steak and went home.

Next morning, we were on our way to Shelborne Bay. We managed to run aground entering the bay, but fortunately it was soft mud, so we only did a little plowing of the sea floor, creating an opportunity for some critters to go forth and multiply in a disturbed zone.

We had smooth sailing to Thursday Island and Horne Island for some R&R. We departed Horne Island, but sixty miles out managed to collide with the large ocean buoy marking the Carpentaria Shoal. We recovered from the incident and ensuing discussions to find ourselves on day four out about 470 miles in the night with a tanker headed toward us. I took early evasive action but was followed by the tanker. We made more course corrections and were followed by the tanker. The tanker, medium size but big enough, did a turn in front of us and almost stopped. We came to a halt and were back-winded and unable to make another course change. We powered up the engine and slowly maneuvered away from this ship, never able to make successful radio contact.

After forty-nine days (June 22 to August 10), with delays from engine trouble, autopilot failure, a minke whale, grounding, buoy collision, tanker games and all shapes and sizes of wind and wave conditions, we finally made it to Darwin—the hard way.

Tipperary Waters Marina

We were anchored in Fannie Bay off the Darwin Yacht Club when we were notified that we had been assigned a slip at the Tipperary Waters Marina. The marina, about ten miles away, is maintained by a lock system that holds the water in during the extreme tidal flux common in this area. We got a late start and, with the current against us, arrived late and had to wait out a tidal change at anchor along with another sailboat, *Trudel*.

We had been at anchor about two hours and resting in the salon when I happened to look out the companionway and see a very large freighter go by. I scrambled to the cockpit and was greeted by two mates on the freighter. They both waved. One shouted, "You are anchored in the shipping channel, and another, even larger ship is headed this way. You might want to move."

Very friendly chaps. With a few more hours to wait, we decided to post a watch in the cockpit and be ready to move if and when the next big ship arrived. *Trudel* decided to do the same.

We had no problems, and eventually we both headed out for Tipperary, farther up the river. *Trudel* was in the lead and had the only map of the area. All we had to do was stay close enough to follow them to the locks. Well, we got behind some slower boat traffic, and when we came around the corner there was no *Trudel* and no sign of the locks. I flagged down a small powerboat with what looked like local folks, and they assured me the locks were much farther up the river. About then we got a call from Peter, the lockmaster, who could see us.

"Where are you going?" he asked. "The locks are on the other side of the river, and you're running out of time. With the tidal change, you'll be grounding out soon."

Judy began every other minute with, "Oh my gosh! Oh my gosh!"

Peter, in a calm voice, kept repeating, "Trust me with the new course heading."

We did, and the doors to the locks appeared in the maze of industrial development; however, the opening appeared quite small.

"The locks are too small and it is all your fault," Judy said and handed me the wheel.

We managed to slip in, and once we were secured inside, the locks were closed and filled with water. As we rose out of the depths, we beheld the welcome sight of other yachts tucked safely in their slips. We moved to our designated slip and called it a day with another experience under our cap. Lessons for the day: don't trust local knowledge, take the time to check out a marina before navigating it, have a copy of the route onboard and don't anchor in a ship traffic lane.

Peter is writing a book about his experience as a lockmaster. We may get a mention. He wouldn't say for sure.

Kakadu National Park

It was 6:00 a.m., and we were already late to join our German cruiser friends for a tour of the Kakadu National Park. It was not yet daylight as we scurried from the boat to the security gate where the shuttle bus waited. In the darkness, we were unable to punch in the correct code to open the gate. I was ready to call it a day even though the day hadn't really started, but not Judy.

"Come on, we can do this," she said.

To my amazement, she swung herself out and around the bars extending each side of the gate with protruding spikes. Well, if she could do it, I certainly had to, and I did—amazing lady.

We found ourselves being shuttled to a large tour bus waiting for us downtown. These were the big buses that had been passing me on the highway for years at high speed with dark windows, a sinister presence on the road. Today we were part of that presence, with its air conditioning, bathroom, music, TV and driver narrating on the wonders of Australia. Not a bad way to travel, and something we will consider when we get back home, whenever that is.

The Kakadu National Park, 257 kilometers east of Darwin, is one of Australia's best-known treasures. The region is noted for its native wildlife and ancient Aboriginal rock art. Our driver was full of facts about the area and the Northern Territory. Twelve percent of the world's supply of uranium is mined here, with trucks pulling three trailers requiring eighty-two tires. We had a full lecture on the life cycle of termites, which have been amazingly successful in Australia. Of some 400 species of termites in the world, a hundred are in this Northern Territory.

We stopped at a huge termite mound alongside the road called the Cathedral. It was over fifteen feet high. According to our driver, all the termites in the world would weigh more than all the people. I heard that correctly and it is true. Anyway, back on the bus, and we were off to the Nourlangie Rock, a special Aboriginal sacred area with many rock paintings. We were allowed to enter the area if we were quiet and respectful and stayed on the designated walkway. This was no problem, as there was a spiritual presence about this place.

Afternoon was a boat trip to the Yellow Water Billabong to observe the wildlife. A billabong is an estuary-type marshland and, much like our wetlands in the USA, has an abundance of birds. But unlike our wetlands, this is the preferred habitat of the saltwater crocodile, and it is indeed a hard act to follow. I tried to observe the birds in all their glorious plumage and behavioral dances, but when the boat was suddenly smashed into by an angry croc that flipped up and fell backwards into the water, it was hard to do any serious bird watching. We only had the one collision, as most of the big boys were hauled out on the shore, evidently taking naps.

We saw one large, active fellow in the water suddenly catch a fish—ten or fifteen pounds—and flip it into the air, catching it in his mouth with his huge tail arched out of the water as some kind of counterweight. Crocs are carryovers from the dinosaur period and continue to be very successful. If they can catch a fish in muddy water with zero visibility using their sensitive detection of movement and their quick jaw reflexes, they will be around for a long time.

Too many croc stories, so I will only tell two recent occurrences. A fellow, out swimming, and was caught by a croc. The croc was evidently not hungry, so it only stuffed him under a log to eat him later. The lucky "bloke" regained consciousness and crawled to safety. Then, just yesterday, back in Darwin, I was over at the adjacent marina when a fellow walked up from the shoreline.

"Guess I won't go swimming today," he said casually. "There are two crocs out there."

Good on you, I thought to myself.

Next stop, Indonesia; I wonder what is going on there?

Return to Darwin

We were about sixty miles out of Darwin on our way to Ashmore Reef and Bali when our Alpa autopilot didn't like the course we were on and decided to set out on its own. After several attempts to reach an understanding, it became clear that we could not go on this way. The low-to-no wind condition was not enough for the windvane, and with over 800 miles remaining to Bali and another 900 miles to Singapore, it would be too much hand steering for even the veteran hand-steering team of the *Nereid.*

Back at Tipperary Waters Marina, waiting for parts and feeling sorry for ourselves, we decided to take in a movie at the downtown cinema complex. We choose a Matt Damon high-speed, high-tech thriller, *The Bourne Ultimatum.* A great movie, third in a series, a modern version of the *Manchurian Candidate* and *French Connection* with flawless high-tech connections on cell phones and computers. All the cell phones connected instantly, no language issues, no call waiting or numbers that didn't work in the area as the chase went on from country to country. We were still having trouble with our satellite phone on country codes and local calling. As for the computer operators tracking Mr. Bourne, there were no forgotten passwords or wrong IDs and no battery or power failures. This whole scene became surreal for us because of our equipment failures and the way we were still struggling with online banking.

Back at the boat with time on our hands, we turned on our small portable radio to check out the local music—usually country western in these parts, but there was also local and international news. We tried to sample the news with our low-tech radio about once a week. Top story this day was that Indonesia, hopefully our next port of call, had purchased two nuclear submarines and some other military hardware from Russia. To put this in perspective, Indonesia is a third- or fourth-world country with the fourth-largest population behind China, India and the US. It was suggested that their navy would be better equipped than Australia's and Australia should do something. I am sure the US has a couple of old nuke subs to sell—just our luck to be in the middle of an arms race. Also on the news, the US wanted future agreements regarding the purchase of uranium from Australia to require the Aussies take it back when we were through with it. This was not a good day for our weekly news sample.

We decided to add another day of news, and the top story? President Bush was in Australia for the Asia-Pacific Economic Cooperation (APEC) conference. He evidently had thanked OPEC instead of APEC. Not a good day for the pres. His aides said he was just kidding with the OPEC comment. They may have a problem with jet lag on Air Force One. It was mentioned that this plane is a technological wonder from which the president can conduct the business of the entire country. I am not so sure this is such a good idea. Anyway, that was the news here in OZ, and it should hold us for some time. We will be on our way by the end of the week, unless war breaks out between Indonesia and Australia.

Update: Our Furuno GPS and Trace Inverter just stopped working.

Decision to Return

It looked like it was not going to happen this season. We were back again in Darwin after a third attempt to break out, much like the prisoners of days gone by when Australia was a penal colony. We were back at Tipperary Waters Marina and, fortunately, had told most people we were just going for a day sail. Some were confused and looked at me with a slight recollection.

"Didn't you just leave for Singapore?" they asked.

"No, you must be thinking of someone else," I replied.

What happened this time was not so much equipment failure, although we still had some of that. The seas were flat, without the slightest ripple to indicate wind from any direction. We had motored for three days and had gone about 250 miles, which meant we would definitely need to refuel at one of the small island communities in Indonesia. We were still dealing with some equipment problems, but none of them were game breakers. We had plenty of fuel to make it to a refueling stop, but something else was continuing to bother me.

The normal fueling and check-in site for Indonesia was Kupang. We had been warned not to go there, as customs was charging ten-percent bonds on the value of boats and keeping them. Kupang was in West Timor, not a friendly place at this time, and it was even less friendly in East Timor, where they were hacking each other up with machetes based on bloodlines and past atrocities by the Indonesians, Dutch and Portuguese.

Indonesia was an exciting place. In the northern part of Kalimantan, the locals were cutting off heads and advertising this manly exercise with two parallel cuts on the backs of their hands. Anyway, we knew this starting out about Indonesia; of course, there was also the pirate issue. We were reminded of this when we contacted two "ships of opportunity" about the weather.

"You know there are pirates in those waters," both skippers said when they heard we were going to Indonesia.

I had to remind Judy that the few reported instances of pirates occurred in the Malacca Straits, which come after Singapore.

Anyway, I had been wrestling with the decision for weeks, and now we had decided to go and were three days out and still no wind. The question kept coming up—why now, and why the rush? Something was not right, but we had made bigger decisions on longer and more uncertain passages without a question of turning back. This time, my uncertainty persisted.

"I think we should turn back," I finally said to Judy, who was excited to be out here and on our way.

She studied me for a moment and to my surprise said, "Okay, I agree. We are going to be too rushed, and we can do this next season."

It is never an easy decision to turn back, and we would question it later. We made our decision at that moment to return and spend the season in Darwin. We would start again next spring, leaving about late May.

The message: listen to your heart, listen to your gut, and listen to your angels. There is always tomorrow.

We definitely needed some downtime with the grandkids, especially while they still thought we were wonderful. We could also use some grounding with friends in the USA. We would like to include some visits to our new friends in Australia. Anyway, our dance card was open except for the months of December, January and February.

The Fall

Our return flight from San Francisco to Singapore was long but had movies and games available on the seat backs in front of us. We watched about five movies which, with today's movie theater prices, just about paid our airfare. The last leg from Singapore to Darwin, Australia, was via no-frills Tiger Airlines; although without the entertainment in the seat backs, it came with a lively group of five younger folks sharing their seats with a fellow named Jack Daniels.

Jack was undercover for the first half of the trip but became more noticeable after several orders of Coke and ice. Revenues lost by the airline as a result of Jack were more than replaced with the increased sale of soda. Later into the flight, Jack could be seen transferring across the aisle after each fresh order of Coke. Jack's friends became more entertaining as the flight went on, offering great belly laughs and shoulder punching, along with umpteen trips to the toilet.

We said our silent goodbyes to our young friends as we departed the plane, and I assumed that would be our last get-together. While waiting for our luggage I decided to use the restroom, and when I walked in there was one of our young friends at the wall. I say "the wall" because in this part of the world the typical individual porcelain repositories aren't that common. Instead, and at this airport, they have a large sheet of stainless steel where you step up on a platform to take your shot. There are no instructions about the platform—whether to stand behind and shoot, or stand on it for a short-range height advantage. Whatever; the wall allows a lot more freedom and creativity. The player can cover more area, write his name or do a walk-along, none of which is possible at the more restrictive porcelain enclosure.

Our young traveler was talking to himself at the wall when I stepped up, and he turned immediately with a big smile to extend his conversation to this new guy now standing beside him. It is not clear what happened next— he may have turned too quickly, at least for his condition—but his feet went out from under him and his head slammed up against the wall. While he still held his more sensitive part, his feet continued to slip and he did a slow-motion slide to the floor, wiping off the wall with his head on the way down. His smile changed to confusion as he slid to the floor, but he did manage to keep talking. His fall was partly broken by his head pressed against the wall, but unfortunately, he came to a rest in the worst place in the airport for personal hygiene.

He looked up at me from the floor, and I tried to formulate an appropriate response. It was an embarrassing moment for both of us. What could I say to someone who has just cleaned the wall with his face? I had done nothing, just stood there, barely able to redirect my own action. He stood, zipped up and shook himself off.

"Are you all right?" I asked.

"The... floor is kind of slick in here," he replied.

I had to agree. He then headed out, I assumed to the sink area to wash off. He may have been in denial about what had just happened, as he did not stop at a sink but went directly out the door into the general population. I hoped he was not meeting someone at the airport. Then again, how did one wash up at a sink for what should have been a major cleanup?

My greater concern was that a fall like that at my age could be fatal. Not the way I would want to be remembered. However, our friend in his prime youth was up and out of there and, thanks to his friend Jack, probably didn't remember a thing.

Humping the Hostess

"I caught a really big fish today. Do you want some? It's all cleaned and everything," yelled Ali, a fifteen-year-old whose parents had recently sold their spacious home overlooking the marina for a cruising life.

We invited Ali to join us for dinner that evening—all was well so far. Later in the day, we met some boaters who had purchased a big-screen TV and wanted to know if we were interested in their old TV for a small fee.

"Yes," I said.

"No," Judy countered.

Since I am still the captain, we compromised on a short trial period.

Dinner was to be at 6:00 p.m., and Ali arrived on time with the beautiful fillets from her thirty-pound sea bass. She insisted on cooking the fish, although her parents had said she should not. Judy, in a most conciliatory way, agreed to let Ali cook the fish on condition that Judy closely monitor the action in the small galley area. Everything was under control and moving toward a pleasant evening with our teenage guest/cook when there was a *knock, knock* on the hull of the *Nereid*.

"Surprise, surprise!" someone shouted. "Guess what we brought you!"

It was our new friends with the used (and larger than expected) TV; and they never went anywhere without their medium-sized black poodle, which was like a third person only more demanding.

So it was to the companionway and up the stairs with the greeting, "Oh, how great to see you again so soon; and you brought the TV. Come in, come in."

Well, in they came: two adults, a large TV and a very active dog. With our table set for dinner, there was only a small space in the galley area to move around. It was suddenly very crowded. I took a seat at the table to relieve some of the congestion, leaving Judy to manage the remaining biomass. Everyone was talking and periodically the dog would start barking.

From my vantage point, the dog seemed hungry. It was actually barking at Judy, which seemed strange at the time—with all the varieties of bodies to bark at, she was the chosen one. It would not stop barking unless a treat was produced from the pocket of its master, whereupon it would roll over to be served, which was tolerably cute.

Ali was cooking. The burner must have been too hot, as there was smoke accumulating, and the dog became more and more vocal. It wasn't total chaos, but it was getting there. Fish smell and dog smell contended for the air space, and the dog smell was winning. Drinks were served, and the chaos continued until our guests realized there was not going to be enough fish to go around and it was time to leave. The fish was slightly overcooked, but under the circumstances, Ali had done an admirable job; she was rightfully pleased with herself.

I asked Judy after everyone had gone home, "Why was the dog barking all the time?"

"Well, Raymond," she answered, "you couldn't see from where you were, but the dog kept humping my leg."

I couldn't believe what I was hearing.

"Yes," she said, "it only barked when I would kick it away."

"But the owners were both right there in front of you. And they said nothing and did nothing?" I said.

"Well," she said, "they did produce treats to distract it momentarily, but then it was back on my leg."

I have decided I really, really do like cats… add to that I really, really like cat owners.

Note on Cats and Dogs: Why do I like cats? Let me count the ways: they don't hump your leg or do it in public, they don't take you on walks to dump on someone's lawn so you can pick it up and carry it around, they don't bark, they don't sniff your bum. And in the hereafter, cats pass through the Pearly Gates to rejoin their masters, while dogs just sniff the gates and take a leak. That is why I like cats. Now, why do I like cat owners? Actually, there are no cat owners; like marriage, it's a relationship.

Byron Bay R&R

We visited with Ross and Laura for a few days before they headed back to Alaska to start a family, or rather continue the family they had already started. We stayed with a dear friend in Byron Bay who had a lovely home in a jungle setting, only a few yards from the beach. Each morning there was a singing contest between about five species of birds. Their songs were spectacular and filled what had been missing on some of our travels. We had expected to hear more of this communication, but only on the shores of Australia did it really happen. The lead singers were the kookaburra and rainbow lorikeets, accompanied by magpies and cuckoos.

The pace was pretty fast in this household and the day usually started with the cappuccino machine. It took a couple of days of instruction, but what once seemed like an endless number of steps was not all that difficult to master. I suppose one could hurt himself just starting out on his own, but with two experienced brewers and a team effort, it all made sense and resulted in an excellent cup of coffee.

We played some cards, in this case the deadly game of Joker, at which our daughter-in-law is a master, as is all of her family. The game requires intense concentration and is unforgiving in the procedures that need to be followed. The cappuccino machine required less attention and was more of a short-term win, while Joker was very competitive—the opposite of teamwork and not the best game to introduce to new friends. However, our hostess proved to be a fast learner, even winning some rounds.

There was some TV time watching cricket—an unusual game, but if one took the time, some of it began to make sense. It also helped to have someone in the room who understood the rules. One of the problems, because it involved hitting a ball with a stick, was the obvious comparison to baseball.

Hitting the ball with a stick—there the comparison ends. Cricket players don't have gloves but cover every other part of their bodies. The batters are all dressed up like catchers, with pads covering their legs and helmets like catchers' masks. The pitcher runs at the batter and throws as hard as he can, but the ball has to bounce once. If the batter hits the ball, he runs down a baseline with his bat. A batter gets to keep hitting the ball and making runs until either he dies or someone catches the ball he has hit. Some games can last for days.

Players are positioned anywhere on the field to catch the ball. The batter can make over a hundred runs before he is out, but when he is out, he is really out and has to leave the field. As for the officials, the American way is to challenge a close call and go jaw to jaw with an umpire and maybe get thrown out of the game. Cricketers never question a call by the official; in fact, any emotional response draws a fine.

Once I quit trying to put cricket into a baseball uniform, it started to make more sense, but it is an order of magnitude of greater complexity than baseball and has its own vocabulary, and it would take more time to become a real fan. There was some strange stuff going on with a little wood piece balanced on two upright sticks behind the batter. It was a big deal if it got knocked off, but the details on that require more study. Anyway, the British Empire had left its mark. Now for some lawn bowling.

Pining Away in Darwin

"What are all these crumbs on my shirt?"

We were visiting friends and sitting out on their patio, overlooking the harbor, with drinks and chips. I had looked down to find there was an inordinate amount of chip fragments on my shirt. Actually, there was a surprising number of small pieces that would have been too much to brush off onto the clean tile floor. I proceeded to pick them off and reenter them. This was a significant marker in the aging process—first, I noticed them, and second, I took direct action to correct the problem, which put me still in the third quarter of life. The fourth and final quarter is when one gets the food on oneself, discovers it or not, but in either case doesn't care or do anything about it.

Another age indicator is the new region of hair management. The hair that once prospered on the top end has been gone for some time. There has been a recent reemergence of these lost follicles in several other places. This has been especially disturbing to Judy, as she is more visually affected. Time previously spent managing the top end is now directed to the eyebrows, nose and ears. Redistribution farther down has not been an issue.

Some serious changes were evident when holding my grandchild; he jerked back to focus on my ear.

"There is a squirrel in Grandpa's ear."

Judy and I are also both concerned with the status of our short-term memories. We now rely more and more on memory boosters like the 3M Post-it Notes. No matter how many reminders we leave ourselves, we still have trouble remembering to turn the refrigerator back on. For example, an HF radio transmission requires turning off the fridge to minimize the interference. We put notes on the computer, the fridge, the wall switch and the galley cabinets, but it is sometimes many hours before turn-on, resulting in much work for Judy.

Also, crossing the streets is becoming more challenging. I look both ways but have trouble retaining the all-clear from the first look, thus requiring numerous looks both ways to come to an informed decision to cross the street.

We are happy to report one discovery associated with the short-term memory, now long-term, in finding our emergency cash. We had stashed a sizeable amount of greenbacks for emergency payoffs, etc., but even with a short lecture—"Now, let's remember where this is"—we soon forgot, and the cash had become a bonus for the next boat owner. Our contingency was that if bad guys demanding money boarded us, we would all look for it together. I am happy to report that the cash was recently found and relocated, and at least at this writing, we both know where it is.

We have been working on the boat, no surprise, but are now focused on the "bright work." Bright work is a boating term for the care and maintenance of the woodwork on a boat, and the *Nereid* comes with a small forest of teak trim. Bright work is really an oxymoron. An example for non-boat owners would be to take your finest piece of wood furniture, strip off all the varnish, sand with 60 to 400 grit, recoat with a minimum of six to eight coats—the more the better—and, when finished, leave it outside in all kinds of weather for a year or two. Anyway, there are books on how to do it, people have gone crazy over it, but (thank goodness) Judy has taken over this responsibility and I am delegated to mixing and cleanup. She has done a fantastic job with eight coats on the starboard cap rail, leaving the rub rail, eyebrow and hand rail still to do—then we turn the boat around and do the port side.

Judy was taking a break at the moment, finishing another book. She has gone from a pre-cruising non-reader to about a book a week. The only downside is that if the book is about some guy who was a jerk, upon finishing the book she might sit there for a few moments glaring at me as if I had done something wrong. Anyway, the burning stare doesn't last long, but it is a time to minimize extracurricular conversation.

My grandson, Gage, age three, has become very protective of his aging Papa. On our last visit, we were in the garage and there had been a mess-up that could possibly have been my fault. In any case, Judy had lovingly called me a stoop and was asking those tough questions: "Why did you do that? Where is it? How could you forget? Don't you know anything?" Well, Gage overheard this grilling and wanted to know what was going on.

"Oh, nothing," Judy said.

"I heard something," he insisted. He then took me aside, and pulling my arm so I would bend down to his level for better eye contact, he said, "Papa, I know some things and I will tell them to you."

In terms of aging, it doesn't get any better than that.

Darwin Side Shows

We sit here in the marina with a "pod" of other boats, our masts sticking up into the sky like lightning rods, waiting for or inviting a strike. Three boats were hit by lightning a couple of years ago and it took out their electrical equipment. The boaters were not hurt. We are ready to sacrifice our electrical equipment if it will spare us.

Electricity is in the air, with a laser light show in the distance that starts each evening about 6:00 p.m. and lasts four to five hours. The entire night sky lights up, and as the light show comes closer, it is accompanied by sound effects, some with bolts of light discharging to the ground. There is no thunder this evening, we are too far

away, so we should be safe. The more exciting moments
are when the activity is overhead, with no delay between
the lightning and thunder. The flashes are so bright and
the sound so loud that for a moment I think I am dead
and on my way to the next world. It takes a few moments
to realize I am okay, my mate is okay, and the boat is
okay. The only after effects are the ringing in my ears and
dampness in my pants.

The light show is followed by a water show.
There is an abundance of water at this time of year, and it
comes down in a big way. It's not really rain but more of
a water dump, like standing under a waterfall. Sometimes
the drops are so large they send up a rooter tail when they
hit. It doesn't last more than ten to twenty minutes, but
anyone caught out is totally soaked in seconds. When it
really gets going, I can't see the other boats. It's as if a
gray curtain was drawn through the marina. We now have
some understanding of the term *monsoon*.

The ongoing show is the crocodiles. This
morning's copy of the *Northern Territory News* has a picture
on the front page of a tourist out fishing with his buddy.
They were in separate aluminum skiffs, and one picture
shows one of them pointing at the crocodile in the water
near his boat. The next picture shows the croc lunging
out of the water and the fellow lunging for the other end
of his boat.

The fellow is quoted as saying, "It clearly wanted
to kill me."

Not really, he was just looking for dinner, nothing
personal. The local folks say the tourist was teasing the
croc by pointing and staring at it. Excuse me! These
reptilian throwbacks to the Stone Age are sensitive to eye
contact and having a finger pointed at them? I don't think
so. However, in Australia, as it was in Alaska, one's
credibility and knowledge are based solely on how long
one has lived here.

To make our stay more enjoyable, we have brought some of the weather under control by adding to the *Nereid* an air-conditioning unit. It was purchased with great reservation and numerous discussions about investing several hundred dollars for a few months' service. First, we tried a large fan to move the warm air about, which was some improvement, but still the general comfort level was that of an extended camping trip. It is with great pleasure and cool body temperature that I am happy to report an air conditioner on a sailboat, at least in Darwin, was an excellent idea and has ranked in importance with food and shelter.

So with gators in the water looking for dinner, a light show overhead with thunderous applause, and torrential tropical downpours, we are happy to report that all is well, "no worries." It's only after staying in one place for a while, like we have in Australia, that we come to appreciate and learn more about it. Even the Aussie sentiment for the song "Waltzing Matilda" has become meaningful, and that is good. Also, the Australian hamburger, which includes a fried egg and beetroot, is starting to taste as good as the burgers at In-N-Out. Saying that—we may have stayed too long and need to get moving.

Historical Electrical Note: Working for the Forest Service, I was caught up on a mountain on horseback in an electrical storm. The air was making popping sounds, and sometimes I felt a little sting that seemed to be coming from my hat brim to my nose. My horse, a veteran of the wilderness, was staying calm, directing its ears forward like horses do when they are curious. This time the parallel ears seemed to set up a polar exchange, as there was a buzzing light between them. This was too much, and my horse made the decision first to get to lower ground and bolted down the mountain. I hung on, and we both survived the storm and the rapid altitude adjustment.

Part 4

Southeast Asia

Chapter 11

Indonesia

Leaving Australia

Australia, we will miss you: the "yeah yeahs," the long-drawn-out "ummmphs" in response to someone saying something interesting, the expression "No worries," a prime minister who speaks fluent Chinese and Cantonese, hamburgers with beetroot and a fried egg, all the words ending in "ie"—footie (football), littlies (children), and sunnies (sun glasses)—with mates all around, great songsters like the kookaburra and the high-energy lorikeets, Aussie TV with David Attenborough and the occasional surprise feature like *"Designing the Perfect Penis."* The most memorable TV commercial was *"Stiff and Stiff Again,"* two guys playing the piano without using their hands, advertising erectile dysfunction correction. We will miss the crocs; the latest newsmaker was taking horses on an outback ranch. Special friends Bill and Lyda, John and Julie, John and Tres, Peter the lockmaster, Nario, Alison and Paddy, Bill and Kerryn, Ian and Wendy, Claus, Claire and Errol, Lex and Joann and that dynamite teenager Ali—all will be missed.

Our departure from Darwin was a low-key affair, no fanfare; last year, after three unsuccessful attempts, we learned to only inform a few close friends of our intentions, thus minimizing the explanations if we had to return. The winds had been light for the last month, and we were worried there was not going to be enough wind to sail, making us depend on the engine, our "iron jenny." We needed to get going to make our annual visit to San Francisco by late August, so we said our goodbyes and motored out of the harbor. We fueled up at Cullen Bay and were on our way by 2:00 p.m. There were only light winds the first day, and we motored ten hours; the second day was more of the same, only we motored for twenty hours.

Day three and about 200 miles out, the weather changed quickly to a new ball game. The SE monsoon that carries the rallies and other boats into Indonesia began its three-month blow. But instead of leveling off at a nice 20 knots, our ideal sailing conditions, it just kept coming and coming and didn't peak until 50 knots. It was then that some of our latest and most expensive equipment began to fail. The new laptop decided it didn't like the COM port setup, and after trying to get the navigation program up and running, it was back to the backup computer. Next to go and equally important was the new $6,000 Raymarine autopilot, which was replacing the troublesome Alpha autopilot after a record three trips to the factory for repairs. The Raymarine might have handled the forces of the new weather system, except the installation had not been done correctly, resulting in the rudder bracket slipping to hardover port.

Judy said she didn't care what broke, what didn't work or how hard the wind blew, she did not want to go back. After hand steering for two hours in these high wind conditions, it was time to take a break, and we did the magical hove-to maneuver that is to park the boat at sea. The force of a back-winded staysail is countered by locking the rudder in the opposite direction, positioning the keel to de-energize the swells, resulting in a relatively restful condition. We went below, and after our naps, the wind screaming, we played cards and did some reading, always checking for possible boat traffic. Judy read an entire book and did the cooking, with some teamwork as needed to open cupboards and fridge doors. With our boat speed reduced now to about 1 knot, we still did about thirty miles a day.

The boat was tossed around in these conditions, but we adjusted. We slept in the salon, the windward bunk fitted with a safety net to keep us from going to the floor. The stove was in full gimbaled swing, the operator with a butt strap to stay in the area. The nav station required the use of the seat belt, once believed to be unimportant. Inside the boat, we were like primates moving through the jungle canopy using the overhead handrails. The most challenging moments were on the head—once inside, close the door and wedge yourself with your elbows and knees to keep from flying out before finished.

One good thing about bad weather is that it can't last, and we were certain it would calm down the next day. We were assured by our radio contacts in Darwin that this kind of condition was always going to let up the next day. Well, it was a record blow, and we were hove-to for four days before the winds dropped to a manageable 35 knots, at which we could set the staysail and let the Monitor windvane do the steering.

Anyway, it took us nine days to make our first stop, Rindja Island, Komodo dragon country.

Jurassic Park, Rindja Island

After nine days at sea, of which four were spent hove-to, we safely anchored at Rindja Island. The day before our arrival was spent motoring with no wind and no autopilot, so we had hand steered most of the day. Rindja Island, part of the Indonesian Archipelago, is home to the nine-foot Komodo dragons. Dragons eat pigs, deer, monkeys and small tourists, so we stayed on the boat.

We waited offshore, safe in the cockpit, for our first dragon sighting. Low tide exposed possible new food potential, but there was no activity on the beach. We were in the world's fourth-most-populated country and not a soul in sight. The morning sunlight slowly moved down the opposite shore. The only sound was the gentle waves breaking along the shoreline, the only movement the slow shifting of our boat at anchor. The first visitor to arrive was a very fat pig with short legs that moved systematically along the beach, sniffing out the new arrivals as possible food.

Our first dragon was small, about four feet long, and appeared just as the sun had started to warm the beach, making what was probably his daily stroll along the sand, not looking from side to side, just straight ahead. He moved like a sumo wrestler, each step deliberate and authoritative. He seemed to be on a mission—first thing in the morning, maybe on his way to the weight room. Maybe it was his turn to do the obligatory walk for the new boat in town—if so, we appreciated it.

The stillness was now broken by a variety of birds waking up, some monkeys arguing and an occasional very loud moaning growl that sounded like a cross between a cow and a lion. It was an impressive sound that had to come from a dragon. The sound could be objectively described from the safety of the *Nereid*, but if we had been on the beach or in the jungle, it would have been terrifying, something out of *Jurassic Park*. It sounded like two dragons in communication, one coming down the trail from the jungle the other coming along the beach to our left. They should have met right in front of us, either to mate or fight or maybe both. The growls continued, but they never appeared. These two dragons were only to be heard and not seen, but it was enough to discourage any idea of going ashore.

The dragon we did see on the beach was a fair size but not the big growlers that can chase you up a tree. We had heard about some more aggressive tourists who hired a guide and staked out a live goat in a jungle clearing, then hid back in the cover to await the slaughter. Well, the goat got off its tether and ran away as several dragons were closing in for the kill. It was then that the dragons, again just like out of *Jurassic Park*, turned their attention to the tourists. It was suddenly everyone for himself, and they all found trees to climb. The dragons tried to climb up the trees after them. The tourists were there for some time but did manage to escape. Their first order of business when they were safely back in camp was to cancel the rest of their three-week vacation and fly home. There was no refund of the advance-paid trip, and nobody cared.

Day Break

Anchored in a quiet cove,
Somewhere off the jungles of Borneo.
Magic of cruising is the early morning stillness,
Crystalline silence when only nature is talking.

Sunlight invades the near shore,
Life not seen begins to awake.
Background chorus of crickets, a million plus,
Following their conductor, all stop on the same note.

Birds are the soloist, somewhere in the event screen.
Twenty different songs, specifically intended.
Most go unanswered but they don't seem to care,
Maybe it's just good morning, is anyone there?

Sun keeps coming, the jungle is warming,
Songsters diminishing, the water picks up the beat.
Occasional fishing boat is now on the move, much work
to do.
Time to set sail, find the next quiet bay and await a new
day.

Ray Emerson
March 1, 2009

Selat – For or Against

Selat is the Indonesian word for straits, where the
sea level between two lands masses tries to equalize out
any differences as quickly as possible. This process can
create some very exciting moments and is further
complicated by tidal flux, prevailing currents and wind
patterns. The pilot book advised that currents could be
strong in the *selat*.

We had departed Rindja Island knowing that we
would arrive off the straits to Bali at night, so we needed
to slow down to arrive at daybreak. As it turned out, there
was no need to worry about those hours of darkness; the
currents took care of that. We had a nice SE wind at 25
knots off our beam; with genoa and reefed main, we were
doing 7 knots. As we approached the *selat*, the *Nereid* was
sailing along nicely. The GPS indicated a speed over
ground of 5 knots, but the chart plotter had us moving
backwards with the current.

I fired up the engine for a sail assist, and with the
engine at 2,200 rpm, which should move us about 6 knots

under normal conditions, we were now only holding our own and occasionally moving backwards. In the first half of the day, going all out with sail and engine, we gained about eight miles. The possibility of running out of fuel and being swept out to sea was discussed briefly.

A local fishing boat, very decorative blue and orange and designed for these conditions, saw our struggle, came up beside us, then moved ahead on the same course. We were behind them; they waited until we were close behind and then maintained a consistent distance from us. We continued to slug it out along with the local boat, and with the help of some countercurrents and tidal shift, we made it to our waypoint at the entrance to Benoa Harbor, Bali. It was very comforting and reassuring to have a local boat near and on the same course—it encouraged us to keep going.

Turns out our fishing-boat escort was delivering some family to participate in the canoe races taking place in Benoa Harbor. We waved goodbye as they headed back down the *selat*. It would have been nice to meet our boat people and spend some relaxed time together, but we will always remember them.

We arrived in Benoa Harbor amidst tankers, fishing boats, tourist boats, square riggers, a large luxury yacht, jet skiers and power boats pulling inflated sea monsters carrying inflated tourists shrieking with joy. In the skies were tourists strapped in para-gliders being towed by speedboats, and all this to the roar of jets taking off overhead from the nearby airport. To round out the surreal diversity of activity was a loudspeaker broadcasting a Muslim call to prayer that no one, at least in this scene, seemed to notice.

Concerning the big passenger jets taking off overhead, we take for granted all this technology coming together. Here we sat with our new computer and new autopilot not working. In fact, most of our equipment only works part time. This is an adventure made possible through backups. I wondered if there were any backup systems being deployed in the skies above us—surely not.

Grounded High and Dry

Upon arrival in Benoa Harbor, a place alive with tourist activities, we headed for the channel to the marina. Partially distracted by the activities, partially less attentive after our strenuous passage up the challenging *selat*, and partially assuming the channel markers were not for real and forgetting that the guidebook said to give these markers plenty of clearance, we concluded all of this miscalculation with a sudden grounding. We tried desperately to back off the shoal, but no luck; the receding tide secured our capture.

Alex, a native boy in his small skiff, was the first to notice our situation and quickly realized we needed more than his help. He said he would contact the coast guard. Shortly afterward, a power boat with a faded orange strip like the US coast guard's and the captain and crew out of uniform made a valiant effort to pull the *Nereid* off the shoal. They eventually gave up, leaving us with the reminder to set our anchors to prevent the tide from moving the boat further onto the shoal.

The *Nereid* took her misfortune like the true lady she is, and with the receding water, she slowly healed over. She came to rest on her port side as the tide went out, lying down easily as if to relax—no damage. She looked like a shipwreck and quickly became a tour-boat attraction and photo op. Tourists lined the rails with their cameras, seemingly enjoying our predicament.

It was a very sad and depressing moment, along with the inconvenience. Life inside the boat was like playing on a jungle gym, trying to maintain a vertical position on a forty-five-degree surface. There was concern that any movement would tip the boat further over onto the mast, but the 7,700 pounds of ballast did its job. I took some preventative measures, closing all the seacocks and the shutoff valve for the upside water tank. Judy decided to do some reading; I did some review of a book titled *Aground and the Technique of Kedging Off.*

I managed to get out and take some pictures and make a few jokes to myself to offset the stress. If I had planned better, I could have done some bottom painting, like they did in the old days.

I hailed a small skiff with a father and son who were fishing. They came over and we reset the stern anchor into deeper water, as I had only carried it as deep as I could wade. They then agreed to reset the bow anchor into deeper water. I dove down and pulled it up, and the son placed it on the deck of their boat. When the father saw the size of the anchor, he changed his mind; he was afraid it would hurt his boat. The son, very respectfully and with a helpless smile, said it was his father's boat and there was nothing he could do. I couldn't argue, but I was impressed with the respect the teenage son had for his father's decision, even though he didn't agree.

He handed me back the anchor and said goodbye, and they backed away. Fortunately, I was still in the water up to my neck, and the added thirty-five pounds made it relatively easy to dive down and reset the anchor.

We waited, and as the water depth returned, the anchors held and the *Nereid* slowly regained her respectable vertical position. About midnight, she was set free. It was time to start the engine, back off the shoal and head for deeper water while retrieving the two anchors. The whole exercise went just like the book described, so we did good. It was then time to find an anchoring place among the many fishing boats and tour boats silhouetted in the dark. After several tries, we found a space with good holding. It had been a long day and we were ready for sleep.

Note: I initially thought the grounding to have been the result of a combination of distractions and poorly placed channel markers. Some weeks later, while enjoying the sunset and an adult beverage with my first mate, she mentioned that instead of following her captain's directions to maintain the present position while the captain went below deck, she had decided the red and green buoys off the starboard bow were guides to the marina. Taking this direct route between the markers had resulted in the grounding of the *Nereid*.

There has been no lashing or reassignment of duties, but the captain will be more vigilant and never take his best mate for granted—she definitely bears watching.

Bali Marina – The Slip

The Bali Marina is very popular, so when we got a call over the VHF from Armando that there was a slip available, we did not hesitate. I had visited the marina only the day before and put our name on the waiting list, so it was a welcome surprise to get a call so soon. We pulled anchor and headed over to the marina, and there was Armando directing us to the first slip, adjacent to the entrance. This slip had a tricky restricted access, with a large catamaran taking most of the maneuvering room. It required a 180-degree turn immediately upon entering, this day against a 20-knot head wind. I had told Armando the day before that I did not want this slip. When he called and said he had a slip for us, I assumed it was another one that had just become available.

There were two helpers on the dock when we arrived, plus Armando, who was in a dinghy to assist. We decided to go for it. Well, in short, we entered the breakwater and couldn't make the turn, and Armando's dinghy was unable to prevent contact with the big cat. The cat, with its heavily oxidized white paint, left its mark on the *Nereid*, along with some scratches to the bright work and waterline. We almost lost a stanchion, but cleared it with some fancy footwork and major leveraging. About this time two other cruisers, a Dutchman and a Frenchman, arrived in a dinghy and suggested some long lines were needed, which I provided and we slowly winched the *Nereid*, stern first, into her new home. We would worry about getting out of this slip later.

Note: Our day of departure a few weeks later was uneventful. With no wind and a single line midship, we were out of there—goodbye, beautiful Bali.

"I Am Hindu, I Am Lucky"

In Bali, every family compound has a temple designed to keep out the evil spirits that make people do bad things, much like Geraldine of Flip Wilson days— "The devil made me do it." There are also large temples for the masses. All temples, large and small, are decorated with vicious beasts that are symbolically keeping the evil spirits away. The placement and design of the entryways are especially important, as these are the portals of entry for evil.

Christianity blames the individual for yielding to the dark side and has a resultant heavy guilt trip. The Hindus believe that humans yielding to the dark side stems from evil spirits getting through their temple defenses. There is no guilt trip, just a need to redesign or add to your temple defense system. Consequently, there is a thriving business in stone masonry, especially temple creatures. Maybe the reconstruction effort is symbolic, but there may also be a mental adjustment, making people feel more protected from evil. Anyway, our guide,

Youdah, when asked about his beliefs, said proudly, "I am Hindu, I am lucky," and he is right.

The Balinese are hard-working people. The wage scale is very low. We had two young men cleaning the rust off our stainless-steel boat fittings for the going rate of $10 a day. One of our workers, Madee, age thirty-four, had a son in high school. Fortunately, food costs are reasonably in line with this wage scale. Our favorite breakfast at the marina totaled two dollars for fresh orange juice and eggs benedict. Dinner for a fellow cruiser and his wife, which included drinks and dessert for four people, was $8.50. One can be a big spender in Bali, at least in one's own mind.

Tipping for services rendered is not expected, and some sources say is not to be encouraged. It is not clear as to the proper thing to do, but my hunch is the non-tippers are just cheap and using the cultural thing as an excuse. I can say that each time we have added something to the bill, it has resulted in a huge smile and expression of gratitude from the recipient. As a representative of our country, it has been a joy to be in a position to help a third-world neighbor.

Kodak Moment in Lombok

Back into the *selat* and headed north to Lombok, we were like Alaska salmon that migrate up the rivers, taking advantage of the back eddies near shore. We were better prepared this time to deal with strong currents, and we knew to search out the eddies that would make travel upstream more efficient, keeping closer to shore and carefully watching our depth. The high point was when Judy, at the wheel, summoned me to come quick.

It sounded like her usual concern for a passing boat or some obstacle in our path, but to my surprise, she said, "Did you see the volcano?"

I had been at the bow, watching for whatever, and I hurried back to the cockpit as she pointed off the port side. There was this surreal presence, a huge volcano with its cone breaking through the clouds. I was shocked—how could I have missed it? I recovered and started snapping pictures.

The volcano was unbelievable in size and the perfect shape. It turned out to be Gunung Agung, which erupted in 1963, killing a thousand people and destroying a hundred thousand homes; however, the Eka Dasa Rudra temple near the summit was unscathed. Sukarno, the president of Indonesia at the time, refused to acknowledge the importance of the eruptions and lost power two years later, probably because he did not respect the spiritual significance of the event.

We arrived at the NW corner of Lombok at Teluk Kombal, 08 24S and 116 04E, and awoke the next day about 5:00 a.m. to a call to prayer and the crowing of many roosters. There seemed to be two groups of crowers, the predawn set and other cohorts at sunrise. Probably the same roosters, really, just with more enthusiasm when joined with the call to prayer broadcasts, making for quite a noise fest. There were overlapping chants or calls to prayer from the adjacent villages and nearby Gili Island. The calls differed greatly in quality, like the roosters, representing a wide range of vocal ability.

While a village has the electrical power to broadcast the prayer, there is no electricity in the homes. There is no running water; the water is obtained from a central open well. The village is very clean, no trash, and the people are healthy and happy. They are quick to catch a joke.

"How much for the whole case of pearls?" followed by "I am a very rich man" was always good for a big smile.

Judy and I had the opportunity to attend a wedding ceremony in a small jungle village. I had the only camera to record the event, and Mohammad, our guide, asked the groom if it was okay to take pictures. He gave his nod of approval. The traditional ceremony, hundreds of years old, included sixteen male dancers with small musical cymbals. They all moved in precision to the beat of two huge drums, eight chime players and three players with large cymbals. It was a Kodak moment, but I really needed a video camera. The dancers moved to the beat, as one with their hands and feet. It was a beautiful ceremony and we felt lucky to have been invited. Mohammad speaks good English and basically runs the marina and many businesses on the side. He arranges tours, water, fuel, whatever one needs.

Transportation around Lombok and the adjacent islands is via longboats with double outriggers powered by a fifty-hp outboard that carry fifty to sixty people. Mohammad set us up with Dream Divers on Gili Island. It was a package deal with one guide/diver, a half-day for $35. Highlights were the coral, cuttle fish or "nautilus" and beaked sea turtles that let you get up close while they crunch away on coral. We opted out of the afternoon dive and missed an unexpected big attraction—a whale shark. Oh well, the real news is of food interest: there is KFC on the island, at a buck a piece.

Note: Croc stories are still coming in from cruiser friends, the latest from the primo cruising grounds, the Kimberly Islands in Western Australia. Some cruiser friends had their dinghy tied up beside their yacht and found it ripped to shreds the next morning. Evidently the slight bumping of the dinghy against the side of the yacht was an irritant to some of the big guys, and they responded accordingly—anyway, so goes the story.

"Keep the Change"

"How do you like your Monitor windvane?" was the question that came in over our VHF radio.

"Great," was my reply. "It has been a life saver, since both of our powered autopilots, the Alpha and Raymarine, are out of commission."

I continued my praise of the Monitor; however, about an hour later we were dragging the Monitor rudder behind the boat—it had broken off. No whales this time or impact noticeable to cause the event. I concluded it was the result of an incident several years earlier in SF Bay, where it was hit by another boat and possibly cracked, and after several years of service and with the incredible timing of my accolade, at last it had rusted through. Now with three self-steering units out and 740 miles to Singapore, we headed for the nearest inhabited island, Bawean, for repairs. We needed to find someone who could weld stainless steel, otherwise we would need to hire additional crew to share the steering.

Finding a welder for stainless steel on a small island was a long shot, but the local folks were very sympathetic and assured us there was someone who could do the job. Motor scooters are the primary mode of travel on Bawean, so we went out on three motor scooters, one with the Monitor tied on the back and the other two transporting Bjorn, a cruiser friend from Malta, and myself.

After two refusals by welders to do stainless, halfway around the island, we found a young man who said, "Yes, I can."

We untied the Monitor from the scooter, carried it into his shop and placed it on the dirt floor. The welding machine was all he had in his shop, but it was all we needed. It took about ten minutes to weld the rudder, and he did an excellent job.

Smiling and nodding approval of his work, I said, "How much do I owe you?"

He said, "Fifty thousand rupees" about $5.

I said in disbelief, "What?"

He replied, "Too much, then how about forty thousand?"

I handed him a 100,000 rupee bill and he said, "I don't have any change."

I said, "Keep the change."

After some thought, he asked, "When you will come back for your change?"

Shaking my head, I said, "No, no, no, not coming back, you keep the change, it is for you!"

He suddenly understood and acknowledged with prayerful gesture and smile.

With lunch for the five of us, service at 100,000 rupees and transportation via three scooters for half a day, the whole deal amounted to $45. And with the trip on the back of a scooter, the picturesque ocean-water scene on one side of the road and on the other the farmers in terraced green rice fields, cutting and thrashing—the whole experience was priceless.

Bawean Burkas

In our travels we have seen many women wearing the traditional Moslem burka, but Bawean gave us a new and fascinating appreciation for this attire. After the repair of the windvane and with the *Nereid*, *Eloise* and *Mischief* safely anchored off shore, all six of us were relaxing at a local restaurant when we were approached by a schoolteacher and invited to make a short presentation at their middle school. We agreed, and all of us were swiftly transported there by six young teenage boys on the back of their motor scooters.

At the school, the girls were in traditional dress with burkas, the boys in clean, open-collared white shirts. In the classroom, the girls were enthusiastic and seated in the front with the boys, more casual, collected in the back. One of the teachers translated our brief presentations. They were not sure where Alaska or Bawean was in the world, nor were they much enlightened after my drawing on the chalkboard. The only English spoken was a counting exercise and the ABCs, which were both recited collectively as chants.

We were seated in front facing the students while the girls watched us intently. If you made eye contact, they would flush with a smile of embarrassment. After our presentations, we were preparing to leave when one girl cautiously extended her hand to us. We shook hands with her, and then everybody, both girls and boys, wanted to shake hands and everyone had a huge smile.

These were beautiful kids, like all kids that age, maybe a tad more respectful. The school and classrooms were very clean but lacked supplies, which we plan to send, and we may adopt this school as one of our causes to support. It was a wonderful experience; these kids were very happy and no one asked or wanted anything. I think they genuinely liked us. With this younger generation, there is hope for the world.

When we all walked into town a few days later, we were still in celebrity status. It was a holiday and only the general store was open for business. We purchased ice cream bars and sat on the storefront steps, all six of us in a row, when our curious onlookers began to assemble. First one by one, then two by two until about thirty or forty, ranging from elementary school age to high school, had gathered a few feet away. No words were spoken, but they watched our every move. Judy motioned one little girl to come sit on her lap, but an older boy, probably her brother, grabbed her by the shoulders and turned her away. When we finished our ice cream and stood up to leave, everyone wanted to touch our hands; it was like an opening of the *Jay Leno Show*—touching everyone's hands.

Later that afternoon, we were gathered around a roadside juice stand when six teenage girls arrived on three motor scooters. They had organized this expedition primarily to see Judy. They were fascinated by her beauty and had to have a closer look and touch her face. The conversations quickly accelerated, and soon there were cell phone cameras out and we were in every combination of picture, everyone smiling and laughing. At one point I was told, "Look this way and smile, I am taking your picture." It was a first for me, being told what to do by someone who earlier that day had been wearing a burka. As for the burka, if the original intent was to desensitize onlookers—I'm not sure it is working.

Our next stop is Kumai, to view the orangutans on the Kumai River Reserve; on Bawean, we were the orangutans, with the locals doing the viewing.

Note: We received a thank-you note from the school for the wall maps of the world and Indonesia. They would appreciate any school supplies. If you would like to help these kids contact: smp1tambak@yahoo.co.id

Mounted on the Lord's Mantle

Our passage from Bawean Island in Indonesia to the Kumai River in Borneo was 177 miles, plus another six miles up the river to the town of Kumai. We had a smooth overnight crossing and headed up the river with about an hour of daylight remaining, which was a bonus because we usually arrive at our destination in the dark. Except for a sharp bend, the river was a straight shot. Unfortunately, the waypoint given in the pilot guide did not agree with my MaxSea charts, which showed us passing overland, near the far side of the river channel.

Nobody was available on the VHF to confer with, so I took an average of the two reference points. As we entered the bend in the river, the depth was okay, but suddenly the keel hit something and a few seconds later the depth alarm blasted, indicating six and a half feet. We need six feet. Before I could take any corrective action, we plowed into the river bottom and were grounded. Not only was the *Nereid* grounded but dug into the mud so deeply that as the tide receded to a depth of only two and a half feet, she didn't list to her side. We were like a toy sailboat, perfectly upright, mounted on the Lord's mantle.

We were now in radio contact with our buddy boats, *Mischief, Eloise* and *Prism*. Christine, from *Mischief,* wanted to round up a tug to pull us off. Ed from *Prism* wanted to survey the area around us with a lead line. He arrived in his dinghy, and we did a bottom survey with a lead line to determine an escape route for the incoming tide. We were like Captain Cook looking for safe passage through uncharted waters. With Ed's dinghy, we pulled 250 feet of chain and set the bow anchor along a possible escape route, then Ed returned to his boat. Judy and I waited for the flood tide that was expected about 5:00 a.m. We were really "stuck in the mud," though, and I was doubtful the incoming tide would be enough to release us.

At the designated hour and to our surprise and relief, the *Nereid* floated free. We retrieved the anchor and were on our way up the river in plenty of time for the 8:00 a.m. expedition into the jungle to view the orangutans. Safely anchored in the river at Kumai, we transferred to fast boats. As we raced up a Kumai River tributary, placing our trust in our teenage driver, I recalled how I had gone from depression a few hours earlier, grounded in the mud, to a high expectation of observing these magnificent animals in their natural environment—the change in my psychic energy was exponential.

Some movement on the trail ahead of us tipped us off to our first orangutan sighting. We waited and watched, and a man-sized, orange, Sasquatch-like hulk appeared briefly then disappeared into the dense foliage. It was an exciting moment. At the feeding area, the orangutans were out in force, and we spent several hours in close proximity, comparing our related behaviors. The orangutans were relaxed and seemed comfortable with our presence. They have amazing dexterity with fingers and opposable thumbs like ours. According to our guide, the orangutan and human genomes differ by only three percent. I have since confirmed this important factoid. This is a big three percent that has extended our habitat far beyond the hot, steamy jungle and taken us to the moon.

There was a stressful moment, at least for the "acting" male, when he heard in the distance what sounded like large limbs breaking. Something big was headed our way, and he suddenly took off into the dense jungle. Our guide explained that the acting dominant male knew those sounds were made by the dominant male, numero uno, *el supremo,* and he was not going to challenge the social hierarchy, at least not on this day. When the dominant male finally appeared, he was huge. Our "acting" had made the right decision when he left.

Our return trip in the fast boats began and ended with a major tropical downpour, or monsoon. Our bodies and clothes, sweaty from the day's activities in the hot, humid jungle, were washed clean in the hour-long deluge of fresh water. It had been quite a day. In twenty-four hours, we went from being grounded, stuck in the mud, to getting free at 5:00 a.m., getting picked up in a high-speed boat at 8:00 a.m., racing up a jungle river tributary, spending the day kibitzing with orangutans, getting caught in a monsoonal downpour, having dinner that evening in the colorful town, walking the streets alive

with people, and returning to *Nereid*, in bed 9:00 p.m.—
asleep, 9:01.

Note: The human genome differs from the common
house mouse, Mus musculus, by only fifteen percent. The
insightful professor Jay Savage, in his book *Evolution*,
begins with: *All living things are the same but different.*

Tanker, Tug and Bad Guys

The last leg of our trip to Singapore was more life
threatening than our grounding and orangutan adventures
at Kumai. On our second night out from Kumai, which
was very dark, I noticed a set of lights getting closer. I
made several course changes, which were duplicated by
the unidentified set of lights. They kept closing the gap,
and not having any success with course changes, I pulled
out our large floodlight and began flashing it directly at
the oncoming vessel. It was coming on fast and, based on
the distribution of what looked like running lights, was a
large ship. I then took the floodlight and flashed it up and
down our mainsail. Our tricolor light, at the top of the
mast, had been on all along; now I was showing them that
light was a sailboat and not some distant star. I then woke
Judy up, and she responded quickly to my request to take
over the steering. I went below and called on the VHF,
channel sixteen then channel seventy-three, saying,
"Tanker, tanker, this is sailboat, tanker, tanker,
this is sailboat, what is your intention?"
I repeated this several times—no reply. Then Judy
shouted down to me, "The tanker has turned sharply to
starboard!"
This was probably the most frightening moment
to date for my time at sea. Judy has these experiences all
the time; she gets nervous if there is another boat on the
same ocean as her. We are not sure what saved us, but

out of options and in the night with such a large ship, we may never have been seen or heard from again. There are stories of similar incidents with the big ships, and one reoccurring explanation is that sometimes the pilot gets bored and likes to generate some excitement, or is just curious to see who is out there with them. Anyway, we are happy to be the ones reporting this incident and will always have someone on watch and wide awake for our night passages.

Our next incident was in daylight with a tugboat pulling a barge on a long towline. From a distance, it looked like we were moving much faster than the tug, and our angle of approach should have given us plenty of room to pass. I did not want to slow our progress by passing behind, and passing under the towline would have resulted in a dismasting—which would not have been good—so we continued with Plan A to pass ahead. As we closed the distance between us, it became apparent that something had to change, as the present dynamic was looking more and more threatening. A course adjustment required a sail change, as we were running wing on wing, which gave us only a small angle in which to maneuver. The lesson here is that an initial decision is based on limited data and that it is important to continue collecting data, check your ego and remain flexible to change your mind. How does a tug pulling a huge load change course?—It doesn't. We decided to slow down and let the big guy pass.

Our third moment of excitement occurred in daylight with no other boats around, except for a native-style fishing boat in the distance that kept adjusting course to intercept us. We have passed many similar such craft, but they were always on their own courses or tending fish traps. This was the first fishing boat we had seen since leaving Kumai, and we had seen no marker buoys for fish traps or anything to indicate this was a fishing area.

Our suspicions continued to accumulate; the oncoming boat had fish traps on deck, but it was noticeably poorly equipped. There were no floats visible for the traps and no line inside them for the 175-foot depths in this area. The three men in the boat were not native, and as they approached, all three of them were watching us. Usually, we have been of little interest to native fishing boats; maybe one of the occupants takes a moment to glance at us and sometimes wave. Something else was strange that I didn't realize at the time, but all three of these guys had similar-style haircuts. Anyway, it was time to start the engine and get more speed; we had been sailing about 4 knots at the time. The man on the foredeck was holding a single small float, the size used to separate two boats when tied up.

As our boat speed increased, there was a moment of decision and they opted not to give chase. They could have easily overtaken us, but maybe when they saw a second person—Judy peering out of the hatch wearing a studley baseball cap—and my buffed body, glazed and tattooed, that they...wait, they couldn't see my tattoo. As we motor sailed away, we discussed our contingency measures. I had my new Borneo headhunter's knife to cut off hands grabbing hold of the *Nereid*'s cap rail. Judy could lock and load the spray bottle of tequila we kept to quiet big fish when hauled on deck, and of course there was always the heavy artillery of smoke flares and phosphorous incendiaries.

We have since learned that there are advisors operating in the South China Sea, financed by our tax dollars to help control piracy. They could have been pirates or pirate chasers. If they were pirate chasers, they should continue to exclude sailboats operated by old people. If they were pirates, the short military-style haircuts may be an attempt to improve their image and be invited onboard. We will never know for sure, which is probably best, but they were interested in something aside from fishing.

Chapter 12

Malaysia

Traveling with the Big Boys

The Singapore Strait had been a classroom in managing high-density ship traffic. All said, we didn't do too badly. When we entered the strait, it was full of ships of all sizes and shapes. Not just the standard oil tankers and container ships—which were huge—but ships that loaded and unloaded, ships pulling barges and mystery ships that looked like they had been designed by Dr. Seuss. The most challenging part of the encounter was trying to determine which were moving, which were just holding in the water and which were anchored. My mate liked to keep tabs on these important details and at one point gave up in frustration with no further communication.

There were designated traffic lanes on the chart where the moving traffic was supposed to be concentrated, but the boats didn't always follow suit. We tried to stay along the edge of this lane, assuming it was like a bike path for smaller and slower-moving boats.

There also seemed to be a lane just for barge traffic. There were many barges pulled by their tugs, some of which moved more slowly than we did. Anyway, we waited for the traffic to clear and then made our move to cross the traffic lane just like a busy street. The other side of the street was filled with boats, which we picked our way through. Most of the big ships were anchored. Many smaller support craft were not and readily changed course as they maneuvered through traffic.

We made it without incident across the strait and up the eight miles of jungle river to the marina at Sebana Cove. The crossing was stressful, something we did not want to do again—at least not right away—but the river was slow and easy to navigate, and we arrived at the marina just before dark. It was always a relief when we arrived at our destination in daylight. Looking back, it was a very exciting day.

We left Sebana Cove after a restful two months. This time entering the strait, we were better prepared, and we handled the high-density ship traffic like the experienced sailors we were. I estimated that moving boat traffic was about ten large ships which were replaced by another ten large ships each hour. Over the thirty-hour passage from Singapore to Port Dickson, in the Strait of Malacca, we saw and kept an eye on about 300 ships, making sure we stayed out of their way. How much my mate had matured since our first crossing could be exemplified by the following: I had taken a little rest in the cabin, leaving Judy to deal with the ships for a short time. I later popped up into the cockpit having overslept.

"How's it going?" I asked her, half expecting a tearful explosion.

"Now don't be alarmed, but look behind you," she replied.

I turned and there was a huge ship moving off our port side, at a safe distance but much closer than expected. She was totally calm and smiling. Without question, we had arrived and could travel with the big boys.

Marina Hopping in SE Asia

The marina and hotel at Sebana Cove, Malaysia, were financed by the Malay government, and they spared no expense. The intent was to attract boaters and vacationers from nearby Singapore. So what we had was a five-star jungle resort with all the charm and convenience of civilization but without the crowd and at Motel 6 rates. There were some unusual folks in these parts. The sultan of Dubai had a small bungalow and parked his boat there. I was hoping to meet him and ask how it was going, but he never showed.

The charm of this place included the hotel restaurant, where for evening entertainment a host of geckos appeared on the walls to catch anything flying by and chase each other for a share of a lucky catch. The grounds around the hotel and the swimming pool had visitors of the small monitor lizard variety. These characters appeared for a warm-up in the midday sun on the patio. The marina ladies who handled the important transactions were in burkas and always very friendly and helpful. It was a short ride on a shuttle to town for supplies and great coffee with the locals and a lunch buffet for five ringgits ($1.50 US).

There were some cats in the area, but they were not that social. They could best be described through an encounter we had with an old fellow selling goods at the market. I had taken an interest in his wares but decided not to purchase, so I made an excuse that it was nice stuff and I would think about it. Well, his time in life and experience told him I was not going to buy anything, and he cut me off with a "Ya, ya, ya."

This had to be said quickly with a slight attitude, and that was what the Malaysian cats were saying to us. When we gave them the standard greeting of "Here kitty, kitty," they didn't even break stride or look at us. They were saying "Ya, ya, ya." They don't have time for anyone's nonsense, too much to do.

After a two-month rest stop that included a trip to the States, we headed out from Sebana Cove without checking the prop or the underside of the boat. I had assumed, since we were in fresh water, that there would be minimal accumulation of fouling organisms. We motored out of the marina and down the river without needing much power, but at the river mouth, where I needed more power to maneuver, it was obvious something was wrong. We anchored, and a quick inspection under the boat revealed a propeller solid with critters. It was too much for a free-diver cleanup, so on went the scuba gear, and after an hour or so of work we were ready for Singapore.

Singapore was clean, efficient, highly regulated and full of oh so many, many people. I couldn't help but wonder how all of these people were going to get into heaven. If they did get in—and they should—it was going to be crowded, but if the folks at Google can copy all the information in the world in the next ten years for our searching pleasure, then I suppose anything is possible.

The western side of Singapore had the famous and luxurious Raffles Marina, and with regularly scheduled bus service to the nearest MTA or fast train, one had access to all the resources and entertainment in Singapore. At the marina, there were some amenities we had not had before, including a newspaper delivered to our boat each day, ice delivered upon request and a six-lane bowling alley. There was an elegant swimming pool and a variety of restaurants. They also had a haul-out yard where one of the Volvo racing yachts was being refitted for the upcoming race season.

We had our main batteries replaced and some warrantee work done on our new Raymarine autopilot. Repairs took longer than expected, but eventually we were on our way up the Strait of Malacca to Port Dickson, Lumut and Penang, and maybe if we got lucky, we would catch up with the Sail Malaysia Rally.

The Rally

We were supposedly in the Sail Malaysia Rally, a 540-mile run from Singapore to Langkawi, Malaysia. The rally was almost half over and we had not made any of the functions, which included dinners, tours and cultural events along the way. This was for the usual reason: boat repairs had kept us out of the events. However, over seventy-five boats had somehow managed to actively participate. Our main purpose in joining the rally was to meet cruisers with plans to do the Red Sea and Mediterranean. We attended the kickoff event in Singapore and made the first leg of the rally to Port Dickson in record time. Our repaired autopilot performing as it should kept us rested, putting the next rally function in our sights.

We got a late start but with an overnight run in the Strait of Malacca, we could make the 145 miles to Lumut. Buoyweather and the grib files indicated little to no winds over the next seven days, but off we charged, expecting to motor all the way. Into the night, the weather went crazy with gusts to 40 knots on the nose and into a current of 2 knots. With only a reefed staysail and motoring full out, we could only do 1-2 knots. After ten hours of tacking close-hauled into the current, we had progressed about twenty miles. It was an exhausting effort and we were using up fuel for little gain, so we decided to heave-to. This procedure didn't work well in a current, and after fifteen hours we had a net loss of ten miles. Our time and fuel were slipping away, along with another rally function.

We finally headed for shore, and by midnight were anchored in the Strait of Malacca, better known as Pirate Alley. We anchored near shore in the dark and kept off our cabin and anchor lights so as not to attract any attention. The next morning, the winds had dropped to 20 knots, and we motored into Lumut at 6:00 p.m., too late for the dinner and the big day of planned activities.

There was an additional tour the next day, and I called the listed contact people in the morning. They put us on the tour, which was leaving at 8:30. That gave us only thirty minutes to make the pickup point in front of the marina. It took that long to launch our dinghy, so I called the marina and asked if we could be picked up at our boat, not a monumental request for a marina. I was never able to get through to the person on the phone that we needed a lift to shore. Heavily accented English and limited communication skills offset the miracle of our cell phone working in this foreign country.

Not much talk was going on the VHF radio, so I went topside to check out the boats and saw a young lady and got her attention.

"Hello, how are you? I see you have your dinghy launched and ready to go."

"Yes," she said, "I remember you from Sebana Cove. How are you?"

"I need to ask a huge favor. We need to get to the marina to catch a rally tour leaving in a few minutes. Would you run us to shore in your dinghy? It is worth a 'slab' of beer of your choice."

"Sure," she replied. "Let me get my husband."

Her man dragged himself on deck, rubbing his eyes, and after a quiet discussion and long pause, agreed to do the deed. We were back in the game, ready to attend our first function!

We were excited, and as we motored in, I said to our chauffer, "I can't believe I had the nerve to ask this favor."

"I can't believe I am doing this," he said.

I reminded him of the slab and he seemed pleased.

We rushed to the marina office and began our wait. Three French couples also showed up, and shortly after that, a pickup van arrived. Turned out it was the actual tour bus, and it only seated six. There was much arguing and noise coming from the French quarter—not the guys, just the ladies. One lady was very upset, saying she had booked this tour and didn't want to sit with three crowded in the back seat. That didn't even include us as participants.

The tour driver spoke little English and zero French. The three Frenchmen didn't want to get involved with their ladies and just stood around, one of them smiling. The driver finally got the idea of what was needed and called for a bigger van. At this point, the French lady said she wanted her money back, which sounded good to me—then there were six counting us, and I would be glad to sit in the middle.

Finally, Judy decided that she was not going on a trip with people who didn't like us. For me that was not a problem, having worked many years for the government. One of the Frenchmen made a serious pitch for Judy to go and said that nobody liked the other couple, and I could see why. Anyway, Judy became more adamant about not going. The conciliatory Frenchman finally gave up, and so we said our adieus, and with forced smiles, we walked away to check out downtown Lumut. Another rally function bit the dust, but there was always the next function at a place called Penang. Weather permitting and putting aside personal differences, we hoped to make the next function.

The Rest of the Story:
I ruptured a disc loading fuel cans in Lumut.
Painfully attended part of the function in Penang.
Major back surgery in Penang.
Missed the last function in Langkawi.
Recovered with swimming and R&R at Rebak Marina.
We did get T-shirts.

Surgery in Penang

Week three and still in the hospital—here for one more day, into a rest home for four weeks, and then I should be safe to return to the boat. In my seventy-one years of active living, I have put my back through some challenging and exciting experiences. However, this time, while handling heavy fuel cans, I twisted my back severely as the dinghy suddenly shifted. I have hurt my back before, but with the care of "Dr. Jude" and with rest and ice packs always returned to operational health.

Before starting this sailing adventure, one of my suppressed fears was to need major surgery in a foreign land or a third-world country. My first choice for any significant procedure was to get back to the USA. This was not an option unless I could make the entire trip lying in the aisle of the plane. After a couple of weeks trying to get the body to repair itself, we decided to call it. I was not getting better this time; in fact, I was getting worse. The pain became so severe that I didn't care who operated—forget the USA, get the janitor.

By the time the decision was made to see a local doctor, I was flat on my back in the salon of our boat and could not even entertain the idea of getting up the companionway steps or any movement at all. Judy made the rounds to some boats in the marina, and in a few minutes there were six guys in our boat. While maintaining my prone position, they somehow managed to lift me out of the salon, off the boat and onto a gurney.

The ambulance ride was a trip with the siren on, so it was definitely first-class handling all the way. We had checked the yellow pages for hospitals in the area and asked fellow boaters, but it was mostly luck that guided us to Loh Guan Lye. This hospital had a specialist for just about every body part. My operation by Dr. Soon Hock Chye was a success, and I felt blessed to have had this procedure done where the doctors and medical support staff were of such high quality. The ruptured disc in my back required trimming and fusing the lower three vertebrate with stainless-steel screws into a titanium bar. I have been out of the hospital for eight weeks and pain free thanks also to my physical therapists Morgan and Ooi Kok Eng.

Judy had to take over some of my responsibilities during this time. These were chores she had purposely avoided, such as checking the engine oil, charging the battery and dealing with shore power disruptions. She also had to go shopping and replace one of the *Nereid* charging systems. Her most challenging aspect of shopping was getting this male-oriented culture to assist a woman who was not with her husband.

She was even approached and sternly reprimanded by an older man on the street with, "Where is your husband?"

"He is in the hospital," she replied, equally stern. No doubt to imply, "You better back off, Jack, or I'll put you in there with him."

Part of my rehabilitation process involved the use of a walker. My experience in the hospital and outside on the street I filed away for future reference. In Penang, as in most Southeast Asian countries, it was "pedestrian beware." I was not even sure a motorist was required to stop if he ran over someone. I must say that I was amazed with the change of attitude and degree of consideration shown to someone with a walker. With my new-found armored vehicle, I would enter a crosswalk or any point on the street, and irrespective of traffic density, it was like Moses entering the Red Sea. While I did not tarry in my crossings or abuse this newly discovered convenience, it was a refreshing take on people, and I hope it translates to other countries or wherever we are in need of the magical walker.

Malaysia prides itself on respecting other cultures and religious beliefs. I will always remember a conversation with one of my nurses that took place during Christmas. I was up and about with my walker in the hospital, and beside me was one of my nurses. We were standing in the foyer watching Santa Claus, Christmas music playing in the background. There was a line of little kids, and they were each stepping up to receive a gift from Santa.

"What would you like for Christmas?" I asked my nurse.

"Oh, I am Muslim," she quickly responded. "We do not have Santa Claus."

"I know," I said, "but just pretend you could have one thing from Santa, anything. What would you choose?"

She thought for several moments, and then suddenly her eyes and face lit up with a big smile. "For you to get better."

Penang: World Food Court

The *New York Times* selected Penang, Malaysia, as the number one must-visit destination for 2009. That was a headline in the local paper a few weeks ago. The *Times* ranked forty-four places to go in 2009. They listed Beirut second, which didn't sound all that friendly, but Phuket, Thailand, was listed fifteenth, and just to put some perspective on this, Metz, France, was sixth. According to the article, adventurous foodies were turning to Penang and eating their way through the lively street-food scenes of what they were calling the culinary capital of Southeast Asia. Anyway, there were plenty of places to eat and we were hoping to sample a few. There was a cultural competition between Chinese, Indian and Malaysian eateries. There were also the usual American representatives, such as McDonald's, KFC and Pizza Hut.

The most skillful and serious about eating were the Chinese. When their order arrived—and it was a sight to behold in complexity—their conversation at the table stopped and everyone got down to the business of eating. There never seemed to be a straightforward passage of foods ready to eat. No—each bite was carefully assembled. This required picking and choosing from the variety before them, then dipping the assemblage into one or several sauces before it could pass entry into the mouth. The tools usually included extra-long chopsticks in one hand and a large porcelain soup spoon in the other. With soups, the spoon was loaded up using the chopsticks, and for non-soup dishes, the spoon helped assemble the bite for the chopsticks. In either case, both hands were constantly working.

Indian restaurants were an entirely different story. They didn't feature the serious focus and workmanship required in assembling a bite of food—in fact, quite the opposite. First of all, there were no tools to bother with. One ate with fingers and used only the right hand. The left hand should remain in one's lap the entire time, which was the challenging part for me, being left handed. At our favorite Indian restaurant, a banana leaf was the plate. We learned to tear off pieces of the bread and meat with our fingers, using only one hand. From there, we dipped the food into the appropriate spicy hot sauce, and then the bite was complete and finger-licking good.

Imagine a family of six or eight, kids, parents and grandparents, all eating with their fingers. It was interesting to see a young couple, possibly on a first date, having a fun conversation while eating with their fingers, or an older couple dressed up for an evening out but again eating with their fingers. Kind of messy, right? Well, each restaurant came equipped with a sink in the main dining area in which one could wash hands and, in my case, it was used before, during and after the feast.

In every case, whether Malaysian food, Chinese food, whatever, we must give thanks to the chicken, although if the bird was small it was probably a pigeon. Where would we be without chickens? If one took the chicken out of the diet of this world, it would have catastrophic cultural impacts. And where were all these fine birds being raised? We did visit the local market, where we saw these courageous creatures in cages awaiting their fate. Judy ran for cover to the vegetable stand, while I stayed for part of the processing. Although the birds were handled carefully, it was not a pretty sight, and for a moment I had a thought that vegetables were the answer, but I have since crossed back over to the fowl side.

There was one culinary area that could use some improvement, and that was the breakfast menu. The standard American eggs over easy with fried potatoes and bacon was hard to find except on the *Nereid.* While there was an abundance of eggs, there did not seem to be a translation for "over easy." Most places didn't offer eggs, but rather served a noodle dish or baked beans for breakfast, and a few promoted dim sum. Coffee had been perfected and was readily available, the best stuff being a Chinese white coffee either hot or iced, usually for about one ringgit. Costs on most items were a few ringgits; the exchange rate was three and a half ringgits to a dollar. A chicken dinner with fried rice and drinks for two went for about twelve ringgits, roughly $3.50. That was on the low side, as we had spent up to 150 ringgits for pizza. The pizza was an Italian treatment with no meat and it was outstanding, but we only did that once.

In summary, the price was right and the food was right and the art of eating was right. Until now, my attention span had become so limited in the process of food selection that I had it down to a few numbers.

"I will have a number three, please."

I can eat a number three without ever really looking at it; maybe I didn't want to look. I could eat a number three or any numbered entree while talking to someone in the car, while on the phone, reading a book or watching TV. Many times I have wished for number three in tablet form so I could, with one swallow, take care of my bodily need for food.

With our extended stay in Penang, I am happy to report a rediscovery of the eating experience and appreciation for food.

Circle of Life

"Dr. Soon said he did not want you to overdo it on this trip. We need to stop for the night," my darling wife reminded me.

We were headed for Rebak, a small island off Langkawi, Malaysia, with a quiet protected marina. It was getting dark, and Pulau Payar, an island only thirty miles from Rebak, was just ahead. The chart indicated buoys were available for tie-up, if the dive boats were not using them. No dive boats, so we headed in. The buoys were there but very close to shore and seemed risky for our boat with its six-foot draft. There was only one boat in the area, a powerboat. We motored up to it and asked about the depth at the buoys, and they assured us it would be no problem. Our depth gauge was presently in its part-time operational mode, so we thanked the power-boater and moved in for one of the near-shore buoys.

We were now experienced with buoy anchoring, slowing down, and holding position to hook the feeder rope, connect our anchor line and secure it to the deck cleat before we drifted away. Not as easy as it sounds, but this time there was an added feature. There was a bird perched on the buoy. I expected it to fly off when I began our tie-up. Much to my surprise, the bird stayed, as if to say, "I was here first, so find your own buoy." Actually, he was not aggressive but more asleep, eyes half closed, feathers a bit worn on the ends and continually adjusting himself as the buoy bobbed in the water. Now we were adding additional motion to the buoy, but he continued to compensate and hold his perch.

I returned about an hour later, checking the noise of the buoy bumping the side of the boat, and to my surprise the bird was still on the buoy. With each bump against the boat, the bird did a major "re-perch" requiring some wing action. I told him I was sorry for the added inconvenience and went below for the night.

Next morning, I went forward to check our tie-up to the buoy and noticed our bird friend was gone. Wait—once back in the cockpit, there he was, feathers still looking worn, eyes half closed. The only new feature was the fresh deposits he had made. The debate that ensued with my mate was an attempt to assess his situation. Was he sick, resting or near the end of his run? We decided to see if food and drink were needed, so Judy put some water in a bowl and I got some of Romeo's leftover cat food, which we are still carrying for some reason, and made our presentations.

He eventually got up on the rim of the bowl but then fell in. He floated there in the bowl for a few minutes, then crawled out. The cat food was of no interest, so basically our feeding efforts failed. He sat there on the deck, still not looking good. Where was a biologist when we needed one?

Our next seminar was based on the assumption that he was sick and needed to have his life ended as mercifully as possible. I had a slingshot but I'm not very accurate, even at close range. I had finished off wounded game birds in my earlier hunting career by wringing their necks. Judy did not agree with any of these options and was totally unimpressed with my hunting experience. Our talk must not have sat well with our visitor, as he suddenly began trying to get himself up on the cap rail, a height of about six inches. He kept trying, so I decided to give him a boost. He was watching me closely but remained perfectly still as I put my hand around him and placed him on the cap rail. I was sure he was seriously sick or hurt. He sat there, unsteady, like he was about to fall off.

I was headed down below deck when Judy shouted, "Raymond, look, he's flying!"

I turned around, and sure enough there he was, skimming over the surface of the water. He touched down twice but kept going and continued on out of sight. His circle of life was on hold; he was still a player.

When is it really over?—One never knows. Good luck, my friend, and thanks for stopping by.

Zonation

"Zonation" was all I said as the *Nereid*, our Valiant 40, was hauled out of the tropical waters of Malaysia at Rebak Marina. The bottom was covered with marine life, but now that name would change to "fouling organisms," a study for some and money for others who would assist this aging marine biologist with their removal. I had once been on a field trip in Mexico with other graduate students where we traveled half a day to a cliff overlooking the ocean. Below us were breaking waves against the layers of marine life attached to the rocks. The instructor gave a one-word lecture: "Zonation."

The hull of the *Nereid* was packed with invertebrates, just like the cliffs in Mexico. Those dominant marine organisms more adapted to exposure were near the water line and included a species of smaller barnacle and some serpulid polychaetes in their white calcareous tubes. Below these dwelled larger species of barnacles and oysters, their upper shells providing home sites for an array of colorful sponges, crustaceans and soft corals. The barnacles were not as accommodating to other species, as they must keep their topsides unobstructed to catch their food. Large tunicates or sea squirts lined the bottom of the keel like Japanese lanterns.

The beautiful zones of marine life all had to go, and we needed help. This would be the first time Judy and I would not be doing all the work ourselves. It was a relief, but there was also some guilt. While two young men scraped away on the hull in the hot sun for 40RM ($10 US) per day, we sat inside with the air conditioner and busied ourselves with other projects. This first crew was very young, with upper arms the size of my wrists. When they applied the scraper after a dose of paint remover, not much came off. Our yard time doubled and the paint remover disappeared much faster than expected.

I demonstrated how to get more paint off with the scrapper using two hands.

"Oh, you very strong," one of them said.

Other boaters came with an abundance of advice.

"You got to keep an eye on these kids or they will take forever."

"You need to fire them and get another crew."

They prepped me several times on what to say to the yard foreman, and each morning right after yoga class I would come back so "enlightened" I would smile and nod approval to my young friends. Later in the day, about the time I returned to normal, everybody had gone home except my wife, and I wasn't about to fire her.

After the haul out and cleaning, the next big decision was what to put on the vessel's bottom. There were the standard discussions of soft or hard ablative paints, but the intriguing ongoing quest was to find the perfect additives. These ranged from the highly toxic and illegal in most parts of the world TBT (tributyltin—you're dead), to more environmentally friendly chili powder. Chili powder left a rough surface, but when "fowlers" considered selecting a treated boat as a home site, they would shun it, almost as if to say, "This bottom is too hot." Chili powder should not be used in Mexican water, where it reportedly may serve as an attractant.

Whatever the formula, it was always interesting to hear the testimonies of those who had the answer for the pesky fowlers. It would be nice if these testimonies came with a control to compare against the test additive. We really didn't know anything about these additives or the paint products without controls. While inconvenient, it could be very cost effective to just do a small area. Ideally the boat would be a catamaran or two-bottom, and we could do one with the full treatment and the other without. That would be a bottom experiment to talk about and worthy of publication in *Cruising World*.

A new crew was eventually brought in to work on our boat. These guys were more physical and the zonal distribution patterns began to disappear. They even removed the multiple layers of old paint, but I was still feeling guilty about not working. Judy set the record straight.

She said in her sweetest voice, "Raymond, the workers don't care what you are doing. You are old."

I looked in the mirror and I think what she was seeing was not age but just facial zonation.

Backpacker Suite

Traveling backpacker style can be very cost effective, plus adventuresome. We were doing some land travel with our stuff in backpacks and, assuming there was no age limit, going where the backpackers went. On our return to Penang for a visit with my orthopedic surgeon and some x-rays of the new hardware in my back, we decided to make this a four-day trip. We checked into the Stardust Guest House, only eight rooms with café, Internet and so forth on the first floor.

We made the room reservation over the phone but they didn't take our names, so we could only hope there would be a room for us when we arrived. Most places required prepay and a name. Our luxury hotel on my first round of rehab, the Bayview Hotel, was 175 ringgits per day. The Stardust was four days for 105 ringgits, about $10 US per day. Of course, there was no pool, exercise room, massage therapy or room service at the Stardust.

I will describe the room, furniture, bathroom and towel in that order. The room was up one flight of stairs at the end of the hall, the bathroom at the other end. The room, about ten by ten feet, was very clean—wood floors, nothing on the walls, two windows opening to the lively street scene directly below. The windows were mostly covered by the outside hotel sign. We could see over the sign enough to know that we were upstairs. It was a no smoking room; however, the outside window ledge was filled with cigarette butts, washed out by the rain so no smell, just the visual if we looked down behind the sign. The door was the weak link in the system, with only the basic push-to-lock knob and enough space around the latch to open it with a credit card, or if a thief didn't have a credit card, he could use a small stick. The special features of this room were the fan and air conditioner, which both worked.

There was a small desk and metal folding chair that served double duty as a nightstand. There were some hangers on the back of the door for clothes. The fan was also used as a hanger when clothes needed drying. The twin beds had fitted bottom sheets—no top sheets or blankets needed in these warm climates. The mattresses were firm. Sitting on the edge near the middle would cause the bed frames to separate and, without warning, suddenly drop the mattress down a few inches. The potential for a sudden change in elevation during sleep or any extracurricular activity was somewhat disconcerting.

The two large bath towels were issued almost reverently at the desk when we checked in. We each had a towel and used it in several capacities: bathrobe, drying, and blanket. The bathroom, at the other end of the hall, was shared by boys and girls. We could wrap ourselves with the towel for safe passage, and upon arrival step into the toilet area or shower. It was always a surprise to see new faces. There were two sinks with mirrors for washing up and personal grooming and a window looking into another hotel courtyard that, on occasion, had some entertainment value.

The towel, of course, was also valuable for its intended purpose of drying off after a shower. It was important to shower early so our towels would be dry at night, when they might be needed as blankets to modulate the temperature settings of an air conditioner seemingly out of control.

The evening time was spent reading and playing cards, and we didn't even miss not having a TV. On prior hotel stays, we would turn on the TV after dinner, and that was it until late night. Judy was apprehensive about this overall step down in comfort from the Bayview to the Stardust and tried to find a good reason to cancel and move back to the Bayview.

She kept saying, "The only thing I am worried about is that I am not worried. There must be something wrong with me."

"Tomorrow I Will Do Something"

This has been my theme or mode of operation for the last six weeks here at Rebak Marina in Malaysia. The doctor said no sailing, only light activities for six months, so that was my excuse. Our daily routine that required some energy expenditure was as follows:

Get up at first light, open up boat, take in birdcalls, check batteries

Go back to bed, await new day, think of something to do

Get up again about 8:30 and see Judy off to exercise class

Leg stretches and back exercises while she is gone

Go back to bed, awaiting her return about 9:30

Get up again, turn on air conditioner, breakfast

Discuss lunch options, read and/or do Sudoku until 11:00

Adjust shade awning

Lunch

Afternoon nap, emails, some reading and writing

Late afternoon, head to pool for swimming, reading and study

Check Komodo dragon feeding area on way to pool

Study pool attire, black with eye slits to barely covering

Card game with my mate, two games, about one hour

Dinner on *Nereid* or catch 7:15 shuttle to big island restaurant

Order nasi goreng and iced coffee

Moonlight boat ride back to Rebak Marina, about fifteen minutes

Return to boat, select evening video, reading, Sudoku,

Evening discussions: grandkids, Red Sea, where to live on land

The birds' early-morning chorus at the marina was amazing; usually five or six especially talented species led the group. Our favorite Australian bird was the kookaburra. Our favorite Malaysian bird was the oriental pied hornbill—not a great songster, but fascinating to study. Up to twenty-eight inches in length, with their huge bills they carefully selected from the trees one berry at a time. If we quietly complimented their beautiful beaks, they would let us get up close and personal. They were very social. Pairs mated for life, and that could be thirty years. The female found a hollow in a tree, barricaded herself in and laid one egg, and the male provided for her.

Being grounded and only using our boat for shelter and close body contact, we planned some trips into the terrestrial world. We had until January in SE Asia, at which time, pirates permitting, we'd depart for the Red Sea.

Our passports were almost full. Running out of blank pages was a very big deal. We recently made a special trip to the US embassy in Kuala Lumpur, the capital of Malaysia, for more pages. While there, we picked up a visa for China that was a four-day exercise. Air travel and accommodations were so reasonably priced with Air Asia that we added a few more trips. We were planning five days in Chiang Mai, Thailand, twenty-one days in Cambodia and Vietnam with another couple, and fifteen days in China. Our annual trip to the US would also include a stop in Paris for a river-barge cruise with grandson Milo, and then we'd carry on to San Francisco to visit our other grandkids, Colette and Gage.

Our trip to the capital had some indicators that
we might be getting too old for this stuff. The taxi driver
could not understand me when I tried to parrot back
exactly the directions he had given me to the Chinese
embassy. He would look at me as if asking, "What are you
saying?" We did this routine several times. The other
negative highlight was an exchange with a vendor in
Chinatown, a young, aggressive entrepreneur who wanted
to sell me a Rolex. He went from a thousand Ringgits
down to three hundred and finally one hundred as we
tried to leave. Wow, a Rolex for only $28 US.

"How many do you want?" he kept asking.

"None," I'd reply.

This was followed with a few more rounds of
"how many."

Finally I said, "How about twenty-five."

He looked at me, shook his head, then said
something about old people that I was going to pursue
until Judy jumped in, preventing an international incident.
And just when I had recently finished a book about the
life of Buddha. Looks like it will be some time before I
move to the next level. If I run out of time, I could come
back as a lower life form, which would not be good,
unless maybe as a cat.

Bye for now. Hope all is well in your part of the
world. Don't worry about us. Judy is planning to bake
banana bread and make caramels. I just need some ideas
on what to do tomorrow.

Mr. Din

"Do you want a good car or a not-so-good car?"

We were talking with Mr. Din, the man to see for
a rental car to get supplies or explore the adjacent island
of Langkawi, a short ferry ride from the marina on Rebak
Island. "Not so good" meant that something didn't work,

like the radio or air conditioning, although most day's air conditioning would be essential. All the basics like brakes and ignition should work. A "good" car should have had all of the above in working order.

Mr. Din was about six feet three inches and didn't smile or say much. If one called ahead for a car, the conversation was very efficient and went something like this…

"Hello."

"Mr. Din?"

"Yes."

"This is Ray Emerson."

"Yes."

"We are coming on the nine thirty ferry."

"Yes."

"Do you have a good car?"

"Yes."

"Thank you, Mr. Din."

Click.

There was no pressure and no competition. He didn't do much but control the keys. The best part of Mr. Din's business was that there was no paperwork or questions asked. He just handed over the keys and pointed to the car. No questions about insurance, driver's license, co-drivers, how one planned to pay. None of that brain-drain stuff. Did your present insurance apply, should you get the extras coverage, would anyone else be driving? It was great. The whole transaction took about thirty seconds. Our only worry was that there might not be enough gas in the car to get us to the nearest petrol station, especially if another boater had used it. If the needle worked on the gas gauge and showed any movement, it was probably good to go.

Returning the car was also a no-hassle, straightforward operation. There was no mileage check or inspection for damage. The only thing that might cause problems was finding Mr. Din before the ferry left to take us back to Rebak Island. When we had located him, we just handed over the keys and, in the case of a good car, fifty ringgits ($18 US). It would take a few more trips before we were confident enough to try a not-so-good car. As it was, we would treat ourselves to a good car. It was ten ringgits more, not a big difference, but the adventurous spirit still moved us, so we would want to try a not-so-good car eventually.

Anyway, all is well in Rebak, Malaysia, and Mr. Din is doing fine.

Two Ladies from Kazakhstan

Our travels have given us the opportunity to meet many different people. These new friendships were formed in Mexico, the South Pacific, New Zealand, Australia and now SE Asia. Some more uncommon places prompted the question, "Is that near someplace I might know?"

The world travelers we met yesterday, waiting for the ferry to take us to the marina at Rebak Island, were two ladies from Kazakhstan. This was the first time we had met anyone from Kazakhstan, which is just south of Russia.

One of these ladies spoke English and translated for her friend, who only spoke Russian. In fact, the other lady was a teacher of Russian. They were both probably in their mid-forties. We sat together under the shaded seating area waiting for the ferry, along with Judy, another cruiser friend and a fellow from India who was not interested in talking. After a few of the usual niceties of beginning conversation, on which Judy as usual took the lead, I decided to enter in.

Keeping a straight face, I asked, "Are your husband's planning to join you?"

After a pause, they replied, "No, they aren't traveling with us. They are in Kazakhstan with the children."

After another thoughtful pause, I said, "You mean to tell me that you two ladies are out here headed for a good time at a luxury resort while your husbands are in Kazakhstan taking care of the kids?"

There was a moment for the translation to sink in, and suddenly both ladies looked at each other and burst into almost uncontrollable laughter, and so did the guy from India. It seemed the innuendos of some jokes were universal.

In my professional life, I gave a scientific paper in Magadan, Russia. Looking out over a very serious audience, I was tempted to omit the jokes, but I didn't. It was amazing to see their stoic faces break into laughter. These people work hard, drink hard and laugh hard. I especially enjoyed giving my paper through a translator, since it gave me time to formulate my next thought or joke. Sometimes my translator, Tatyana, would look at me after I made a joke with some doubt as to what she should do. I would nod for her to go ahead, a routine that always helped to set up the joke. On the last day of the conference, she came up to me with a concerned smile.

"Dr. Emerson," she said in her heavy Russian accent, "I think with the press here today, it would not be good for you to make your jokes."

I don't remember now, but I may have taken her advice, or she may have done it for me.

While working for the government in Alaska, one of my assignments was to visit the native villages and explain some of the pros and cons of exploring for oil in the marine environment. One of my standard jokes in my slide presentation was a picture of the tidal action with Judy jogging on the beach off Ventura, California. The theme was natural forces cleaning a beach. The next slide was the very same tidal action without Judy, and my comment was that she had been swept out to sea. Again with a translator, there was always a delay and then a ripple effect of realization that it was a joke. Anyway, there is a universal thread of humor connecting all of us. We just have to not be afraid to look for it and enjoy it.

If I should see the two ladies from Kazakhstan while they are here at Rebak, I might pose another question: "Is this trip Mafia funded?" These were two tough ladies, so if this is my last communiqué, it means there are some consequential limits to international humor.

Roast Beast

Fiesta Del Toro
Fire Roasted Bull
Three drinks included

The above advertisement appeared in the *Langkawi Link*, a local weekly newspaper, usually about six pages. The feature article on bloodletting using leaches was unrelated to the bull. Price per person was fifty ringgits ($14 US). We decided to go, and it was a short ferry ride to the site of the feed. There were about fifty of us just from the marina, all cruisers, all hungry and always thirsty. For many it was a no-brainer decision—a hunk of meat with three drinks. Since the *Link* advertisement was also for their readership, it attracted another fifty folks. So there were about a hundred people there, plus the cruiser factor, i.e. some hadn't eaten all day. That's *mucho carne* for one bull, and I was concerned that maybe we needed more bulls or a small herd for this crew.

When we arrived at the site, the hapless beast was on a huge rotisserie and charcoaled black from the slow roast. Supposedly it had been cooked in the ground for two days and a third and final day above ground. Cooking something this big was always risky. We knew from previous experience in Alaska, at a wedding where a large pig was buried for several days with some hot rocks. They didn't dig it up until the day of the event. We were all standing around when this steaming carcass was unwrapped. Turned out it should have stayed in the ground a few more days, as it was definitely not ready for serving. The organizers were out of time and by then the groom didn't care, so a few hardy Alaskans began caving off huge pieces to finish cooking on barbecues that suddenly appeared. There was some discussion about in-ground cooking in a land of permafrost—again, the groom's thoughts were elsewhere.

According to Lyda, our local expert from Colombia, in her country they cook the beast in the ground with the hide and hair still on. The hair not being singed or burned when it was excavated meant that it had cooked at the right temperature. Lyda said this method could yield some very tasty results, but there were usually considerable complaints about hair.

As for the Langkawi method, it was cooked to perfection and, unbelievably, they offered all-you-could-eat. In about forty-five minutes, the roast beast on the rotisserie was reduced to a skeleton. It looked like it had been hit by a school of terrestrial piranhas. While the three drinks deadened some of this visual sensitivity, there was a feeling while in the queue that a war chant or some primal dance around the fire would be appropriate. The visual effect was too much for Judy and she refused to eat, touch or look at the offerings.

The first ferry back to our boats was at 10:00 p.m., and we were ready; the next departure was not until midnight. We were definitely showing our age. Even though the company and conversation were delightful, it was time for us to go. There was going to be dancing and a drawing for prizes, and after three drinks, some of these lovely people were just getting started. One nice thing about aging is that it comes with reduced energy and desire to party. The only change we would make for next year's roast beast, if we happen to be here, would be to bring our own barbecue sauce.

"Only Texans know how to make barbecue sauce," Judy says.

I have found she is usually right, and that's no bull.

Chapter 13

Thailand

Romeo Lost and Found

We were on the western coast of Phuket, Thailand, anchored off Nai Yang Beach. Once a day we climbed into our dinghy, *Romeo*, and headed for land. We were like the marines hitting the beach, and it was always different and always a challenge. Tidal flux, wave action, fishing boats or long tails anchored, the various stages of preparation, ongoing advice and the maneuvering skills of the dinghy skipper were some of the variables. Wheels had to be put down. Timing the final approach and exit from the dinghy just before hitting the beach was often of some entertainment value, especially to the comfortably reclined tourists on the beach with nothing to do.

It was usually just the two of us obviously older mariners. I was always amazed that no matter how chaotic the landing process and ensuing struggles to pull the boat up the beach, no one ever bothered to offer assistance. The bigger the crowd, the more we were on our own. If we had capsized and were struggling to keep

from drowning, I would not have been surprised if the
onlookers had remained steadfast onlookers. This was a
wakeup call for our cruising lifestyle; if we can't land the
dinghy in a crowd, without help, then it's time to return
home to the widescreen TV.

This day we tried something different and landed
a considerable distance down the beach from our usual
site. The water was calmer here and less crowded, making
for an easier landing. Our favorite eating place was a
restaurant where one rested on soft cushions with
triangular pillows and were served like in the days of
ancient Rome. I always asked Judy to peel me some
grapes, but she always refused. Usually we could see the
dinghy on the beach, but this time we were too far away,
which was okay since we had never had a problem leaving
Romeo anywhere.

The real problem was the brew. Chang, the local
Thai beer, had an alcohol content of 6.4%. Chang was
only served in a large bottle, and one must have some
self-control, because it was quite refreshing on a warm
afternoon. After a few hours, a pizza and a beautiful
sunset, we realized we would need all our remaining
faculties to get back to the boat.

We hiked the sandy beach to where we had pulled
the dinghy onto the beach, or thought we had. It was
gone! Now, it was high tide, the beach chairs were
stacked and put away and everyone had gone home.
There was no moon this April night, and our torch, to
light our way on a dark beach, was in the dinghy.

After a brief moment of discussing the demerits
of Chang beer and "I told you so…" and "Why did you
park so far away…" we decided to postpone these
questions.

"We haven't gone far enough," Judy said.

I countered with, "We've gone too far."

We decided to control our growing panic and
make a plan. We agreed to walk in opposite directions

along the beach for ten minutes and then return. Without wasting any more time, Judy went one way down the beach and I went the other.

I soon came upon an older-than-me native fellow who was watching me.

I asked him, using my best broken English and pantomime, "Have you seen rubber boat here on beach?"

Without breaking his gaze, he yelled something.

A woman, younger-than-me, possibly his daughter, came over the berm from one of the family restaurants near the beach. She could speak some English, though not enough for a coherent exchange. She in turn called out to someone else, and in moments a girl in her early teens appeared. She spoke perfect English. It took three generations, but the message was clear: there had been a dinghy on the beach, but it was gone.

"The tide peaked two hours ago and swept it away," she said.

We had no way to get back to our boat. The young girl offered to let us sleep in their deck chairs for the night. I tried to imagine Judy doing this, and then realized I hadn't seen her and she should have returned by now.

Now I had a new problem. My mind shifted from the loss of a replaceable object to the loss of an irreplaceable mate. I moved as swiftly as possible, walking quickly down the beach, as running at age seventy-one was no longer an option.

"Judy! Judy!" I shouted.

I moved through the darkness in the direction she had gone. As I yelled louder, the surf noise seemed to increase and cancel my calls. I began to panic. In forty-seven years of marriage, there have been occasions when we didn't want to talk to each other, but this was not one of those times. It was the first time in our many years and adventures together I had ever called her name in fear of having lost her. Minutes before, I had been consumed with the loss of a rubber boat—how ridiculous that had been. I had wondered at the time if our situation could get any worse. Now I had the answer. Yes.

Just then, she suddenly emerged out of the darkness with a big smile.

"I found *Romeo*. Somebody moved her higher up the beach."

What good news! But the best news was standing right before me. It was time to return to our boat and call it a night. I told Judy what had happened when we parted and that we had been offered beach chairs to sleep on for the night. I was not surprised when I got that raised-eyebrow look.

"Are you kidding me?" she said. "You must be out of your mind."

That's my girl and I love her dearly.

Note: We never found the Good Samaritan responsible for saving our dinghy, but we know he's out there… Thank you for your random act of kindness!

Thailand in the Heat

No one starved and no one cooked. It was too hot to cook, and we ate out one or two meals every day. The food was excellent, and there were floating restaurants on the coastal waterways, tree-house restaurants in the city and hundreds of little family-run restaurants everywhere. In the shopping malls were all the major franchises: KFC, McDonalds, and Subway. The best, and by far most cost effective, were the little family-run restaurants. Our favorite place was near the marina, and we usually had a fresh lime drink, vegetable fried rice and one of several main dishes like curry chicken, ginger chicken, etc. The total bill usually ran 130 BHT—that translated in real money to about $1.85 each. Tipping was optional, but when we did there was always a smile with folded hands that added a final touch to our dining experience.

The *Nereid* was lifted out of the water at Boat Lagoon, and what was only to be a depth-gauge refit became a variety of repairs plus a new paint job. All the contractors here were excellent. Our paint job, I thought, looked good, but Mr. Oh, our painter, was not happy with the Valiant's trademark blue stripe and repainted it to his satisfaction at no extra charge. First names were short; Mr. Oh had a great crew with names like First, One and Yew. He was the only one who spoke English, although we struggled yesterday when he said he wanted to "launch," which didn't make any sense. We were weeks from launching. He thought he was saying "lunch."

We rented an apartment at the marina, and it turned out to be a nice break. We had a TV, air conditioning and a bathroom with a shower. The shower was especially appreciated, since my body can produce a full sheen of moisture in a matter of minutes depending on the activity, such as walking or thinking too hard.

We purchased a folding bicycle from another cruiser, and it came in handy since the boat and the market were a good walking distance. On all of my travels on foot or on wheels, I tried to talk to the birds. The common myna bird was the primary voice at the marina. They proved very smart and always called out a welcome. I am sure we were communicating, and it was not just the heat.

We were enjoying our apartment and it's TV with its seven English-speaking stations to monitor. It came with a remote control—the present-day enlightenment tool. The challenge to enlightenment was to control one's mind or ego, according to the Buddha. The Buddhist monks, in their spiritual quest, did not have TV, but traveled their path through meditation and yoga. As I spun through the channels with my remote, I kept my mind under control. If my thoughts began to wander into the self-perceived complexities of my life, I just sought another channel of interest.

Other present-day enlightenment tools were card games, Sudoku, and video games, all of which could hold one's mind in a suspended state of being "here and now." Endless hours spent on these activities might not be a total waste of time—what do you think?—or was it the heat?

We took advantage of the physical and mental conditioning common in this part of the world. The Thailanders gave a rigorous two-hour massage that could be painful if one didn't say something or cry out. The challenge was to find the level of pain that was bearable but still offered some gain. This punishment cost 300 BHT ($9.00 US). For the mental workout, we became Reiki students, channeling some life force. This can even be done from a distance, so if you felt unexpectedly good last night, it might have come from us. This mind stuff fit nicely with some of the Buddha teachings, so all was well on the eastern front.

Note: Also available in the market was a popular chemical physical/mental booster called M150, which I tried. It was about like a Starbucks cup of Joe, only it had very little caffeine. The active ingredients according to Google were inositol and taurine, a sulfhydryl amino acid—more later—maybe.

Chiang Mai

We walked with the elephants and lay down with the tigers. We were tourists in every way. Our first tour began the evening we arrived in Chiang Mai with the cab driver from the airport. We were whisked away to a night safari, expecting the roar of wild beasts and nighttime activities we had read about. Unfortunately, these beasts were not doing much hunting. In fact, most were sleeping, a result of overfeeding. There were a variety of herbivores from various parts of the world, and being vegetarian, they didn't have much time for sleep, so they were active around the tour vehicle. The tour guide was pleasant, but her English was so heavily accented it resulted in little information exchange. I did have a few minutes with a very awake seven-month-old tiger that wanted his bottle of milk. I held the tiger and his bottle on my lap while he guzzled his prey.

Next day, we found ourselves on the back of a very large Indian elephant named Kopak. While Kopak had a handler sitting on his head and guiding him down the trail, there were times when Kopak was the handler of the handler and would decide he needed a good scratching of his side along the trail wall or some nourishment. He would reach over the side of the trail for tender shoots that he would pull out and then slap around until the dirt fell off and the shoots were ready to eat.

We had to trust that Kopak was as opposed to falling off the side of the steep trail as we were. His big moment was with a branch of mangos on the trail that the handler wanted him to leave, but there was no question who was in charge. We watched him carefully strip each mango from the branch and consume it. If Kopak had been with Hannibal, they would still be en route, but his speed in this jungle setting was perfect for us.

Back at the elephant camp, we were treated to some tricks and even a soccer game. Each team had a goalie and two strikers. The finale featured six of the more artistic pachyderms, all about two years old. They walked into the arena, each carrying a box of paints, and at their own easels they each did a painting. One would have to see this to believe it. All of the paintings sold before Judy could get one, so we settled for some prints from the gift shop.

The tigers were in another park, good idea, and for 320 Thai Baht ($9.00 US) one could get up close and personal for fifteen minutes. I bought a ticket and signed some kind of waiver. It was a very exciting fifteen minutes. The handler emphasized the importance of not touching the head or front paws, no problem. They were sitting or lying down, and we could pet them and even touch their tails. Petting them shook loose a few coarse hairs, like with any cat. One of the tigers, named Paula, let me touch her back feet, and she extended her claws, which were very impressive. She was lying against a wall. I gently pushed her so I could get behind her. She rolled away, then there was a very serious deep growl and she rolled back, and I knew better than to try that again. Thank you, Paula, it's your space and you should have it. The park photographer got some excellent pictures, but Judy's photos taken from outside the electrical fence and standing on the second balcony of the adjacent building were not that clear, but no way was she getting closer.

Every mode of transportation came with a complimentary tour guide, which was okay initially, but after the tour there was an obligatory visit to some craft shops. The cab drivers got a gas credit for each customer they brought in, and even with a strong, "No thank you," one could still end up at a shop. Once inside, Judy was too nice to say a meaningful no, and I had to stay nice, so I couldn't save us. If we shook our heads and said no, they just rolled out a few more rugs. We resisted the rugs but did come away with some other coverings.

There were night markets, a Saturday market and a Sunday market with a lot of everything and yet the same things. We bought a flute that was beautifully demonstrated and supposedly hand carved. That evening, we discovered the shipping address was Yahoo.com. Market highlights were the foot massages, half an hour for 60 Thai Baht ($1.75 US), which left one rejuvenated to continue shopping.

Thailand is predominately Buddhist and there are many elaborate temples in Chiang Mai. We visited several. There was even a small area at the airport with a sign that read "For Buddhists and Novices." There were temple services in the open-air parks. A monk would sit up front facing a golden image of Buddha, and tourists could join the locals at any time. After the service, the monk would join his audience and talk with them for as long as they wanted. He blessed each one, and they came away smiling.

According to the book *Present Day Buddhism*, by Karen Armstrong, Buddhism is primarily ego management through yoga and meditation and goes back to about 500 BC. Egos seem to be about the same or getting bigger. We haven't made much progress. Judy was interested in my doing some ego management. I could get into this, except folding my legs and getting up can be a problem.

If I ever drop out of this game, it will be to a place like this for a chat with Buddha.

Ant Wars

"Raymond, these ants are back again and they are driving me crazy!"

We had been at war with the ants on the *Nereid* for most of our travels. They were never in great numbers, nor were they large in size, but they were very fast and well organized, and the location of their base camp has remained a mystery. My darling mate, who has spent more time on the front lines at the galley sink, countertops and food storage areas, has expended considerable physical and mental energy. I had been relegated to the rapid response team, so when

"Raymond" and "ant" were used in the same sentence, I mounted a swift attack. My hunt-and-kill mentality had served us well in Alaska, but I was noticeably ineffective with this much-smaller game and was now expected to respond only with supportive verbal disgust.

We were attempting to secure our living area, and they were like terrorists with their hit-and-run tactics. Individual scouts could appear anywhere on the boat and could usually be neutralized, while large numbers could quickly converge on a food target and run for cover upon discovery. Careful remote observation could reveal their lines of communication and deployment, but never their headquarters or command posts.

We were waging a war we could not win and chemical weapons were not an option. We had the advantage of size and technology and controlled the air space above them, but their superior numbers and knowledge of the terrain kept them in the game. We had been unable to find their leaders, who remained safe in the many inaccessible parts of the *Nereid*. We would think we were winning the war one day only to wake up to find them attacking an obscure food particle or to have somehow penetrated a Ziploc Safe Zone.

We wanted to negotiate a meaningful peace, but invariably we would discover they had moved into a new area that was not to be shared. We were too vastly different to have any meaningful dialogue, and not really interested in communicating with lower life forms. Besides, some of our fellow boaters would not be happy with us if we were somehow able to negotiate a lasting peace. So what to do as the transgressions and violence continued?

The answer came loud and clear as I was sitting in the head; I noticed an injured ant trying to climb over the barrier to the shower. This fellow would struggle vigorously for a few seconds, lie perfectly still and then resume his frantic effort. He was of one mind, but with each attempt he would fall back exhausted, in need of rest. He continued to try, giving it all he had, and I identified with his plight. His energy expenditure was from the same biochemical process that I had working for me, only never with his intensity. We were the same but different. It was a very peaceful moment of understanding and enlightenment.

I recently read something by Eckhart Tolle about being here and now.

"We should not kill the spirit that lives within every creature and everything," he suggested.

He had something there. At the risk of sounding too weird, I wanted to thank my struggling friend whom I did not harm or help, but at least for the moment, the war was over. I just had to talk to Judy.

Note: Ants greatly outnumber humans, about 10,000 trillion to 6.7 billion, but we are about equal in total biomass.

Mindfulness

You only use about three percent of your potential brainpower—at least, that was what I used to tell my students, years ago.

Thus, always in quest of more brain function, I set out to learn to meditate, and what better place than with Buddhist monks in Thailand? Also, I wanted to check spiritual enlightenment off my to-do list. So Judy (who was always interested in spiritual stuff) and I set out for a ten-day silent retreat in the jungle at Suan Mokkh, about 200 miles NE of Phuket, a place made famous by a monk named Buddhadasa Bhikkhu. He thought capitalism was a catalyst for greed and was thus listed in the US as a communist in the '70s. He died in 1993, and I agree with him but wish I had been more successful. The retreat was only 2,000 BHT, or about $60 US, making it affordable for this limited capitalist.

Some rules of the game for the ten days: no talking or contact with others (about sixty of us), up at 4:00 a.m., in bed by 9:30 p.m., two vegetarian meals per day, yoga exercise one hour, assigned chores one hour, instruction one to two hours and eight hours of standing, walking, sitting meditation, focusing on breathing for a state of mindfulness—not an easy task. Along with the ego, it was recommended to check in cameras and also watches, as a large bell would be hammered when it was time to get up, change classes, eat, etc. As I dropped my wallet and camera into the sack to be locked away, I decided to include my watch. Ten days without a watch and without speaking to my mate would be a trip in itself. It would be a new record since our earlier days of marriage, when we went for several days without speaking to each other, but that was not a spiritual exercise.

The men and women had separate sleeping and eating areas, and in a short time I realized how much I missed Judy's voice and our conversations. It was always a treat to see her and catch a glimpse of her meditating. We sometimes walked briefly together and I would look at her, something we were not supposed to do, as it was said to take one's mind down bad pathways. I wanted to know how she was doing, but she would, with the sweetest smile, put a finger to her lips as a reminder not to break the silence. I did not speak, but my meditative state needed to be recovered. Actually, if any woman came into my line of sight, I was supposed to look away. I even observed the monks-in-training doing this, especially with Judy.

In the dining hall, the men and women were separated. It was self-service and there were two or sometimes three large pots. One picked up a bowl and dished up a rice-barley mix, a few lettuce leaves, some cooked cabbage and a cup of hot water. That was the breakfast/lunch meal. The first day, I took only a small portion of the rice-barley, which looked like gruel for prisoners. The following day it looked much better and I filled my bowl. When everyone was seated, we read a short prayer or verse and we all began to eat together, yet each was very much alone. When finished, each of us washed our bowl, spoon and cup. Dinner was more of a stew, with no meat but with potatoes and carrots and a slight curry flavor that was greatly appreciated. I wanted to ask if there was going to be a dessert tray, but there was no talking, no complaining and no questions.

Separate male and female living quarters, of course, and we each had our own room, about eight by eight feet with shuttered window and bars like a jail cell. The bed was a concrete slab with a grass matt and wooden pillow. One was issued a mosquito net to cover the bed and a light blanket to cover the body, which I used to wrap around my waist to reduce the pressure of the hard surface on my hip—like sleeping in the woods with a depression in the ground for my hip. This was my new sanctuary, and by the end of the day I was ready to sleep on any surface.

One of my problems was with the flashlight I had brought from the boat. It had never failed me, but it did not work from day one. The backup system consisted of a candle-powered lantern, which gave off just enough light when walking at night to warn of potential danger from snakes, scorpions and large centipedes. Matches were a problem as a result of the continuous monsoon rains, which made everything wet or very damp. When the matches would not light, I tried to follow someone with a flashlight. We changed classes every hour, and in the early morning and late evening, everyone was groping along in the dark to the next class.

The rain was so intense the trails became flooded, and we sloshed along with or without a light, sometimes guided only by the reflective surface of the water on the trail. The noise from the rain made it difficult to hear the morning bell to wake up. I missed my first class on the first day—the guilt I successfully meditated away. The next morning, with rain noise continuing, I tried harder to hear the bell. I did not want to miss another class and did not want to disappoint Judy. Two different times I got up, crawled out of the mosquito netting, opened my door and looked to see if anybody was moving around. Still not sure, I would light the lantern, walk down the path and check a few doors for padlocks to see if my neighbors had gone to class. No padlocked doors, so I returned to my room and to bed, wondering why I had turned in my watch.

The most challenging secondary effect of the rain was that the wet, polished concrete floors became extremely slippery. I had visions of taking a hard fall and breaking my hip like old people do. I was overly cautious and switched my mental focus to not falling. In the end, my closest call was not from the rain but came unexpectedly from a freshly mopped floor in the dining hall, where shoes were not allowed. I came around a corner after washing my bowl and hit this glassy surface in my bare feet. I went skating across the floor into the ladies' eating area. It was not possible to maintain a tranquil state of mind at this time. I did manage to come to a stop without hurting myself or someone else and to keep the silence. There was a brief exclamation within myself that went something like, *Holy shit! That was close.*

Judy was not so lucky and fell on the fourth day.

Shortly afterwards, she took me aside and broke radio silence, fire in her eyes. "Raymond, I am leaving. You can stay, but I am leaving!"

I was having considerable back pain sitting for hours without a back support, so I assured her I was ready to leave. Judy also had other tolerable challenges, like the large spider she would usher out of her room but which would quickly return, evidently taking advantage of the Buddhist rule "take no breath." Killing anything was not the spiritual way. She also had a variety of other spiders and insects (small breathers) sharing her room. Her mosquito repellent was not effective and she had numerous bites, but the game breaker was her fall, as she could no longer bend her legs into any sort of meditative posture.

It was an unbelievable experience, and we practiced our meditation and mindfulness on safer home ground. We enjoyed our time together and conversations even more. When we recovered, and as long as we were in the neighborhood, we were thinking about a return trip or a spiritual retreat in India—still needing spiritual enlightenment and increased brain function.

Finally, I should mention that anyone is really missing out by not spending a few nights in the jungle, under mosquito netting, during a tropical monsoon.

Silent Movie – Observation from Judy

For over a year, Ray and I had wanted to attend a Buddhist meditation retreat. We read *The Buddha*, by Karen Armstrong, talked with boating friends who had attended retreats multiple times and slowly were convinced it would be a good idea to spend time in quiet reflection and contemplate the meaning of life. No real plan was required to attend. We just had to show up at the temple on the last day of the month, fill out a short form (name, age, country of origin), pay 2,000 Baht (about $65 US) to cover food costs, have a short interview with a monk or nun and we were in.

The interview went something like this...

"Silence is required for the entire ten-day retreat. If you need to ask a question…write it on paper and give it to one of the nuns."

"Okay," I said, "I'm here to learn to quiet my mind."

"Men and women have separate dorms and there will be no contact with the opposite sex."

"Okay," I said with a smile. After forty-seven years of marriage, it would be nice to have a break from Ray.

"No eye contact should be made with men and especially with the monks."

"Okay," I said with a smile, thinking, *I'm sixty-six years old...I'm sure I won't be a threat to anyone's chastity.*

"We rise at four a.m. and lights go out at nine thirty p.m.; no lying down between these hours."

"Okay," I said, still with a smile, but wondering how this was going to work.

"A vegetarian meal will be served each day at eight thirty a.m. and twelve thirty p.m."

"Okay," I said, wondering how Ray was going to handle this one.

"Take no breath. That includes snakes, spiders, centipedes, mosquitoes and ants."

"Okay," I said, hoping I could comply. Mosquitoes?

The interview was suddenly over, and the nun pointed to a key and said, "Silence begins now."

I wanted to say, *But wait, aren't interviews a two-way street? And I have to say goodbye to Ray!*

I could feel a very big adventure had begun, so in silence I picked up the key and was off to find room number 124. The women's dorm was built around a lovely grassy garden. My room was at the back of the compound and near the toilets/washing area. No showers, only bucket washing...no big deal; living on a boat taught excellent water-conservation techniques. The lock on 124 worked easily. I entered the small room and marveled at the unusual bed. A gray cement slab with four legs...thin grass mat...mosquito netting...wooden pillow. I started talking to myself, thinking things like, *they must be kidding…no way could anybody sleep on this.*

I suddenly started laughing, *I'm in jail!* The only luxury was a lantern with candles and matches.

At 4:00 a.m., we were awoken by a large bell, not the farmhouse dinner bell but the kind seen in old Chinese movies. The sound was beautiful. Our ringer played for ten minutes with a variety of tones and volumes. It was a very pleasant way to start the day. In the dark, we all headed to the meditation hall. The hall had a sand floor complete with red ants walking single file, spiders building trap doors and fifty wannabe Dalai Lamas sitting on coconut mats. We listened to the history of Buddhism and how to meditate for about one hour while in cross-legged position. Then we meditated for one hour. Next was walking meditation. This was walking in a very specific way: one foot at a time, not picking up the second foot until the first foot had completed its step and was securely on the ground. It was very slow and intentional and made us think about every movement. Next came yoga. Really it was just stretches and a little tai chi. Then back to sitting meditations. I was so glad for breakfast, not so much for the food but for the rest from cross-legged sitting.

Breakfast was quite a scene. Men on the right side, women on the left side, even the food dish-up areas were segregated. The food was simple. We had rice porridge, bananas, papayas and green leaves that looked like part of a florist's bouquet. I ate the porridge the first day; after that I stayed with the fruit and leaves. After breakfast came chores. Chores took only about thirty minutes.

After chores we had free time, which most people used for bathing, washing clothes or practicing walking meditation. I, on the other hand, went directly to bed. The bell called us back to the meditation hall at 11:00 for more instruction and cross-legged meditation. Then lunch. Again, I was more excited about resting my legs than food. We had steamed rice, yellow curry with tofu, potatoes, carrots, string beans and the florist's leaves again. Each meal was a variation of this menu, but pretty much the same. We were reminded at the beginning of the meal that we were eating to maintain the body and not for pleasure. And we were also cautioned not to take more food than we needed to maintain our bodies.

After lunch, we again had free time. I'll let you guess what I did with mine.

At 2:30 p.m., the bell called us back to the meditation hall, where we had instruction, sitting meditation and walking meditation until 6:00 p.m. Then it was back to the dining hall for a cup of warm liquid. It tasted like weak chocolate, and that was the end of food until the next morning at 8:30. Then back to the meditation hall until 9:00 p.m.

If I got bored with meditating, I could always watch the bugs biting me. I had thirty-five mosquito bites the first day. Citronella oil did not work in the jungle. Oh, my kingdom for a can of OFF!

Our days started in the dark and ended in the dark. That sounded okay until I added the fact that I was in the jungle and there was no attempt by the powers that be to keep any animal out of the temple area. I instantly recalled the story about the country mouse and city mouse. I decided I was definitely a city mouse.

It started raining just as we arrived at the temple and it didn't stop. Sometimes it was just a mist, but most of the time it was like being in the bathroom shower. The paths were flooded. My feet were wet and wrinkled for three days. All my clothes were either damp or wet. I gave up changing. Thank goodness Ray had insisted I bring an umbrella. After the second day, my matches were damp and would not strike. Of course, Ray, being a Boy Scout and sea captain, kept his going the whole time. I had a very small flashlight that saved the day.

This reminiscing may sound like complaining, but it's not. I will start my complaining now.

Most of the spiders in my sleeping area were the usual garden variety, easy to sweep out of the room and too small to get excited about. Even the small tarantulas were willing to find other shelter. However, on the third day, my eye caught movement from the open door to under the bed. I grabbed my flashlight to investigate. I could not contain my shock. My heart rate shot off the charts; no way could I maintain silence.

"What am I going to do?"

"How am I going to get this thing out of here?"

"Where is Ray?"

The spider now under the bed, where I slept, was huge, teacup-saucer size. Really, I'm not exaggerating. No one responded to my verbal outburst. Suddenly, I heard the bell calling us to meditation, so I locked the door, leaving the spider in the dark.

I found it a little more difficult to keep my mind focused that afternoon. I knew my new roommate was getting under the mosquito net and sleeping on my blanket, or maybe under it! This was the first time I had wanted to meditate all night. I'd take ants and mosquitoes over monster spiders anytime.

When I once again unlocked my bedroom door, checking everywhere for the unwanted guest, I became even more upset because I could not find it. I slept with my flashlight. I say "slept," but not much sleeping occurred that night. The next morning after breakfast, it came to visit again.

This time I stayed calm, got a mop with a long handle from the bathroom, and proceeded to herd it out the door. I could see it much better in the outside light. It had thin black legs and a body the color of sand with a black chevron design near the head. I was quiet proud of myself for getting it out of my room and still obeying the "take no breath" rule. My glee lasted about five seconds, as I watched in horror as the spider climbed the wall and reentered the bedroom through a small decorative opening built into the wall. We did this dance several times and then I heard the bell. Now I was through with rules! In a soft voice, I told the spider he'd had his last chance.

"If you are here when I get back, you are DEAD! Do you hear me? …I mean it. I am going to break the rule; do you understand me?" And once again I locked the door, leaving the spider in my bedroom.

My adventure ended with good news and bad news. I fell on rain-soaked cement the morning of the fourth day, and by early afternoon my right knee was the size of a cantaloupe and the ribs on my right side were becoming more painful with each breath. Unable to find any sitting position tolerable and with the pain increasing, I decided I needed to leave. As I packed my few belongings, I wrestled with what to do about Ray. Should I tell him I was leaving? If I did, he might insist on leaving also, even if he didn't want to. Should I not tell him I was leaving? If I didn't tell him, he would worry when he didn't see me at the meditation hall. If I left him a note, he would be upset not knowing for sure how badly I was hurt or if I was going to be okay negotiating taxies, buses and trains getting back to Phuket.

I found Ray as he was entering the dining hall and broke the silence. He confessed that his back was very sore and he was thinking of calling the retreat short. I quizzed him every which way to be sure he wasn't leaving just for me. I was convinced. As Ray packed, I retrieved our passports and cameras and arranged for a taxi.

The good news was I learned so much about myself during these four days. I learned I liked myself, and I loved Ray more than I had thought possible. I learned silence was good. I learned nothing was black and white but rather a million shades of gray. I learned everyone had their own truth—mine might not be yours.

I decided the retreat was very much like the theme of the MasterCard commercials…priceless.

My silent movie was over, but I hope to see it again.

PS: The spider lived to see another day.

Conning the Duffers

"Excuse me. Could you tell us where there is a money changer? This is our first day in this country and we need some local currency for a hotel room."

We were in a modern shopping mall in Kuala Lumpur, the capital of Malaysia, a short plane ride from Phuket, to get our visas renewed. Visas couldn't be renewed in the country one was living in, which made for good business.

The mall was a very upscale shopping center, and we were making our way through the throng of people. We were doing more hand holding these days but not shuffling along like duffers. The nice-looking fellow and his lady friend may have seen us a bit differently, as we were the least likely among the multitude to know what was going on—although Judy had recently cut my hair and trimmed my beard, so I was looking good, and she always looks good, so maybe we did look like we knew the score. Whatever, we were flattered that they had selected us for help.

"We have just arrived from Turkey," the man said, "and want to know if there is a bank or money changer in the mall."

We didn't know of any in the mall, but the place was huge. I tried to think where they could go but could only come up with the airport, from which they had just come. Judy, always ready to meet new people, was excited to talk about our desire to visit Turkey.

"Could we see an example of the local currency?" the man asked.

Judy started to open her purse when I had my first clue that something was wrong. She had only a single twenty-ringgit bill, worth about fifteen cents. He seemed excited to see the twenty.

"Could I see a higher bill?" he pressed. He took out his wallet and partly pulled out what looked like a new one-hundred-dollar US bill. He had a stack of these new bills in his wallet.

Later, Judy admitted they had been too green in color.

"Do you know the exchange rate for the local currency?" he asked, but he didn't seem too interested in the answer.

His enthusiasm and effect of helplessness in a strange land began to change as he fondled the lowly twenty-ringgit bill. My wallet at this point was not going to produce any "higher" bills. He handed Judy back her money and, nodding and smiling, we said our goodbyes. As they disappeared into the crowd, we went over what had just happened.

They had travel experience and had just come from the airport, where banks and money changers were numerous. They were from Turkey with a wallet full of very green hundred-dollar US bills. They had to be counterfeit to make this exercise profitable, which was why the exchange rate didn't seem to matter. We had been selected from a host of potential affluent locals as easy marks. The final and most devastating fact was that we looked vulnerable; maybe they thought we were duffers. We then tried to look more alive by standing straighter and walking faster.

Afterwards, I wished we had let this play out a bit further, like by touching a new hundred-dollar bill, then holding it up to the light and asking, "Where did you get this?"

The only con job that we followed to the end happened in London, England, years ago, when we were definitely not duffers. A nice fellow named "Jimmy" showed us around the palace grounds and we watched the changing of the guard, and then he went for show tickets with our $80. It took only about one minute in the pub, waiting for him, before we looked at each other with the same realization—Jimmy was not coming back. A great memory, and periodically I wonder how he is doing. He may be living in Turkey.

Walking the Dog

New Year's Eve, and it was just the two of us. It was early, about 6:00 p.m., when we left our apartment at the marina and headed for our boat. Last New Year's we were on the other side of Phuket Island, anchored in Patong Bay, watching spectacular fireworks from our cockpit with friends. We planned a low-key affair in the cockpit this year, with our boat tied up safely in the marina at Boat Lagoon. We had some things to celebrate; our cockpit table was finished after taking months to complete and costing almost as much as the boat, and it was beautiful. Also our boat was for sale, and we wanted some quiet time to reflect on what had been an amazing eight-year adventure. We began with a bottle of excellent champagne and followed it with two bottles of wine. We felt secure within the familiarity of our boat that had carried us safely halfway around the world. We reminisced about our travels and talked about the grandkids and our plans for after the sale.

It was only 10:00 or so when we decided to head back to our apartment. We maneuvered our bodies out of the cockpit and headed down the narrow dock finger alongside our boat. At the end of the dock finger, there was a sharp right-hand turn onto the connecting dock.

Judy was ahead of me and progressing nicely. She seemed all right. I thought I was all right too, but when negotiating the turn, I lost it and went into the water. As I surfaced, my only thought was the collection of debris I had seen in the immediate area, of which I was now a part. I grabbed onto the edge and pulled myself out of the mess onto the dock. Judy was pulling on my shirt and demanding to know why I had gone into the water.

I shook myself off with no explanation, as I was surprised myself—this was a first—well, actually a second, as months earlier I had ridden my bike down a ramp that was quite steep. I went too fast. When I hit the bottom of the ramp, the basket on my handlebars bounced off into the water. I could see the basket resting on the bottom, and as I stretched to retrieve it, I rolled head first into the water. I cut my nose, but more importantly—nobody saw me.

Nobody saw me miss my turn this night either, I was again following Judy down the dock and to the ramp. The next few moments were a bit fuzzy. There was no logical explanation—no turns or curves, just a straight shot to the ramp. I remember reaching for the railing of the ramp and being within a few inches when the railing, at first as if in slow motion, began to move away, and I found myself back in the water again.

Judy was speechless this time but went to work clearing a path. When I surfaced, I was separated from the dock by the bumper and mooring line of a large catamaran, *Mango Moon*. Judy pulled the bumper out of the way, leaving only the mooring line, which I had to climb over to reach the dock. I repeatedly tried to swing my leg over the line and repeatedly failed.

After each unsuccessful attempt, Judy would say, "I am going to get help." This made me try harder, as I was in disbelief and too embarrassed to bring in a third party. Disgust with myself and fear of discovery helped me make a final supreme effort that just got one leg over the line, so I was able to pull myself onto the dock a second time.

Finally together again, we proceeded up the ramp with very little discussion onto the main dock, which was about ten feet wide and should have been no problem. I was exhausted and fell a third time, this time staying out of the water.

As I lay momentarily on the dock, I pleaded, "Can I rest here for just a few minutes?"

"NO!" Judy said in her loud voice. Then in her quiet voice, next to my ear, she said, "If you don't get up, I am going to leave you here."

That didn't sound like too bad of a deal at the time.

Anyway, I raised one arm and asked her to help me up.

She said later, "I tried to lift you but got no help, just your extended arm in the air."

She then instead began pulling me by my shirt collar, like a dog on a leash. I did manage to get onto my hands and knees, but that was the best I could do, and in this simulated dog posture began to move slowly down the dock toward our apartment.

We traveled together this way "walking the dog," with me occasionally requesting a rest stop just to lie down for a few minutes, which was always met with my handler's response that she would leave me. If I slowed too much, there would be a jerk on my shirt collar, so I kept moving, my head down, tracking my slow journey over the planking of the deck. Looking up occasionally, I could see our objective near the lighthouse at the end of the dock; however, there were now two identical lighthouses side by side. My handler was not interested in discussing this problem and just kept pulling me along.

Days later, I paced off the distance we traveled together in this manner and it came out to 425 feet. That was a long way for anyone at any age, especially on a dog walk.

Back in our apartment, we assessed the damage. My body had taken on some cuts and gashes going into and crawling out of the water. My knees had taken a beating on the walk, especially my right knee, which was bleeding, but my pride was the most hurt. How to explain this extensive bodily damage to our friends would later became a concern, and we talked over such options as saying I had been in a motorcycle accident or sidestepping the whole thing by saying I was very sick and confined to my room. I remained in our apartment for three days. We eventually decided that if I wore three-quarter-length pants that would cover the knee damage, and a hat for my head and shirt covering my arms would do the rest.

It was an embarrassing moment, and we felt fortunate that we had returned to our apartment undetected. We have kept this little adventure to ourselves, and in private moments I am sometimes referred to, depending on the situation, as lead dog, good dog, bad dog, etc. We were grateful that our adventure had gone undetected—that was, until about a month later. We were having a lovely meal at the Galley, a dockside restaurant from which we could see our boat. Our usual waitress was especially friendly this evening.

"You very funny man." She smiled. "I am looking for a man with sense of humor." She then asked, "How old are you?"

Now that seemed strange. I had joked with her from time to time, but to ask my age seemed unusually forward for a local girl.

When I ordered our second and final round of Chang, our Thai beer of choice, I said to her, "Don't sell us any more, or we will have to sleep here tonight."

She laughed and said with a big smile, "Or you have to…" She then pantomimed a dog walk.

We were both shocked! Judy had not gotten her dog home that fateful night undetected.

My response may have saved the day as I eventually said, "Oh, yes, you must have seen us the other night when I pretended to be a dog and Judy was walking me home. We had a bet that I couldn't go that far on my hands and knees."

She nodded and, with a big smile said, "Yes—you very funny man."

I was not going to document this life-threatening event, and while it has some entertainment value, I realize that I was lucky both times not to have surfaced under the dock or hit my head on an outboard prop on the way into the water or suffered any number of unfavorable outcomes.

"Dad always gets lucky," Ross has said many times.

I hope that is true. I know our kids think we were too old to be out here, halfway around the world, and should be closer to their home on safer ground. It was a sobering experience and reminded us that there was more to worry about than Somali pirates.

Note to Loved Ones: This account has been written while casually watching the upheaval in Egypt on TV with the sound off. It's probably only a coincidence, but a line just came across the bottom of the TV screen stating that Charlie Sheen had entered rehab. I don't plan at this time to join Charlie but will check in with him if this dog ever goes for another walk.

Part 5

Homeland and Side Trips

Chapter 14

USA

R&R in San Francisco

After an eight-month cruise across the South Pacific and a grueling twelve-hour flight from New Zealand to San Francisco, we were ready for some rest and recuperation. We arrived in SF, were met by loved ones at the airport and were whisked away under sunny skies, surrounded by happy faces. Our daughter, her husband and their two kids, our beautiful grandkids, were all smiles, and even with their house undergoing major renovation, we were all happy to be together again.

We had advance reservations and tickets to Disneyland the following week. All was well, except the kids had just gotten over colds from their school, but we were just in time to catch them. I recovered; Judy did not and ended up going to the UCSF emergency room. The doctor concluded she was okay. It was just a cold, and her chest pain was probably a pulled thoracic muscle. This news carried us to Disneyland with the grandkids, where she got worse and didn't want to leave the hotel. The kids had a great first time in the land of make believe. We stayed in the hotel and watched unbelievable episodes of Jerry Springer.

Returning to SF, she was not getting better, and we had her checked by another doctor, who determined she had an advanced case of pneumonia. We were in one of the many little rooms waiting for the doctor to come in, and she could hardly talk at this point. She motioned me up close and whispered, "You know you will have to move off of that chair when the doctor comes in." No matter what her condition, Judy is always more concerned about others.

It turned out her illness had advanced to where they had to open her ribcage to remove pockets of infection. She was hospitalized for two weeks. She controlled her pain levels with morphine to be administered as needed. She would sometimes overdose, and I would become a darling companion. Only by the second week was she interested in eating and wanted to watch an occasional TV show. Still worried about others, if the TV was turned on she insisted it be very low volume so as not to disturb anyone. The volume was kept so low that I would have to put my ear near the speaker.

The nurse came in once and saw me and asked, "Are you alright?"

"I am just watching the show," I replied.

"Well, why don't you turn up the volume?" she asked.

After one week in the hospital, Judy was doing much better. I was okay; I did do one thing new for the first time just the other day. When I was getting dressed, I evidently put my underwear on backwards. When the time came to access, it took five minutes of searching to realize what had happened. I don't know if this is a new trend, but just in case, I may start my trips to the bathroom with some lead time.

So far on this trip we have not been able to do much, in this case R and R has taken on a new meaning—rescue and recovery.

R&R in Spokane

Once a year, we locked up the boat and headed for our terrestrial home, in this case Spokane, Washington. Our alternate base of operations was San Francisco, where grandkids, our daughter and her husband resided. The visit to SF was always greatly appreciated, as we were still heroes to the grandkids, and I dreaded the day when they were to discover Papa was overrated. Anyway, our stay gave the parents a break and some help with whatever was needed. The accommodations were somewhat restricted with a full house, leaving us the foldout bed in the front room. Sometimes this created a privacy issue, but the chance to greet the kids as they came down the stairs from their bedroom to our bedroom was ideal.

Spokane was a different story. With no grandkids around, we stayed with other relatives; in this case, my brother Richard, a bachelor, and Judy's sister Mikel and her husband Bill. Both house sizes were similar, with numerous beds and baths. There were two late-model cars in both double garages, and the houses were equally equipped with the standard amenities of stove, fridge, etc. Both houses had huge TVs in the front rooms, but here the similarities begin to drop off significantly.

We stayed first with Judy's sister, even though they'd had numerous phone conversations; there was still important late-breaking news that must be shared immediately. Mikel and Bill had retired from the teaching profession and were fully prepared for the new incoming class, which even included entertainment and some dinners cooked ahead of time. Bill had a small distillery going in the basement and a fully stocked wine room. We also had access to one of their vehicles as needed. There were some limitations on TV and the best and largest set was dedicated to continuance of their programming, as it should have been. If we wanted to watch something else, there was a TV in the basement. The ongoing or continuing programs were reality and game shows like *Dancing with the Stars* and *The Biggest Loser,* a contest where the biggest loser of weight became the biggest winner—go figure.

The time to leave and spread the joy of our company to my brother's place came with the realization that the playing field was going to change. The happy bachelor home afforded us our own room but no other amenities. The house was immaculate but there was no food or drink or car. The fridge had only a few things and any serious consumption meant eating out, usually at a diner called Waffles Plus. Water was available but was not to be heated on the range. Only the microwave was used to heat water for tea or coffee. The new range had been used only once, to heat water for the hummingbird feeder. Both cars were to be driven only by the owner and should not be touched unless absolutely necessary, especially the Porsche Boxster.

My brother was amazing in that he could talk about anything while following what was happening on TV and playing solitaire on a laptop. No game shows appeared on this TV, as it was dedicated to old westerns and sports. Fortunately, with the miracle of cable, any or all of these programs were available at any time of the day or night. Eye contact was rarely made and usually in conjunction with more startling events on the TV. The TV was huge and produced life-sized figures. We viewed some all-time favorites, including many hours of *The Big Country.*

The range in comfort and accommodation was stimulating and entertaining, but we were happy to get back to the routine on our boat. Actually, when we thought about it, we were probably the strangest of all after many years of living on a sailboat.

The planned entertainment with Judy's sister was a real celebrity, Glen Yarbrough. He came on stage and announced, "I have just lost my voice and also my band that has been opening for me." He had also lost his looks since taking the picture on the brochure. He told some stories but forgot the endings. He also had trouble remembering names and places and his wife backstage or a band member would help him. His new band saved the night, if the audience had no expectations.

At the end of the concert, he said, "I have ten more concerts in Washington State, so please call your friends and let them know I am coming." We only wish someone had called us. The Limeliters were great in their day and so was Glenn, but it was time for lights out.

I had assumed that traveling to see family and friends from our distant anchorages of the world would bring us a celebrity status and translate to taking us out to dinner or, in this case, Waffles Plus for breakfast. It turned out that being the oldest meant picking up the tab. One trip included seven adults and two kids.

We weren't really celebrities. No one was that interested in our sailing adventure, only when it would be over. And, as Judy reminded me, "Raymond, when your folks visited us, your dad always picked up the tab." That was a long time ago. I had forgotten—thanks, Dad.

Number 24

With Judy now well on the way to recovery from her bout of pneumonia, we spent considerable travel time using the municipal transportation system in San Francisco—an excellent system on which, for fifty cents (as seniors), we could spend the whole day traveling about the city with free transfers to connecting routes. Another great feature of the bus system—if we missed a bus, it was only ten minutes until the next one.

We had access to a car, but there were few parking places in this fine city. Oh, there was parking on some hillsides steep enough that if someone decided to push the car over at the top of the hill it would bring down the whole row. Also there were streets where parking was allowed only on certain days, and others only at certain times of the day. For these reasons, we opted for the bus, in our case Number 24.

The first seats in the bus were reserved for the handicapped and seniors, for which we qualify on both counts. This section placed us across the aisle from people with canes and walkers, ranging in age from sixty-five to 105, it was hard to tell. Then there were the handicapped; many had been that way their entire life, yet they struggled on. What was their place in the grand scheme of things?

All this said, there was something else. It was the realization that there were a lot of people out there struggling much harder than we were. It never was a level playing field, and that had always puzzled me. There were so many less fortunate—I saw it in their tired, hollow stares. They seemed lost and some probably should have been in an institution or at least had a caretaker. Not many kids take care of their aging parents. I had to wonder if the person sitting across from me who was partially blind, somewhere between fifty and eighty years old, had any kids, and if so, where they were. There was a lady on this particular ride who was frowning almost ghoulishly and spent the whole time talking to herself. Then there were school kids riding the bus for three blocks who should have been walking off some of their junk-food intake.

Riding the bus gave us a new value system. Most of the people were not in a recreational mode; they were there by necessity or going to and from killer jobs with time schedules, leaving them tired and broken with little chance of life getting better. So here we had a sampling of the less fortunate, those with these bitter jobs, others wishing they had jobs, and of course, some still trying to beat the system and not wanting to work.

Our problems now seemed so much more manageable than those around us. Whatever was going on to make up our final grade could be a big surprise. I graded my kids when I taught school on the perceived potential of the individual students. If a student came with many talents but failed to use them, at least in my class, they received a lower grade than the less-talented kid who worked hard—something like "from each according to their ability."

Bottom line, I might be in more trouble than anyone around me, as I have been given many skills and many opportunities. I have been getting by on credit, the payments for which are overdue. I need to find some payback activities while there is still time. If there is something going on after this, I would like to be there. I know the people on Number 24 will be.

Team Effort at 1.25 People

With Judy's bout of pneumonia, now well on the way to recovery, and with me approaching my big seventy, it had become more and more apparent we would need a team effort to get to the finish. On average, my contribution—depending on the subject matter—was about 0.50, or half a person, in cognitive functioning. Judy was closer to 0.75, so together as a team, we came to about 1.25 or one and a quarter folks. This worked out about the same as during our prime time years together as high achievers, when we were each operating at about 1.25; that would have been 2.50, or above average, for two people. Unfortunately, we were more independent then and didn't need to work together that much. Our team average then was about the same as it is now at 1.25. We felt as long as we stayed above one whole person with our combined efforts, it would keep us on the road or at sea, and out of the home.

There were still many things out there to do and see, but with our extensive life experience and waning youthful curiosity, we were comfortable with a 1.25 team effort. It was the little things that were becoming more challenging and annoying. On our recent trip to Bellingham, Washington, via Alaska Airlines, we had a problem with the lunch—in this case, some childproof-packaged gourmet pretzels. My flying days would be over when it was no longer possible for me to open these little packages before the plane landed. Another challenge on this trip was the timed lock on our room at the Quality Inn. With the credit-card-style key, there was only a fraction of a second to do my swipe and hit the door handle. It was not possible standing alone, but with my swiping and Judy hitting the handle, we were able to access our room, just like the regular people.

One thing that changed in our favor was our ability to schedule doctor's appointments. Before our sailing adventure, we were put on the wait list with everyone else, sometimes six months before an appointment. Now, having returned for checkups with our medical teams at Stanford, we only needed to identify ourselves and the receptionist would ask, "Are you the older couple sailing around the world?" Our status affirmed an appointment of our choosing would magically appear. Usually the attending and doctor wanted to hear about sailing before we got to the exam.

I took this fame to a new level just the other day when asked, "What do you do out there at sea with all that time?"

Instead of talking about how much work it was, I simply said, "Oh, we are writers."

It was pretty cool, especially when considering our 1.25 operating system.

Kindergarten Science I

Science class in kindergarten? That's right, and we were invited to help. Our grandson Gage, who attended kindergarten in SF public school, brought home a lesson outline. There would be a lecture and a lab exercise, just like in real school. The subject for these five-year-olds was polymers. There's a TV show called *Are You Smarter than a Fifth Grader?* or something like that. In this case, are you smarter than a kindergarten kid? While admittedly I have an advanced degree and an A in organic chemistry, it was only after a review of an Internet encyclopedia that the lesson came together.

The teacher referred to her twenty students as scientists, and I was introduced as a visiting scientist and guest lecturer. The hardest part of the presentation was getting my legs to fold up so that I could sit on the floor. I was offered a chair but refused this and eventually settled on the floor with my fellow scientists. With the kids' Tinkertoys, I demonstrated the transition from atoms to molecules to polymers. The lecture ended with polymer recycling, and there was even a question about DNA.

For the lab, we formed small groups of five scientists per table. My group consisted of Gage and best friend Jackson, both active doers; Grace, an observer; Nicolo, mostly concerned about my pronunciation of his name; and Remy, possibly a project manager someday, who kept asking, "What do we do next?"

The initial experiment was to cut up a Depend diaper, dip it in cups of water and watch the uptake. My team decided to see how much water it would hold before cutting it up. The Depend loaded with polymers held a full quart of water, information I filed away as relevant for later years.

The team was doing well until we added some food coloring to trace the water. Unfortunately, it was a lemon yellow that translated immediately to my fellow scientists as pee. Now, there were only five kids in my group and I had no trouble talking to twenty kids, but no matter how small the group, when working with yellow-colored water and a Depend, I could only do damage control. Jackson did his own experiment, squeezing the saturated mass until it broke, and suddenly polymers in simulated pee were everywhere. At this point, these scientists were back in kindergarten and enjoying every minute of it.

Evidently we did well; I know Judy did, because her group seemed to be in orderly pursuit of knowledge the entire lab period. There were several parents that sent in complimentary emails saying that they had learned about polymers from their kids. When I thought about it, we didn't have kindergarten. Our kids had attended but hadn't had science, and polymers had just been discovered. These little scientists even had their own lab books to record their observations.

It was fun, and we were invited back to help with next week's science lesson. The topic was ultraviolet light and global warming. Hello! UV? I couldn't believe it. It was only kindergarten and in the public school system, but they seemed to be getting it.

The future of the planet looked good.

Kindergarten Science II

We previously reported our success in the classroom teaching our grandson's kindergarten class about polymers and the following week about ultraviolet light. For our third and final week of classroom instruction, we were informed ahead of time that the lecture section would be presented by someone else, possibly a visiting kindergarten science teacher, but our assistance with the smaller lab groups would be helpful. There was some relief in not having to prepare a lecture, and I looked forward to another scientist's presentation. In this case, the subject was critters living in a pond environment.

When we arrived in the classroom, we didn't find the structured activities we had experienced in the previous classes. The teacher was in control but she seemed less organized. It was Friday, and when she saw us, she could only muster a tired smile of acknowledgement. She eventually came over and asked if we were ready to present the lesson.

We had not expected this, but before I could head out the door, Judy said in a calm voice, "Yes, and I will read to the main group about ponds while my husband prepares the laboratory exercise."

Each student was to have his or her own sample of pond water to observe and study. There were small plastic hand lenses for close-up work, and the classroom aquarium was to be the source of sediment and water to look at. While Judy was reading most beautifully to the little scientists, I took a sample of the sediment and water to see what there was going on. The results were not promising, as I could find nothing of a living nature. Hard to believe—a classroom aquarium with no life forms.

"It doesn't look good," I told the teacher.

"Not to worry," she said. "If you tell them there is something there, they will see it anyway."

This did not seem to be a very scientific approach, to imagine the results. I wasn't going to take my fellow scientists down that path, but we assembled at our lab tables and everybody had a cup of aquarium water with some sand in the bottom. They laid their hand lenses over the tops of the cups and found a focal length at which to observe their pond samples. With twenty individual biomes being observed, it wasn't long before one of the kids began to get excited.

"I've got something! It's a worm doing the cha cha!"

The other scientists scrambled from their seats and rushed over to take a peek. It was a very exciting moment for everyone.

They went back to their own samples, and some were very impatient and complained about not finding anything.

"Scientists have to be patient," I explained, "Some scientists wait all their lives hoping to make contact with some life forms in outer space." Then I added, "It is important not to disturb the samples, so the critters feel safe to move around."

In a few minutes, another discovery was made, this time a small snail. Just about everyone who was patient and didn't disturb his or her sample found something. It was especially fun to see those who hadn't found anything right away patiently waiting and suddenly exploding with excitement when a small critter was found. It was even more fun for this old scientist to be a part of these discoveries.

Note: One of my most intent and quiet little scientists was Gracie. She was the last to find something. She reportedly told her parents that she wanted someday to be a scientist.

Pit Bulls and Sushi

We are back in San Francisco visiting the kids and getting some R&R. Last year, Judy had a serious bout

with pneumococcus, and we were lucky to get out of here alive. Last night we called in a babysitter for the kids and went to one of the many restaurants for dinner.
Restaurants are becoming more challenging these days. At my last restaurant experience, it was too dark to read the menu, so I had to wing it. My son-in-law is in the restaurant business, and he and my daughter usually know what they plan to order before we sit down. This time the light was good, but the menu unreadable. The only word I recognized was sushi. I waited to see what others were ordering, but that didn't help.

"I will have this," I said, pointing at random.

"Very good choice," the waiter responded.

We ended up sharing each other's orders, so the risk factor associated with my random point was lessened considerably. I had no idea what we ordered, but most of it was fish or some affiliation. The stuff that did not appear to be fish had a presence of fish or a sense that fish were in the area when it was being prepared. Anyway, the wasabi leveled the playing field, making everything palatable by bringing all the creativity together under one dominant taste sensor—hot!

Our entertainment outside of eating was the video store. My usual routine was to walk the six blocks to the video store each evening. I needed to start carrying a cell phone and, by closer communication with Judy, minimize returning with feature films we had already seen.

Last evening I was safe in that we had decided on the final season of *The Sopranos* and I knew exactly where those videos were in the store. I said my hello to the manager and headed to the back, where *The Sopranos* were waiting. What should have been a routine pickup suddenly became life threatening. Standing exactly where I was headed were two people talking, which was fine, but each had on leash a pit bull. The pit bulls were not talking and both were watching me closely.

They were probably thinking, "This guy looks old, let's take him."

Since San Francisco is in love with its dogs, it's not a big surprise to see dogs in a store, except pit bulls. Pit bulls are not normal dogs. We had Labradors in Alaska and they were only interested in handouts, a place to pee and retrieving. A pit bull just stands quietly, daring a person to make a move. I thought for a moment, was an episode of *The Sopranos* worth risking my life? Since it was the final episode and I had already come this far, I decided to go for it.

I do well with cats and horses, but lately dogs have been barking at me for no apparent reason. In any case, undeterred, I proceeded to the rack and the two pit bulls. We all three watched each other closely. I did not dally but grabbed my video and walked at a normal speed to the checkout.

"Do you know there are two pit bulls in the back of your store?" I asked the checkout gal.

"Oh, really?" she replied. "They shouldn't be there. I will ask them to leave in just a moment."

I doubted she said anything, and I wasn't going to hang around. Nobody wanted to be labeled a whistle-blower on pit bulls.

Some aspects of R&R in this fair city—the food, the wild beasts on leashes—were more life threatening than any of the islands nations and countries we had visited so far. That was good. If we could continue to handle these R&R challenges in SF, we should be good to complete our circumnavigation.

Parking Lot Slip

"Who has to go to the bathroom?"
"Nobody?"
"Okay, let's go."

"No, we don't have time for shoes. You will be fine."

"Just get in the car!"

We made almost daily trips to the small market only six blocks from the house, but steep terrain and short time frames often found us piling into the car for a quick run to the store. This time, we were too pressed for time to round up all the shoes, so the kids went barefoot, which was no big deal, except no shoes meant no going in the store.

The usual seating arrangement was Gage, age six, and his sister Colette, age seven, strapped in the back seat, and with Judy in the front, we were ready to go. We parked in the store parking lot and Judy went in alone with her list for the evening dinner menu. With her promise to return, I had only to contain the kids in the car during her absence. The kids were great, but at this time of day, after the pressures of adult supervision at school, our roll as supervisors—handicapped by a familiarity index—had basically been reduced to gamesmanship and crowd control.

Judy had been gone about one minute when Colette announced she had to go to the bathroom. I thought she was kidding since we had just left the house, but she assured me after questioning she only had to pee; still not good news, and without shoes, our options were limited.

"There's no problem, Papa," she said as if sensing my indecision, "I know what to do."

Whereupon she opened the back door, then climbed into the front seat and onto my lap. Smiling sweetly, she opened my door, and with a perimeter now partially secured, she proceeded to slip off her pants. There was a man waiting in his car parked beside us who seemed to have fingered out what was going on before I did and suddenly decided to go into the store.

She was giggling and talking, and as I partially held her in position, she let it go. Her initial trajectory almost hit her underwear and required a quick adjustment to a more laid out position, which I helped her with. Everything was going nicely until she slipped and one foot went into her creative deposit. She was laughing and, in trying to save her foot, I pulled her onto my lap, but evidently she had not quite finished. The extra ended up on my pants, to the glee of the kids, especially Gage, who had now moved from the back seat to the front to get closer to the action.

Colette, still giggling, finished and pulled up her pants, and I swung her across my lap into the car. Her foot, still damp, brushed across Gage's face, and he went from finding this a laughing matter to finding it a major concern and immediately wanted something to wipe his face. They were both put into the back seat about the time Judy arrived with the groceries.

In our worldly travels, Judy has shown creativity in similar situations, but always with agonizing uncertainty and fear of being discovered. Comparatively, her granddaughter acted confidently and decisively, with only one bare foot going into the puddle. After a short question-and-answer period with Judy and some talk of who was to blame, it was time to get going. As I backed out of our parking place, I was surprised at the extent of the mark we were leaving. It was an impressive-size puddle for such a little girl, and it didn't even include what was on her foot, her brother's face and my pants.

Sudoku and Opera

We were in Spokane, catching up on football—the kind with padding—and horse racing from the comfort of a recliner at my brother's house. During our stay with Mikel and Bill, they had brought two new, surprisingly unrelated recreational pursuits into our lives. The first was the numbers game Sudoku, reportedly a brain stimulator. It is a fun exercise but has the potential addictive aspect of small achievements, motivating you to seek out more challenging versions. I had only done a few of the simpler matrices, and it had taken longer than I cared to admit. It would be some time, if I stayed in the game, before I was ready to use this as an intelligence index.

The other new entry into our lives was much more difficult to explain. "There was a contestant on the British version of *America's Got Talent* who sang opera and was amazing," Mikel announced.

I was suspect of her judgment and enthusiasm. *America's Got Talent* I had watched before, but it was nothing to get excited about, and an amateur singing opera was the perfect setup for some good laughs. She had recorded the event and now turned on the recorder and TV.

"You won't believe this," she said.

The audience, not exactly opera buffs, was not wanting or ready to hear opera. They were there to be entertained. The contestant was introduced as a salesman of cellular phones with the name of Paul Potts, an appropriate name for some comic relief. He walked out on the stage in his wrinkled suit, out-of-date tie and budget haircut. He stood quietly with an anxious smile. The camera panned across the three judges and they all looked either amused or ready to roll their eyes and make with the wisecracks. The piece he had selected was "Nessun Dorma" by Puccini. I had at least heard of Puccini so my expectations as I was sure most of the audience was only curious at best.

He began to sing, and it took the audience only a few measures into the piece to begin clapping. In a few more moments, as he began to demonstrate his vocal range, they were standing in applause, many with tears in their eyes. It was amazing. These were not opera fans. I had never really cared for opera myself, and here was a humble man singing in Italian and in less than a minute I was hooked, as were those in the audience and also the three judges. How could this be? What universal language had tapped into the soul of all those present?

It was great that we could all be touched when something was genuinely good. Mr. Potts was able to bring us all together for a moment of beauty. He stood quietly when finished with humble uncertainty of what he had just done as the audience and the judges stood and continued to clap. We have since listened to the same piece by the master, Pavarotti, and it was not quite the same—too confident, too precise and too strong. The magic of Paul Potts was not just his singing but also his humble courage.

Thank you, Paul Potts, for taking a chance and wanting to sing opera. We will be taking you sailing.

For All the World to See

We were in the thick of choosing the next president to lead this country for another four years. What a process. The coverage on TV was excellent; the candidates for both parties were still undetermined, and there was a host to choose from. While the candidates struggled to find positions on the issues that they believed in and what they thought the people were looking for for these next four years, there was one overriding theme—all were trumpeting a call for change. Change in our foreign policy, education, immigration, economy and taxes. Each candidate represented a point of view, some changing their positions as they searched for what the people wanted and ready to articulate these points to win.

As the nation and the world watched our process unfold, what were we seeing? The most powerful country on Earth was dissatisfied with itself and looking for new leadership. The people were going to the polls in record numbers to support the candidates whom they believed could best implement these changes over the next four years. Only a few states had been counted at the time I was writing this, with no clear front-runners, and so far the prognosticators and opinion polls had been wrong. We were definitely in for some changes, but at this point those changes were still being defined. The uncertainty was not just in these primaries but in the final outcome. Most presidential elections come down to the wire, and often the news agencies are wrong in predicting the final outcome.

Our system is not perfect, and the forefathers did not intend the decisions of leadership to lie with the main populace, thus we have in our pledge *to the republic for which it stands*—a fledgling democracy may have needed more representation by the experienced and educated. Now, though, with our better communication and education, we were evolving more and more into a nation *of the people, by the people, and for the people.*

While the candidates and their constituents fought it out, the important part of all this was that the people were searching for a leader who would bring change for a better, kinder, more peaceful world community. That person would get four years to try, and if they did well they could get another four years, but that was it. There was no military uniform hanging in the closet waiting for a body that would take over the system. Irrespective of some of the negativity of campaigning, the overriding intent was to find a leader of whom we could all be proud—it shouldn't be that hard, but then again, nothing great comes easy. Our system is not perfect, but it is one of the best, and it is out there for all the world to see.

No Pets Allowed

We were in Bellingham, Washington, where this circumnavigation adventure had begun. This was where our leftovers from the sale of our Alaska household goods were stored, along with a vintage Jaguar E-Type. We were staying at the Quality Inn where we had always stayed, but this would be the first time without our cat, Romeo. There had always been a sign at all the entrances that said "No Pets Beyond This Point," but that really didn't apply to Romeo, since he was not a pet but an important member of the family and a sailor.

In the past, after checking in, we would wait in the car until the coast was clear and then wrap Romeo in a blanket and transfer him to the room. Several additional runs were necessary to bring all of his support materials—cat box, water dish, food dish, canned food and sack of dry food. Sometimes we shared the elevator with others, and I was always afraid he would make a sound during those critical moments of transfer, but he never did.

Once we were safely in the room, the "Do Not Disturb" sign would go on the door and Romeo would make himself at home on the couch or chair. Occasionally, he would try to get out to check the neighborhood, and we would have to open the door carefully coming and going to keep him in the room. He got lots of sleep time and always liked to get up early.

He didn't like being alone in the morning and would wake us up slowly. It went like this: he would jump up on the foot of the bed, and then proceed with slow, cautious steps toward the head of the bed while watching intently for any sign of wakefulness. I would lie quietly as he approached, pretending to still be asleep, and he would position himself about six inches away, watching, and turn on his motor—a loud purr. After a minute or two, he would slowly extend a paw and gently touch my face. At this point, he was hard to ignore.

The most challenging part of our motel experience was when our stay was ending. We had learned from our days in Alaska, when it was time to visit his veterinarian, to not talk or even think about going until he was secured in his car carrier. Otherwise, it could be a major search in the many nooks and crannies of the house to find him.

It was the same in the motel room. This was more baffling, because the motel room did not offer that many hiding places. Sometimes he was under the bed and had positioned himself in the middle where he couldn't be reached and he would just look at us. It was necessary to find a long blunt object to move him out. If the bed was not an option, we would assume he must have gotten out of the room, and sometimes we did a quick walk through the halls. However, a more thorough search of the room would find him jammed up against the wall, in a tiny space, behind the refrigerator, the dresser or the couch. All we would be able to see were two eyes looking up at us.

I admit, Romeo, I never figured out what you really wanted in these situations. You didn't want to get in the car, but then didn't want to get out. You didn't want to go into the motel, but once in, you didn't want to leave. Whatever was going on, it was fun, and we miss you terribly. I know there is something going on out there at the "Big Motel," and it may have a sign: "No Pets Allowed." If it does, just wait for me. I will get you in.

Changing Priorities

We moved around a lot in our earlier years, and initially the selection criteria for a shelter were primarily price and convenience to and from the workplace. With the arrival of the kids and the need for schooling, we selected neighborhoods on the quality of the schools the kids would be attending. We had come a long way; there were many moves, including Sacramento, Altadena, Pasadena, Catalina Island and Livermore, California, along with Anchorage, Alaska. In some places there was only one school, like on Catalina Island, where the kids were bused from the Isthmus into Avalon. Anchorage, Alaska, required the most research as there were five high schools to choose from, and the results of that study were Diamond High School for Taylor and a great elementary school for Ross.

We were back in Spokane visiting old friends, starting to plan where to live after our sailing adventure. Spokane was a possibility, but this time, instead of being guided by the quality of the neighborhood schools, we had new selection criteria. Now, the questions were how far it was to the nearest emergency room, what the average response time was for a CPR team and what their success had been at resuscitation. Also an inspection of the hospital and emergency room would be appropriate, including noting the staff-to-patient ratio and the attitudes of the doctors. Doctors who factor in your age when recommending treatment should be avoided if possible. A walk through the hospital seemed wise, especially during the night shift to see if there was any care going on or just kibitzing at the nurses' station. If there was no night shift at all, then a patient would be on his own, another important consideration.

While in Spokane, I called up an old friend whom I used to hunt and fish with. We were in high school together from 1951 to 1955. I didn't expect to find him, but he was listed in the phone book. I had talked to Don on the phone about twenty years earlier. He had been going through some marital challenges and had invested in a racehorse that ran a beautiful race but had trouble finishing. Don and I had double dated to the senior prom, my only social function in high school, but had logged many hours on hunting trips.

When I called his number, someone else answered, it was another hunting buddy, Jimmie. He and Don were still doing things together after all these years and were planning a trip to Portland. We agreed to meet at a restaurant; as I walked in, Don was standing and smiling. I did not recognize him at first, but then the voice along with the smile left no doubt. It was a positive ID and a great reunion. He was the same kind, considerate, crazy guy with a sense of humor I had known in high school.

The aging process does not change the quality of the person, only their presentation. We talked about some of our hunting trips together and some of the new adventures over the years. It was great to find old friends and renew some memories. Along with the medical criteria, family and old friendships would be a priority in selecting our next land-based home.

Chapter 15

China

Gathering, Gasping and Pushing

We visited China, the awakening sleeping giant. The country has a population of 1.3 billion hardworking people, most still walking or riding bicycles, but ready to drive and accumulate some stuff. They have taken care of each other and are now ready to experiment with the entrepreneurial spirit of capitalism. The highlight of the trip was the Great Wall, which President Clinton described as "amazing." We would agree and also include the "amazing" people.

There is very little English spoken in China. Stepping off the plane came with an abrupt realization that we couldn't communicate. There was not a taxi driver in this populace that spoke English. If we gave the driver a note written only in English, he would glance at it briefly, then hand the note back with a smile and a gesture to get out of his cab. It was important when leaving the hotel to get a note from the desk clerk in Chinese detailing where we wanted to go and the name of our hotel in Chinese to return. Even the universal golden arches of McDonald's were displayed only in Chinese.

Once we learned to get things translated, we were good to go. We handed the taxi driver the translation, and with only a brief glance he nodded and we were off. While motoring along with a driver, there was time to study the note with its extremely intricate characters that made no sense. Of the sixty-four TV stations, even the few in English had Chinese subtitles, again of such complexity they were impossible to recognize. There are over four thousand different characters in their alphabet, which unfortunately may not be user friendly in a digital age, so the sleeping giant could be in for some changes.

Discovering where the English is out there could be exciting. Several times we found ourselves lost and needing directions. I would begin, much like someone begging for food, "Excuse me, do you speak English?" I said this quickly as these people were on the move. Someone would stop, usually right away, and offer to help. At this point, there would be what I would call a gathering. Everyone wanted to help; sometimes, loud arguments would break out as they worked to resolve our problem. Around this more active perimeter would be the curious listeners, everyone very serious and concerned. Gatherings peaked at about ten or fifteen people. I recall one very old man on his tiptoes straining to see what was going on. There were other times when people stopped and offered to help for no reason other than that we must have looked old and confused. When we return from this sailing/traveling adventure, we plan to be more receptive to the traveler who may be in need.

Our train trip from Beijing to Shanghai was fast and crowded. We were the only people obviously from another land. It was interesting to sense our minority status when walking to the club car. At the relatively smooth high speed of the train, it was still challenging to walk. I stopped once to let a lady coming my way pass, and as I paused, the fellow close behind me took the opportunity to pass me. People don't like to wait. Getting out of an elevator could be entertaining as the mass getting on met the mass getting off.

The modes of transportation were exciting, since everyone ran the traffic lights to an ongoing concert of horn play. Pedestrians were on their own. The taxi rides were one of the more death-defying experiences routinely available in China. Judy usually made gasping sounds each time she perceived a close call, wherever we were. I had yet to experience her concern. However, on the Chinese front I had two gasping experiences as our driver refused to yield to a bus that wanted the same space.

The queue, or respectfully waiting one's turn in line, was not practiced. Some fast-food counters were fast only if one had the energy or desire to hold his position in the mass. We just had to keep our feet moving at all times to create some space.

"You must push," a little Chinese lady said to Judy as the crowd continued to pass, then pulled her along to demonstrate.

This reminds me, all the public space was landscaped and planted with flowers and trees. Even the space between two lanes of the highway was a continuous hedgerow with flowers, usually roses or peonies, and this continued for miles, and they were beautiful.

There were two deficiencies—breakfast and tea. We expected the breakfast to be different, but the teahouse was a surprise. The main attraction of the teahouse was the ceremony—special pots, temperature of brewing, various blends—but in the four or five preparations we sampled, the end result was always disappointing. The liquid had only a slight coloration. This finished product tasted almost like tea. It was such a fine taste or, as I found it, a weak taste, that instead of tea it was more of an idea—not worth the effort for such a tiny flavor experience. Excuse me, but it's back to the old standard Yankee Lipton.

Shopping for whatever could be challenging. If the merchandise was not going to be discounted, we expected a relaxed where-is-a-clerk affair. If discounts were waiting, the slightest interest in something created quite a scene. In these places, it was easy to become afraid to hesitate or even glance at something. The initial price would be outrageously high. When we tried to get away, they followed us with a hand calculator, yelling, "Enter your price." To escape and not cause a scene, Judy happened upon the perfect response. She simply put her finger to her lips, meaning quiet in our home, and the salesman-assailant would stop in midsentence, bow and, smiling, back away—amazing. This armed us to venture into many market places.

China was a surprise. We had expected a country less friendly, not happy with the game of life, but that was not at all what we found. However, the people didn't like or would not talk politics. Any question about the brave individual who stood in front of the line of tanks in Tiananmen Square was met with frowns.

"I don't know. I didn't hear anything about that."

More important to them was a kind of team spirit, no hard feelings surrounding past events. In the mass of moving bodies on bicycles and pedestrians, collisions were rare but inevitable. One occurrence I witnessed was a cyclist hitting a pedestrian, weak brakes maybe, but the pedestrian stopped the bike by grabbing the handlebars, resulting in light contact. There was no eye contact made, the parties hardly breaking stride or losing a turn of the sprocket. No energy wasted on road rage or an angry exchange, not even a warning glance. No big deal. It was more important to keep moving.

We were treated like celebrities, many times asked to have our picture taken, so we routinely exchanged photos. I mentioned to a British fellow, equally taken with China that I could become a Socialist. He agreed and added that when we returned to our respective countries, we should start our own China-appreciation cellblocks. China and its people, like the Great Wall, must be experienced to be believed.

Did we like China? I guess one could say that.

Flavors of Beijing

We arrived in China with no plan except to visit the Great Wall, all four thousand miles ready and some parts waiting since 260 BC. We visited the Badaling area and realized we wanted more, so we returned to the Mutianyu area the next day. It was amazing. However, to our surprise, our biggest challenge and study area turned out to be the restaurants and food selections. As people around us enjoyed themselves at their tables of food, we were on a continuing quest to refine our selection process. It was like a treasure hunt, and if we stayed in the game, we would be rewarded beyond our palate's finest dreams. We could not count on what other patrons were eating; while their choices looked delicious and were enthusiastically consumed, these were evidently acquired tastes.

Three classes of menus defined themselves as our search for memorable food continued. The simplest menu was posted on a wall or in a window and was written only in Chinese. These places were closer to our concept of fast food. The menus listed only a few items and we would point to what we wanted. The next class of menu was a regular menu in Chinese and sometimes included an English translation. The accommodation stopped there with the selection of entrees. The first item on the menu could be "cow stomach" or something else commonly known but not on a Western-type menu.

The most comprehensive menu had entrees described in Chinese and English with a color photograph for each. These menus were offset by too many choices that could discourage even the boldest Westerner. On one menu there were photographs of acid cabbage fish, hare blood soup, drunk fish of grandma, delicious flesh, sliced pig's ear, stir-fried pig face, stir-fried flesh, husband-wife lung, broiled wraps of flesh, pig's large intestine, mixed goose intestine, and two canine entrees: dog broth and mixed dog. I never could seem to get across my question about mixed dog. Were we talking mixed pedigree, which should be less expensive than purebred, and was it fresh or frozen?

Our most challenging restaurant experience was in a very popular place close to our hotel. It started to fill up with locals about 4:00 p.m. On our reconnaissance for food we never saw any tourists in there, which is one of our main criteria for choosing a place to eat. When we entered, it was packed with the locals except for one table, which we secured. The menu was without pictures and very limited. Everyone seemed contented with the three or four choices, so what the heck. Our beers arrived. China had great beer, which helped catalyze the uptake of marginal choices. I did a quick study of the bowls on the tables on my way to the counter to place our order. The bowls and their contents all looked the same but probably were not.

I should mention that a crowded Chinese restaurant at dinnertime was very noisy. There was no sound-deadening on any of the surfaces, so we were treated to reflective continuances, causing a shouting match between Judy and me. Add to this the numerous exhalations of the smokers, and in the noise and haze, our bodies and senses became altered. I paid for two bowls of something and wandered to the pickup window. Behind the counter sat two very large pots of a hot liquid. Okay so far, but then something strange happened. The cook reached under the counter and pulled out what looked like a piece of meat—possibly liver that had been torn in a few places, maybe once a pull toy between two puppies. I stood mesmerized as he quickly chopped this material up with a large cleaver and deposited the pieces swiftly into the two bowls of hot broth. I returned with the bowls to the table, where my darling waited. I started on my beer while Judy examined her bowl.

Please remember the context of what happened next. Judy is considerate of other people's feelings to a fault. After a few minutes, she took her first spoonful.

"I am not eating this," she said with a forced smile. With that, she put down her spoon and reached for her beer.

I took my first large spoonful with some meat, and as I was working it in my mouth, I realized it might indeed have been liver, but very tough.

I have neglected to mention that when Westerners join locals for an eating experience, they nod approvingly and wait with great expectation to see the visitors' reactions. The social pressure of the crowd and my ego pushed me to a second and third spoonful, as my audience nodded in approval. What I would have given at that moment for a built-in plastic liner in my clothing to which I could discretely relocate my food! Smiling, I could have loaded up the liner and left. I reminded Judy that it was going to hurt these people's feelings if we didn't consume more of the food. She looked at me incredulously.

"Knock yourself out," she said, and ordered another beer.

I couldn't keep eating, and we finished our beers and left the scene. It was not the end of the experience, as there was an aftertaste that lasted into the next day, probably the brain trying to take charge of the decision process—"Don't go there ever again."

In summary, the food that is awaiting one in China can be the best ever. Our repeat orders of chicken with peanuts in an incredible sauce were indescribably delicious. The Chinese have learned to cultivate a much larger percentage of available land by necessity; likewise, they have to be more efficient in the use of protein. Just as a Westerner may enjoy a good hot dog, the sum of some parts, the Chinese have conditioned their palates to enjoy the parts. Protein is protein, from any part of the animal, in any part of the world. It's just a bunch of amino acids specifically organized which, when consumed, are reorganized.

Unfortunately, we did not have the time to acquire a taste for many of these parts, but unquestionably, the flavors of Beijing are worth pursuing.

Blossom's Suitcase

Our travels have taken us to some surreal places, sometimes leaving us in an altered state. Enter our visit to Beijing and the train ride to Shanghai. Judy had a dream the night before departure about a suitcase left on a luggage carrousel belonging to Blossom. Her dream seemed real—maybe our trip was a dream and Blossom's suitcase was real.

We arrived at the train station, found the ticket office, talked through a narrow glass opening to a person who spoke no English and purchased two tickets to Shanghai. After several wrong turns, we found our way to a train that seemed to be waiting for us. The train looked like a bullet and was ready to go. We found our seats, loaded backpacks and two carry-ons into the overhead and sat down. The couple across the aisle had a baby who studied us through very narrow dark eyes. He was adorable. We had just gotten settled when two young people arrived and wanted our seats—how could this be?

Checking our ticket stubs, we found it was the right train, the right seats, but the wrong car.

We grabbed our stuff and raced for the exit. We found the right car; all the seats were taken except two. As we sat down, the doors closed and the bullet was off—time to relax. I reached for the in-train magazine; it was all in Chinese, but on the cover was the smiling face of Angelina Jolie holding diamond-studded chopsticks.

Most of the people around us had brought food. While we had brought plenty of stuff, none of it was edible. I noted that the woman beside me had three bananas; I would wait but keep track of these. We prepared ourselves for a fasting exercise. There was an electronic reader board monitoring the train speed which showed 323 kilometers per hour, about 200 miles per hour, but there was no noise or sensation of speed— could have been a dream. A stern-looking woman dressed in a blue uniform with star-studded shoulders came down the aisle. She had a clipboard and was taking notes but never said a word. Maybe she was looking for Blossom's suitcase. I decided not to bother the lady beside me for a banana.

As the train raced silently along, the scene outside our window was unreal from a Western context. There were green rice fields everywhere; someone had planted every square foot of area, even right up to the edge of the train track. There was no evidence of farming equipment, but considerable work had been done. Some houses connected by a dirt road with a few people here and there presented a very peaceful setting. What would it be like to live there, the expectations, pleasures? It was an idealistic portrayal of rural life from another time.

After gazing out the window for a while, I decided it was time to end our fast and set out to explore for food. I found the lady in the uniform. She spoke no English, but after some creative pantomime I got the idea that food was available eight cars away. I moved through the dimly lit cars, every seat filled with unfamiliar people who all seemed to be watching me. A few were asleep or trying to make a comfortable bed in a seat not designed for sleeping. This was especially notable with some of the larger people who didn't quite fit in the seats—a wonderful photo op, but probably not appreciated or real for that matter.

I found the club car; the lady behind the counter acknowledged me with a nod, but no words were spoken. I did another creative pantomime, this time of the hot dinners that were being sold.

"So what you want are two of the hot dinners," she said in perfect English.

I acknowledged with surprise her excellent English and she smiled.

The train stopped along the way, and people would hurry on and off. We continued on, never knowing where we were or how much farther it was to our destination. The few announcements and the messages on the reader board were only in Chinese. This continued until there was a stop where everyone was getting off. We sat still, wondering if this meant we had arrived in Shanghai. When the lady in the uniform saw us, she motioned us to get off as well.

"Quickly," she said.

We collected our stuff and headed into the next Twilight Zone.

Late disembarking, we found only a few people in the distance going somewhere. We decided to follow them, as all the signage was in Chinese. We went down a long, dim hallway and up some stairs and came out on the street. We were met by a host of pseudo taxi drivers in a clamor of broken English. We showed them our note with the hotel designation written in Chinese. The first driver coming out of this night scene wanted fifty yen, the second sixty yen, and the third a hundred yen. Not happy with the floating prices, we wandered around and saw what looked like a sign for buses which sent us down some stairs, where we found the real taxis and buses.

There were two very long lines of people with their stuff, being loaded into taxis. The two lines seemed endless as they serpentined though the dim alley. Taxis, six abreast, three on each side of the passage, were rapidly loading with a loud slamming of doors in a haze of exhaust fumes. When we finally got in a taxi, we found ourselves separated from the driver by a plastic shield, so we never saw his face to know if he was real. He did not speak, only glanced at our note, and we sped away into the night, hopefully not to death and destruction, but to our hotel.

We arrived at the hotel around 10:00 p.m., and it looked like it was closed or had been condemned. I asked Judy to stay in the taxi while I checked it out. There was a large metal gate that had been pulled down across the hotel entrance. I pulled on the gate, and when it did not move, I began to worry that we had been duped on our online reservation. Through a window, I could see a woman moving around some tables. I banged on the window; she looked up and then, as if I didn't exist, continued what she was doing.

I tapped on the window again as a strange fellow appeared beside me.

"Do you need massage?" he asked in broken English.

I didn't acknowledge him.

"I have some very nice girls for you to see." He persisted with "It will only take ten minutes."

I am not sure if that was an insult, but he then asked me, "Who is waiting in the taxi?"

"My wife, and this is supposed to be our hotel," I said.

He handed me his business card, which had a picture of some girls on it, and said, "The night entrance to the hotel is around the side of the building."

It was the climactic moment of this surreal adventure to be arguing with a strange fellow about a massage and meeting some girls while trying to get into a hotel that appeared closed and with Judy anxiously waiting in the taxi with the faceless driver.

Blossom's suitcase may never have been recovered, but we are relatively sure the trip from Beijing to Shanghai was real.

Chapter 16

Cambodia and Vietnam

Golden Temple

The Golden Temple was where we stayed, the temple ruins of Angkor Wat and Angkor Thom were what we came to see. These temples were constructed over a period of six hundred years, from 802 to 1432 AD. The temples are endless and a source of pride for Cambodians in what was once called the Khmer Empire. We did three straight days of "templing" with a guide who transported us to and from via *tuk tuk,* a motorcycle hooked to a trailer designed for passengers. *Tuk tuks* are economical, open-air, comfortable and practical for the crowded streets. We would go many miles and spend many hours in these vehicles with our Australian mates Bill and Lyda.

The temples in and around Siem Reap, Cambodia, are magnificent, the largest being the temple city of Angkor Wat. This temple city ranks in grandeur with the Great Wall and the Pyramids. All of these temples were made possible by the abundant rice production in the

Mekong Delta, which boasts an amazing three rice crops per year. With this ready food supply, there was time to think about religious issues and make war upon neighbors. Each king had to have his own temple, and there are so many temples aside from Angkor Wat, a visitor needs to pick and choose.

Hinduism, which originated in India, was the area's initial religious direction. Later, Buddhism became more popular, and many temples were changed over to the more simplistic Buddhist symbols. In some temples, both the Hindu and Buddhist were represented, showing the meditative pose of the Hindu with crossed legs and knees raised while on an adjacent wall was carved a Buddhist in a meditative pose with knees lower to the ground. It was these little tidbits that made hiring a guide worthwhile. We found we could tour a temple much more quickly without a guide but come out not knowing much. Many of the guides were college kids working to make some extra money; they spoke very good English and knew their subject. We had travelled this far and it was not the time to save money by not hiring a guide.

These temples were the primary reason tourists come to Cambodia. We had planned three days of touring temples and were about templed out when we realized another temple was calling, and that was the Golden Temple, the hotel at which we had booked our stay in Siem Reap. We ended up spending another seven days enjoying Siem Reap, along with the staff and comforts of the Golden Temple.

At the Golden Temple, we were met by a large statue of the Hindu god Vishnu with his four sets of arms extended; most of the other décor was Buddhist. Most memorable was the staff at the Golden Temple. The happy waiters and waitresses were working on their English, evidenced with phrases like "Are you okay?" for good morning and ending sentences with "my darling." I was responsible for "my darling" and tried to explain a more conservative context for usage, but I was still hearing "my darlings" when we left. There was a tradeoff in that the staff was ready to help with our Cambodian language skills. Their graphical language is sometimes more efficient than or equally efficient as English, for example the word *Cambodia* has one symbol for each syllable; thus the word *Cambodia,* with eight letters and three syllables, needs only three symbols.

Cambodia was definitely the place to buy a Buddha statue if one was in that mindset. The market was loaded with Buddhas of all kinds and sizes. Our shopping for a Buddha was ongoing and came down to two places. One shop owner got a little perturbed when I kept asking questions (if you can imagine). That was good, since it helped me settle on the other shop, where the lady was more spiritually centered. The final three were hand carved in jade. My selection has some imperfections and leans slightly to the left, both features I could identify with.

I didn't want to negotiate the price of a spiritual piece, but the vendor kept coming down and each time ended with "Good for you, good for me." Anyway, for $35 US we have another person with good vibes watching over us on the *Nereid*.

Cambodians are hardworking, like the waitress that gets up at 6:00, peddles to work on a bicycle and during her lunch does schoolwork. We would be eating out and suddenly find someone under our table checking our shoes for possible repair opportunities.

There are so many Cambodians in need. For only a few hundred dollars, one could sponsor a student though the University of Cambodia. This pays for the books, fees and a tutor for the academic year. The University is the trustee and they administer the funds for educational purposes. It's a small price to pay for so much potential return and would be a truly "Golden Temple Experience."

Note: If you care to donate, go to the website, www.cambodiatomorrow.org or send a check to:
Cambodia Tomorrow
195 Santa Ana Avenue
San Francisco, CA 94127

Trains, Buses, Boats, Rickshaws

The three weeks and a thousand miles from Siem Reap, Cambodia, to Hanoi, North Vietnam, saw us in a variety of conveyances: vans, river boats, buses, trains, sleeper buses, *tuk tuks* and rickshaws. Our only bad experience was early on with a driver on the way to Phnom Penh, a journey of about nine hours, in an overcrowded van. We were packed in tighter and tighter as more and more friends of the driver were squeezed in along the way. From Phnom Penh we did a Mekong Delta tour to Chau Doc, Can Tho, and Vinh Long. The ride into Ho Chi Min City (Saigon) was via a large, modern bus that seemed to sweep away any opposing traffic. From Saigon, we continued in another comfortable bus to the coastal city of Nha Trang, then on by train to Hue, near the DMZ.

The train was very old and slow, but with the *clickity-clack* over the rails in the background, we had a chance to observe rural life in South Vietnam. Our initial impression of the train, even though we had upgraded to a sleeper for four, was not good. When we first rushed on board, our compartment had not been cleaned or the sheets changed from the last occupants—slippers scattered about the floor, some still warm from the previous feet—but new sheets arrived and someone swept the floor. We were a bit disappointed in our arrangements until we walked to the dining car. The cars with only upright seating were packed with people, kids and noise. After that, we felt pretty good about our place. Satisfaction is sometimes relative to the suffering of others—what would Buddha say about that?

The dining car served some basics and a variety of drinks. Periodically, a cart of food would stop in front of our sleeper. Most interesting was a cart with hard-boiled eggs. We purchased four, and as we removed the shells, we realized each had an occupant that in a few more days could have removed its own shell. As the ladies gasped, Bill took out his Swiss pocketknife and began a dissection to identify body parts. It was definitely a duck, with a bill and traces of feathers. We had seen these beauties in the market and weren't ready for them then, and we were still not ready. We Westerners relish the beginning and the end product—why so fussy about the middle?

In Hue, Vietnam, we came to rely heavily on a rickshaw. We had ten minutes to find a bank before it closed. Like a major river crossing, we were suddenly stopped by a huge intersection with six or seven streets converging. There were no traffic lights and no pedestrians trying to cross. A rickshaw driver was dozing in his rig near the corner. I woke him up and showed him the bankcard where we wanted to go. He had one bad eye that looked past me, but motioned us to get in. He pulled out a board that tiered from the main seat, indicating where Judy would sit—almost on my lap.

Judy studied this seat then our older driver who would be peddling us across the mad rushing river of vehicles and said, "There is no way I am going to get into that thing."

I wasn't surprised at her assessment and said, "I am going anyway. Give me the bank stuff."

She started to give me the paperwork, then realized that would be riskier than the rickshaw ride, so while engaged in a conversation with our Savior about my intelligence, she climbed in.

We launched immediately into the intersection and, suddenly, we were challenging the traffic in all directions. The driver took a direct route and the traffic seemed to open a path for us to travel. We arrived five minutes before closing and I asked him to wait. When we came out of the bank, our driver had found a friend on a motor scooter to assist on the return trip. Surprisingly, the motor-assist driver had a similar bad eye, and together their inner eyes looked directly at me with an outer eye to each side. I wondered if their skewed outer eyes gave them a wider field of vision, which could work to our advantage on the crowded streets. We were definitely ready for the return trip.

Crossing the intersection this time, we were challenged by a much larger truck, but our pair held their ground while Judy covered her face. With our rickshaw driver peddling and his friend on the motor scooter pushing, we made it easily; at least, I thought so. The trip cost more than normal, but I didn't mind paying each driver for their combined effort and visual advantage.

Kalashnikov AK-47

Shooting ranges were available throughout Cambodia and offered a wide variety of weaponry, including the AK-47, M-60 and B-40 grenade launcher. After twenty-five years of civil war, the military had followed up, making this stuff available for a price. Said price was by the bullet or grenade. Shells for the AK-47 were fifty rounds for $50 US. At that price and the rapid rate of fire, the tab could go up quickly. There were some additional add-ons that could include live targets, in this case chickens and, for the real killer, cows. This info is listed in the Lonely Planet guide to Cambodia and concludes with the following: *There have been rumors that it is possible to shoot live animals at these places, such as chicken and cow. Naturally, we in no way endorse such behavior. Does it ever happen? It is a possibility, as Cambodia is an impoverished country where money talks.* Good to know that we had some options at the range if we really felt the need for some bloodletting.

There just aren't that many places in the world where one can experience shooting an AK-47, at least not legally. I was curious about this world-famous weapon and my ability to shoot anymore following the installation of an expensive heart monitor/defibrillator we now call Sparky. Being left handed and with Sparky located in my left shoulder, I have always wondered if I was now totally defenseless. I needed to know my options in a shootout with bad guys and automatic weapons.

I had sold all my shooting hardware when we moved from Alaska. I remember loading all my guns into my pickup, driving to the gun store, sitting in the parking lot with my babies thinking long and hard and then driving back home with them. This happened three times before I went in and made the deal. I have always opposed the sale of semiautomatic weapons to the general public and would never own one, but Cambodia seemed to be saying, *Shooting is okay and thank you for your support.*

It was a forty-five-minute ride to the shooting range, and that was by far the most dangerous part of the experience. Having been caught in traffic, we arrived around closing time, and I was ushered into a poorly lighted room with weapons scattered around on the floor. The AK-47 barrel was still warm from recent activity. It was lightweight and had been well used. I explained my shoulder limitation. We agreed I could hold it in the fold of my left arm. The assistant, a large fellow, had his arms around me on my first few shots. The recoil was okay in this modified position; the most dramatic effect was the noise. Even with ear protection, it was very loud. The topper of the noise, however, were the single shots followed by short bursts of five to ten rounds. I just had to hold down the trigger and the rounds poured out of the barrel.

It took less than ten minutes for the whole exercise—a fast fifty-dollar history lesson. There was some smoke and a smell of gunpowder in the air, and I had managed to hit the target. As I handed back the weapon, I had a flash of Robert Duvall on the beach in *Apocalypse Now*, when he said, "I love the smell of napalm in the morning. It smells like victory."

There were chickens roaming the grounds, but I didn't ask.

"Only One Dollar" – *Teacun*

Cambodia is in need of one dollar. Everywhere you travel, prepare to be asked for one dollar. So many things are only one dollar; after a while, when out of one dollars, the best response is *"Teacun,"* which is Cambodian for "No thank you." Not an easy thing to do sometimes, and at other times, it can be easy. When being hustled by a group of kids, it can be a game.

Walking along, one hears "One dollar, one dollar," and if one responds with "I have no money," some reply with "You are in a *tuk tuk,* you have money, borrow from your friend, ask him for a loan."

Got to hand it to these kids, they are learning some English. Many will try a more personal approach.

"Where you from?"

If you start answering these questions, be prepared for the hard closing.

One of our friends responded to "where you from" with "Timbuktu."

The kid, without missing a beat, said, "How about Tim Buck Three."

These conversations take place while on a fast walk to a place of interest.

Along the way, one will also hear, "I remember you, buy from me when you get back, okay?"

If one casually says yes, one must be ready to do business with this person on the return.

It's not bad. It's actually fun and important to keep it fun. We bought many things along the way. Some items will be treasured for their value, others for the conversation that made it all happen.

One of the most impressive drop-dead approaches was the photo plate. As we were returning from a temple ruin, one of these young entrepreneurs handed me something, which I glanced at and started to hand back when I realized it was a decorative plate bearing our picture. What a shock. At some point unbeknownst, we were photographed, and in a matter of minutes, the image had been transferred to a souvenir plate. Now, this was serious merchandising. With the quality of the subject matter, it was harder to say no. They had obviously done some work and gone to some expense. We bought two of these plates, one with me and one with Judy. One plate got broken accidently, so we did what our Australian travel mates Bill and Lyda did—we posed for a plate picture, and we can have more made if anyone would like one.

One effective approach was a mother with children holding a small infant, while her two- or three-year-old with big eyes and hand out continued to say probably the only English they knew. "One dollar." Another example: Late in the evening, we were sitting at a restaurant. A kid came to the table carrying a huge stack of books. He was maybe eight years old and out on a school night selling books. Another time, late evening, a little girl, about nine years old, was out selling dental supplies. I am sure she would rather have been doing something else, but with a pleasant smile, she asked if we would buy something. Well, she hit the jackpot at our table with Judy, the hygienist, in charge of dental needs. Lyda and Bill had no idea there were so many things they needed to keep their teeth.

Sometimes to escape the harangue we had to pay them off. I did a "pay to go away" to a little boy about five years old with a bill of a hundred something that I realized later translated to only 2.5 cents. He looked at the bill with a frown and some older kid laughed, so I upped the amount to a thousand, or 25 cents, and that seemed to make the difference. Good to know these kids had their limits. On another occasion, we were trying to get away and the entourage of one-dollar people followed us up onto the sides of the *tuk tuk*. One kid in particular was hanging onto the side and looked like he intended to stay. As we started off, I threw some bills out the back, and he was gone. Bill did the same thing another time when on foot, throwing some coins, but without the motorized escape he was mobbed by more kids.

Sometimes I would respond to "Where you from?" with the true answer of USA or Alaska.

One preteen girl quickly followed with, "How is your new president doing?" She mentioned Michelle and the girls and then asked, "Have they decided on a name for their new puppy?"

I gave her one dollar—no purchase necessary. She then disappeared and in a few minutes returned to hand me a drawing of a lotus flower with the following handwritten note on the back:

Hello! Very nice to meet you
My name is Tie – nice to speak
with you – I hve you flower for souvenier.
I with you good luck with your job
and all your family. Thankyou
for you coming to see our country
I like you smile

I hope you like my flower.
I hope to sere you again.
I hope you keep it forever.
I hope you don't for get me.
I'm very happy to meet you.
From Tia good bye.

Grasshopper

Huge quantities of crickets, cicadas and other critters were purchased in the markets of Cambodia for consumption. A young girl in the seat adjacent to ours, nicely dressed and groomed, returned to the bus after a rest stop with a plastic bag of these bugs, presumably to munch on over the next leg of our trip. She was in her late teens or early twenties and seemed okay. She was traveling alone, but I don't think that had anything to do with her apparent fondness for insects.

These crickets looked like grasshoppers. Some folks removed the two large legs, leaving the smaller legs as part of the package for consumption. Once, I decided I was ready for one of these—timing was important. First, I allowed a few seconds for my audience to assemble. There was a twitter of interest to see if I was really going to do this. At this moment, I didn't really know if I was up to the task. I had to remind myself that vast numbers of these beauties were being consumed all over Southeast Asia.

The most exciting moment for everyone came with the placement of the item on my tongue. I slowly slipped it into my mouth for the full effect. There was a moment of disbelief with audience participation consisting of gasps, groans and, "He did it, I can't believe it." Now it was just a matter of chewing up what was in my mouth.

The ensuing crunching sound was not audible to the audience. As my taste buds came in contact with what felt like debris, I experienced a weak licorice flavor. For the big finish, I did an eye roll and started to fall backward.

"Go all the way to the ground, then crawl away, like an insect," the vendor suggested.

This vendor also had a huge basket of large cicadas ready for consumption. These were twice the size of crickets and he suggested removing the wings, which left the more substantial body parts. Another interesting entrée were the golden snakes mounted on a stick. These delectables were about twelve to eighteen inches in length and one would be a meal in itself. Our vendor had only about six of these, each on a stick—neatly stacked. The presentation was nice, with the stick piercing the body in about four different places to give a 'snake on the move' look. These beauties came complete with the head and evidently did not need to be cleaned, which would not be the easiest thing to do anyway, so it was best to eat the whole thing—maybe not the head. I planned to sample one of these, but we had to be on our way the next day, with no time to return to the market. Gosh darn it!

Cambodians have a great sense of humor. We were entertained by two fellows on our bus who were watching an episode of *Mr. Bean* on the TV monitor. Mr. Bean was at a swimming pool and went up on the high dive to impress the ladies, but he lost it up there and went through all the Mr. Bean motions of fear and trembling getting down, and not a word of English was involved. These two young men thoroughly enjoyed every minute of his antics and we enjoyed them for it. It was encouraging to know that with comedy, as with music, we shared a universal language.

We have that same universal connection with most foods—grasshoppers may be an exception.

Tunnels, Mines and a Pothole

At Củ Chi, just outside of Saigon, there are 250 kilometers of tunnels that were used effectively by the Viet Cong against the South Vietnamese and Americans. The tunnels have very small openings, about fourteen by fourteen inches, and we had to put our arms up to get in and out. It was no place for someone overweight or with claustrophobia. We saw some grizzly booby traps and bomb craters. The resourceful and tenacious spirit of the Vietnamese has to be admired and respected. The effectiveness of these tunnels in frustrating the South Vietnamese and US was a testimony to the massive effort of bombing, shelling and defoliating that occurred here. There was an American tank on the grounds that had been disabled by a mine. It was depressing, watching the video blaming the Americans for everything.

The most disturbing ongoing reminder of the conflict was the number of amputees. Cambodia is still loaded with land mines that were put down in the mid-1980s after the war, initially by the Vietnamese to keep the rebel Khmer Rouge contained in Thailand along the 700-kilometer border. When the Vietnamese withdrew, the new government laid landmines to protect against the Khmer Rouge. The Khmer Rouge also laid landmines to protect their holdings. The result of this post-war madness is presently about twenty-five thousand casualties. The present-day casualty rate is about thirty per month, down from a high of three hundred per month in the mid-1990s. There are many street vendors and even musical groups with missing limbs, all victims. Some have devised ingenious means to help themselves get around. Our business and donations were greatly appreciated and their presence reminded us to stay on the beaten path.

We visited the killing fields in Cambodia. Pol Pot took over Cambodia after the Vietnamese withdrew to set up his version of communism, which resulted in the death of one million (some estimates say three million) of his own people. We visited the memorial and saw what looked like enlarged graduation pictures of the faces of people who were killed. Looking at the pictures of these victims was hard to do, and after a few hallways of faces—we had to leave. This experiment in communism lasted only a few years, but some of the administrators of this travesty still go unpunished. Pol Pot himself was merely confined to a two-room house and died a few years ago. Several books have been written on this incident; one of the best is *A History of Cambodia* by David Chandler, available for a few dollars from any of the amputees selling books.

De-mining efforts are ongoing under the Cambodian Mine Action Center (CMAC and the Mines Advisory Group (MAG; www.mag.org.uk), as are efforts to ban the production, stockpiling and sale of land mines (ICBL; www.icbl.org).

Two Flags – One Vietnam

Vietnam, now one country, flies two flags; both have red backgrounds, a star on one and a hammer and sickle on the other. In Saigon, I asked a young street vendor what the two flags meant on the building across the street. He knew the flag with the star was the Vietnamese flag but wasn't sure about the other with the hammer and sickle. Music and singing was coming from the building in question. In the foyer, I saw people signing up for something. As I entered, a healthy fellow moved toward me gesturing to stop and not go any farther. Just think, at my age and still a threat; it was a good feeling. I found out later it was a meeting of the Communist Party.

The Vietnamese are determined people who have been in conflict with their neighbors for centuries. Major powers have taken their licks here, including China, France and the United States. The victor can tell the story any way they want.

In Vietnam, the story is presently being told as follows:

Once upon a time, the peace-loving people of Vietnam were living happily, when along came the Americans and dropped bombs on them from their big planes high in the sky. The defenseless people with their families built tunnels and learned to survive underground. They had few resources, so they learned to make booby traps that would wound and kill the Americans. Even the children learned to fight and kill Americans—the children were very brave. Eventually the Americans gave up and went away.

Another version of this story is as follows:

Once upon a time, there was a North and a South Vietnam. One day, the North decided to attack the South because they wanted to be one country under communism. The South did not want communism and asked for help from the free world. America initially sent equipment and advisors. This was not enough, so they sent troops, and after losses of over fifty-five thousand, the Americans gave up and went home. Many South Vietnamese were killed; those who escaped are living in the USA and other parts of the world. They would rather live in their native country, but it is still too risky to return.

Trademarks of the Vietnamese people are the bamboo hats, squatting down on their haunches when waiting, and the ladies' long flowing clothing called *chon sans*. In the north, the roads are better and the streets less congested. It's almost like Saigon is a ghetto compared to Hanoi. There doesn't seem to be an equitable distribution of capital expenditures between the north and south. Hanoi has manicured shrubbery separating new highways—Saigon, only old highways in need of repair. In Saigon, some English is spoken—Hanoi, almost none.

Ordering a cup of tea in Hanoi was a major undertaking. After we had finished our meal at a restaurant, the tea still hadn't arrived. I ordered again, all with my best smile. They seemed to understand, but what arrived was a single glass of very weak iced tea. I ordered again, and after a while, a pot of hot tea arrived. This time the tea was undrinkable as the pot was half full of tea leaves, enough for fifty cups—maybe the war wasn't over.

On our bus ride from Hue to Hanoi, we met a young, well-traveled college student from Hanoi.

"Did you vote for Obama?" she asked. "There must be a lot of pressure on him to solve the world's problems." She volunteered that she did not vote and said, "There is only one party in Vietnam, so what's the point?" She then said, "The party leadership is so old that most of their energy is spent trying to stay awake." She followed with, "Some of these people are seventy-two years old," which was right on the money for me.

I had to agree that staying awake at seventy-two was not always that easy.

Chapter 17

France and Ireland

Paris (Bonaparteville)

We practiced our French on the *Nereid* for a few months before departure, and I knew we had arrived when Judy started correcting my pronunciation with a slight attitude of "The word is…" Attitude was important since we were going to Paris, and I was reminded of this as we were finding our seat on the plane. I was placing one of our bags in the overhead.

"Why don't you put it there?" said the lady with a French accent and a definite attitude…so I did.

Attitude, delivered properly, can be very disarming and humbling. During the flight it was hard to hold an attitude, since we were seated in the second-to-last row of the plane and thus shared everyone's travels to and from the toilet, along with some of their success there. Sometimes there was a queue to overhear the gushing blast. The French lady that had helped me with my bag remained unaffected by this activity, and we both knew she should be seated in first class. It was a final touch, just prior to landing, that they sprayed the cabin with disinfectant. They sprayed everyone, and not just those at the back of the plane. So already there were two all-time firsts on this trip: being told by a passenger where to put my bag and being sprayed with disinfectant.

We did the hop-on–hop-off bus tour and covered most of the places of interest. Napoleon is the main attraction. He definitely made this town. As a young artillery officer he was once given an evaluation by his superiors that "under the right conditions, he could go far." De Gaulle had a small statue, but almost everything else was a result of the little big man. The art collections, opera house, Arc de Triomphe, the Musée de l'Armée where he was buried, surrounded by many of the original cannons. I could almost feel the history of these artillery pieces, the power, the noise, men pulling them into place. They were an integral part of *La Grande Armée*.

He amassed the largest art collection in the world. He sent back to Paris art treasures, gold, silver, precious stones from all over the world as his success on the battlefields continued. He even sent back the captured cannons of the enemy and had them melted down for monuments depicting his victories. Everybody loves a winner, but losses in Egypt where he had to leave an army to fend for itself, followed by unsuccessful campaigns in Spain and Russia, reduced the treasure return and, eventually, the high body count was unacceptable even for a self-appointed emperor. His countrymen left him with a small kingdom on the Island of Elba, from which he eventually escaped. Then he had to be put on St. Helena, an even smaller island with no kingdom.

The highlights of Paris were the art museums, primarily the Musée du Louvre and the Musée d'Orsay. They were crowded and the entrance fee was not cheap, but crowds were lined up and waiting. The people were of every nationality, age, size and shape, and once inside they moved in respectful silence. Some of the masterpieces covered entire walls, making them spellbinding by sheer size, even for the kids. The Louvre could take several days alone, but the star of the show was not wall sized but quite normal sized and set back a few feet, where she smiles, bemused at the assemblage of people, and goes by the name *Mona Lisa*. There was always a crowd ten to fifteen individuals deep, some waiting to move closer, others holding cameras over their head taking pictures. Kids who did make it to the front stood staring. She is magical.

On the opposite wall from the little Italian lady was the largest painting in the Louvre, *The Wedding Party*. This huge scene of activity shows the newlyweds at one end of the table and maybe something going on with the best man, and at the other end of the table are several servants working with large containers and pouring their contents. Jesus is sitting at the center of the table, staring straight ahead, looking slightly annoyed. Mary is sitting beside Jesus, enjoying herself, holding an empty wine glass and looking like she is saying to him, "I know if we run out of wine, you can make more." The artist had successfully added a human touch to the miracle process. I wondered who commissioned this and whether they were pleased?

The self-portrait of Van Gogh in the Musée d'Orsay was also popular, with people of every description waiting to get closer. There were people having their pictures taken beside a masterpiece—this is me with Venus de Milo, holding up two fingers making a 'v' sign. If they have slide shows of their trips for their friends, I imagine they start each picture with "this is me with Van Gogh" or "this is me with Rembrandt." I suppose with the miracle of Photoshop the possibilities are unlimited.

We visited Monet's museum with his famous room-size daylight of seasonal changes of water lilies on a pond. It took a few moments of study to appreciate this life work by the Father of Impressionism. Picasso has his own museum, which was his house in Paris. I don't remember any of his works nor could I describe them if I did. We tried to understand what he meant before reading the title of the work. Rodin also had his own place. Picasso was into the human form, as was Rodin with his sculpture. Beside the very popular work *The Thinker*, a memorable real-life scene was a mother from the USA with her two boys who were evidently inspired by Rodin's work to wrestle. She had her hands on their shoulders.

"There will be no touching," she said in her very best authoritative voice.

I don't think she was getting through, but I do know the French lady on the plane could have quieted them. Anyway, Paris was an amazing place, and if one didn't appreciate art going in, that would change before going out.

French River Cruise with Milo Magic

Eastern France is famous for its slow riverboats and the fast cars at Le Mans. We did the slow boat with Milo, our new grandson, only eleven months old and already floating a river in the Anjou region of France. We joined Milo and his parents for a one-week, 142-kilometer river cruise.

A river cruise was an excellent way to see the French countryside. After a brief orientation of the boat, we were on our own. It was a lot easier than sailing. The twenty-two locks on our cruise kept the river nice and slow, which for a sailor was an adjustment, since we were always trying to get somewhere before the weather changed significantly. The only weather was a warm, light breeze. After negotiating a few of the locks, there was really nothing to worry about, except maybe to wonder when we would eat.

Eats were a simple arrangement of baguettes, cheese and something with raspberry jam for dessert. A more serious effort would produce crepes with a variety of toppings. Milo had some tastes of the local cuisine but for the most part preferred what he brought from home. He had all he wanted and it was readily available. The only time he really got excited was when one of us was off the boat and helping with the locks. He became very animated and loud while pointing at the person and had to be assured we were not leaving anyone—obviously a brilliant child. Aside from eating and keeping track of everyone, he learned to sort through Judy's purse, and there were some things he could open and some he was not permitted to open. He soon learned to recognize what was off limits and would hold it for a minute, study it, shake his head then hand it to Judy—yes, obviously a brilliant child.

People were fishing along the riverbank, but we never saw a fish being caught. I think the important thing was they had a line in the water while resting in the shade of a tree. The slow-moving water reminded us of Australia, but without gators. The most excitement came from the potential bait community. Blue dragonflies buzzed over the surface like fighter planes protecting the mother ship. They were especially active in the heat of the day, when the work force in France was resting or fishing.

Each little community was gathered around a large church, some built in the twelfth century. Inside were the rows of wooden pews seating up to 175, sunlight coming through the stained glass windows extending up the walls to the archways, and life-size statues below the windows. The original wooden pews and confessional booths showed the wear from years of use. The church still had a presence, but active leadership consisted of a visiting priest every other week. Maybe they didn't need the church as much as before.

Milo Magic wanted to spread his happiness to everyone. In a crowd, he would select a subject and introduce himself with a big smile. The subject might be the least likely to respond, like a worker or professional person on a crowded bus. Within minutes, the subject, seemingly sad or despondent, would be drawn out, unable to ignore this magical man with his smile. This was all followed by more eye contact and, eventually, a full approving smile, and the subject was on board with the likes of this new generation. If the subject was especially hard to reach, Milo would shift into his magic act of peek a-boo. I never saw anyone resist this.

Still in recovery from major back surgery, I borrowed Milo's BOB, Baby on Board, a three-wheeler designed for jogging parents. The parents had headed for the famous Château du Plessis-Macé, and while Milo was asleep with Judy, I headed out for the chateau, pushing the BOB before me. It relieved my back enough for me to continue my walk. I didn't find them or the chateau, but what I did find was that I could still have conversations pretending Milo was on board. It was also easy to engage someone for directions to the chateau, as there were no signs on these back roads. I even flagged down a car—such was the power of the BOB—and they probably would have driven me to the chateau or anywhere if there had indeed been a baby on board.

It was always interesting to see a shift in the familiarity index when they realized this old guy was out on the back road pushing a baby carrier with no baby. I didn't really expect the magic to work without the man, but I was glad to give the French something to talk about—things were just too quiet.

Dublin Duffers

On our way from Paris to San Francisco, we stopped off in Dublin, Ireland. We traveled on Aer Lingus, the Irish airline. With a name like that, we knew they would be either very good or very bad. They were good, and it was especially relaxing to find ourselves around more people speaking our native tongue, although it was not the King's English, but close enough. When we landed in Dublin, the feelings continued as the airport bookstore and personal facilities all suggested English was spoken there. We had enjoyed Paris immensely, but it was hard work to stay in communication and get through the daily activities, since we didn't speak the language.

I got the feeling right away that life here was simpler, and no one was judged on his international prowess or speaking ability. This was the land of a thousand pubs and still counting, while unfortunately—or fortunately—the number of churches was decreasing. This was probably good, since the history of tolerance for other people's beliefs had been bloody. The nearest church to our hotel in the downtown section had only four registered patrons when the Pope decided to let it go. It was currently an information center for tourists and tour guides. In spite of the commercial activity, it still felt like a place of worship, with the high arches and stained glass.

We did a tour of the Powerscourt Gardens and places where some famous writers and poets had lived, but the primary entertainment was Damien, our tour guide. The Irish love their poets, writers and thespians. Damien, all Irish, was seventy-two and drove the tour bus while pointing out things of interest. He carried on a continuous monologue with himself in two different voices. An example: "Damien! Yeeees. Why are we going to this next place? (Dramatic pause.) Well, I don't rightly know. Do you have to go to the bathroom? I told you

before we started it would be a long day. Who are these
people on your bus today, Damien? I don't really know.
Damien! Yeees. Should you be driving at your age? Oh,
shut up!"

He was the star attraction, so if you go on a tour,
you need to go with Damien.

There were many pubs and they needed refilling,
just like the patrons. To see this restocking activity, it was
worth getting out early. There were beer trucks
everywhere unloading their wares. Kegs were being rolled
across the streets and on the sidewalks. The teams of keg
handlers did this for years, nothing fancy or technical, just
brute manpower with much noise and conversation.

The pubs were old but well maintained. The
exteriors of adjacent pubs were in contrasting bright
colors for the benefit of their regular customers. Inside,
there were at least ten beers on tap. Some even had two
or three taps at the individual tables. That allowed each
patron to run their own tab so there was no waiting to be
served.

Two or three of those tappers would be products
of the local Guinness factory, where fifty percent of the
city's labor force was employed. We did the obligatory
tour of the Guinness factory and it was hugely impressive.
The tour ended in the tasting room on the top floor and
came with a panoramic view of the city. The closer a
product is to its site of origin, the better, and Guinness on
tap at the factory was at its best—so I was told.

The highlight or most memorable part of our
tour, and not listed in any of the guidebooks, was the
early morning and afternoon pub clientele. These were
the duffers, old guys, gathering with a group of their
friends, some just sitting quietly at a table by themselves
with a pint of ale in front of them. They seemed content
to reflect about what could have been or just enjoy a
relationship with their pint. They usually couldn't help if
asked, but they loved to be of assistance. If they couldn't

help, they were eager to call in someone in their crowd who could.

In the afternoon, they would yield their seats to the younger crowd then head home, happily thinking about tomorrow's pint.

Chapter 18

Italy and Greece on the *Princess*

The Crown Princess
(No worries with Captain Nick Nash)

When Judy's sister wanted us to meet them in Italy to go on a large cruise ship in the Mediterranean for two weeks, I was not excited. The *Crown Princess* was big and fast, with endless feeding and entertainment for fifteen days and traveled to Italy, Greece and Turkey. There were three thousand passengers and crew who greeted us. She was a big princess at 952 feet by 118 feet and skipped along at 22 knots. That's about 233 *Nereids* per deck, and there were seventeen decks, making about four thousand *Nereids* in surface area—instead of man lost overboard, it was man lost on board.

We saved a bunch by booking an inside room, as we had seen our share of ocean water and sunsets. The inside rooms were soundproof and motion proof, so in the morning when we caught the elevator and came on deck at the fifteenth floor for breakfast, we were hit by the bright sunlight and movement of the sea. If she had pulled into a new port in the night while we slept, there was a beautiful port setting for an added jolt to prepare us for the breakfast buffet with its plethora of choices. I found it best to first tour the food before making any choices and then to grab a platter (skip the average-size plate), load up with my favorites, then head for a table complete with stunning view.

Lunch was soon to follow and, amazingly, we were again ready to eat. The primary exercises between feedings were finding our room, playing cards and exploring inside the boat. When in port, we explored outside the boat: some ruins, shopping and then a return to the *Princess* for some serious evening dining. There were nine different feeding areas on the ship, featuring different specialties from international to the basic burger and fries. Every night was a five-course meal with a variety of appetizers, soups, salads and several main entrées from which to choose. If we survived, a separate dessert menu was presented with variations on ice cream, cake and creative stuff like cherries jubilee and baked Alaska.

It was a food lover's paradise. One felt initially as if there was a competition to consume or to be all that one could be. There were serious eaters aboard and some of these people were on their sixth or seventh cruises, which in some cases correlated with body weight. In our short stay, we added some significant poundage. It gave a whole new meaning to a ship's specification of gross tonnage. By the end of the cruise, I could barely fit into my pants, and Judy had rounded out some—but looked even more attractive, if you can imagine. I wondered, while caught in the moment of a feeding frenzy, if a fellow passenger were to drop dead into his plate, if anyone would stop eating or just give a passing glance as crew hauled him from the dining area.

It is a credit to the design of the *Princess* that each bathroom was equipped with a power-flush toilet. Earlier ship designs with standard toilets needed a special crew standing by ready with plumber's helpers to keep things moving. Along with the modern-day power-flush, if anyone was having serious discomfort from overeating, they could form a partial seal with the legs together that would create a vacuum assist.

Waste disposal is a work in progress and there are no regulations beyond the 3-mile limit. We had on occasion sailed into these personal signatures. Hopefully, the next generation of cruise ships will recycle this material into a biofuel, initially as hybrids and eventually to be totally powered by their own biofuel.

We came to love the *Princess* in many ways but mostly for her convenience. The *Princess* brought with her what most passengers take for granted. We had no worries about charting a course, anchorages, anchor holding, launching a dingy with a motor to reach shore, provisioning, customs and immigration officials, port captains, boat repairs, watch schedules, other ships, fish traps, drinking water, fuel, electricity or weather changes, all of which were the concern of Captain Nick Nash.

But other than the above "no worries," travel was similar to aboard the *Nereid*, which is still our favorite lady. The *Nereid* is significantly more cost effective, and we don't always want to share the experience with a host of strangers. We had an excellent time on the *Princess*. Besides the food, the entertainment was outstanding, the workers were always fun and this ole salty sailor and his mate plan to do another *Princess* cruise, and that's no shit.

Note: Friends of the Earth Cruise Ship Report Card (2013) compares 16 major cruise lines and 162 cruise ships. The Princes line did pretty good with a final grade of B. Report available at foe.org/cruise-report-card.

Rome, Athens and Beyond

"We can make room for two more, Raymond," Judy directed. "Step back so they can squeeze in."

We had just arrived in Rome, Italy, and were in an airport elevator headed to the exit level. The elevator was empty when we first got on, but it began filling up quickly with little people until we were now making room for the last two. I was at least a foot taller than anyone. They were all women, several carrying infants, everyone smiling.

Judy was commenting on the lovely babies when I felt something in my pocket and, as I shifted my body to check, I felt a little hand coming out. I then realized why we were packed into the elevator. This was our welcoming party to Rome, the little women were Gypsies, all about the same height and dress—the cute little babies, an effective distraction in the overcrowded elevator. There was nothing in my pocket, but we would have helped them out if we had known up front—maybe not to the extent they intended.

We spent four days exploring the glory that was Rome, the main feature being the Coliseum, with its arena, gladiator rooms and wild animal holding areas—I sensed the crowd of seventy thousand cheering the fate of a fallen gladiator. The purpose of the Coliseum, aside from entertainment, was to cultivate the warlike spirit of the Romans. Ancient Rome was not a good time to show up as a Christian—some were even burned to light up the gala bashes.

We had to leave Rome for places like Tuscany to find the magic of Italy. We converted from beer drinkers to wine after sampling the fruit of the vine in Tuscany. Our other awakening was the pasta—it tasted better in Italy. We treated ourselves to glasses of Chianti with our pasta, and it was worth the trip from anywhere inside or outside the Holy Roman Empire.

Athens, Greece, was equally impressive, its history violent not unlike Rome, but the ruins of a more intellectual intent. The Acropolis on the hill was not a fortification, but a place to think and discuss the problems in the Forum and the Parthenon. Places where Plato and Socrates contemplated the meaning of life and how to improve the plight of the citizens. Athenians believed that prosperity could only be achieved if they worked together—obviously ahead of their time.

The many rivals, instead of killing each other, were brought together to compete; that was the concept of the first Olympic Games, and it remains so today. Instead of sacrificing men's lives, Athenians were entertained by playwrights and had the first actor— Thespis. One feels warlike in Rome and intelligent in Athens. Modern Greece changed my quality of life, as I went in a tea drinker and emerged a coffee/espresso drinker. If short of cash, one can just take the coffee standing up for half price as a result of the limited seating. That deal could include something to eat as well.

Beyond the Italian and Greek experience was Ephesus in Turkey. Once the capital of the Roman Empire, it left many temples and structures. The Library of Celsus, the most outstanding, is a two-story structure that housed many scrolls, keeping them safe from moisture, a testimony to the importance of the written word.

Other places of note in our fifteen days of land travel and fifteen days aboard the *Princess* with ten ports of call, covering 2,611 miles, included Pisa, an engineering mistake; Pompeii, a day in the life of the rich and famous; Santorini, with its the blue-capped churches and site of the now-famous Blanco ride; and Venice, with its expensive gondoliers and the opera house, which we plan to revisit someday.

Whatever your plans, don't let this short account deter you—just do it—you can't go wrong. Oh yes, and if the little ladies are at the airport near the elevator, load a pocket with some extra cash. We will reimburse you— Thanks.

Table Talk

The most challenging and stimulating aspects of the *Princess* cruise were not listed on the web page or in any advertisements. In some cases they exceeded the glory of ancient Greece and Rome, and they occurred in the dining room, disguised as friendly guests. While we have sailed the world and have met many interesting people, our experience with some table guests reminded us that all was not well on the home front.

We were always a party of four when we entered the dining room. We would request a table for six or eight and then await the arrival of our mystery guests who would join us for dinner. The two-thousand-plus passengers from all parts of the world made for enjoyable and stimulating exchanges. We always felt the world was on a unified track for peace, acceptance and respect for differences of opinion, with two exceptions—both from our own country.

The first was Bob the dentist from San Diego, retired at age fifty-four. He and his lovely wife were doing a tour of various religious points of interest around the world and had recently returned from the Holy Land. They did not plan to visit South America because, living in San Diego, she had had enough of "those people"; also, they were both convinced that the US could be energy independent if we would free industry of regulations and drill for oil in the Arctic Refuge. He had a litany of factoids from Fox News and was sure everyone in healthcare was unhappy with President Obama.

When he found out Judy was a hygienist, he later took her aside and asked her, "How is it to live with someone who was not in healthcare?"

I am sure it isn't easy, but it is not because of healthcare—that would be a much longer story and ongoing. He believed any kind of socialism was just a modern-day form of communism.

Bob was scary, and I would not want to be in his dental chair if he found out I voted the other way. I was reminded of *Charlie Wilson's War*, the scene where he visited some constituents in Texas and came away with the realization that the enemy was not in Afghanistan but much closer to home.

A similar experience occurred with a retired professor from Ole Miss. His lead into his subject of concern was directed to a Canadian couple who had joined us.

"How do Canadians feel our new president is doing?" he asked.

A brief pause and they said, "We appreciate his energy and ability to get things done and wish we had someone like him in our government."

There followed an awkward silence, and so I asked, "How do you think the president is doing?"

Ole Miss took a deep breath and, with great professorial confidence, said, "Let me just say that when he walks into a room, he is the least experienced in the room."

Nobody was saying anything, so I finally said, "He may be the least experienced, but probably the most intelligent."

I had to leave early and meet Judy to catch a live magic show. She was eating with her sister, who didn't like to be around lobster, and this was lobster night. I couldn't pass up lobster, and besides, I would have missed Ole Miss. I was able to keep my cool, which is very important as any change in my bio-fluids can turn my shaky left hand into a *Doctor Strangelove* scene in which I risk stabbing myself with a lobster claw.

As I excused myself, I said, "I have the feeling we are on opposite sides of the aisle, but the important thing is that we work together."

As I left the dining room, I was glad the Canadians had been at the table, and for some reason I was glad to be aboard.

Note: The USGS (2010) estimated the NPRA oil resource at 896 million barrels or about 10% of the 2002 estimate as a result of recent exploration drilling revealing gas occurrence rather than oil. This more recent estimate would only be enough oil to fuel the US for 45 days.

Champagne Trail with Blanco

"Mule rides up the steep cliff to get to Santorini are way too dangerous, and I have seen people fall off and break a leg, so I highly recommend the tram."

These words from the morning orientation on the *Princess* were fresh in my mind as we approached the long line of fellow passengers waiting for the tram. We fell into line and prepared to make the best of it. An old fellow was shouting something about only ten euros and pointing to the loading ramp for the mule ride up the cliff. Nobody was paying him any attention.

As the line for the tram moved slowly along, I recalled my experience with horses and mules in the Park Service and Forest Service and how I had always had complete confidence in both, especially the mules, which were smarter and more agile on narrow, steep trails—the line moved on. I knew Judy had limited riding experience; her sister had spent many summers in Montana on a cattle ranch, but that was years ago, and even she was not interested in renewing her riding skills this day—the line crept on. Judy had said earlier there was no way she would take the mule ride after hearing that legs had been broken, but then my mouth took over for my brain.

I said almost apologetically, "Do you want to take the mule ride?"

She replied quietly, with a smile, "Yes."

I couldn't believe it, but then she is always full of surprises. We said our goodbyes, agreed to meet our fellow travelers at the top, and headed to the loading ramp. It was a big operation, maybe twenty-five mules on the trail, another twenty-five in the holding area— supposedly a forty-five-minute ride to the top. The scene was chaotic and I thought Judy was going to change her mind, so we did our usual dance for life threatening situations where I said, "Looks okay."

It was a short line, and ready or not, we were mounting up with handlers holding our mules. I thought she was getting on, but as I was led away, I turned to see her still standing on the ramp. I thought she had lost her nerve. I tried to turn my mule, which did not want to go back.

"You must go on," the handler directed.

"I need to wait for Madame," I replied.

"Madame is coming," he insisted.

I pointed and yelled, "No, she is not coming. I can see her with her yellow hat. She is still on the ramp."

He kept pulling my mule forward as I kept trying to turn around. Farther up the trail and free of the handlers, I did turn around and was heading back but was stopped again, this time by an angry handler. I tried bribery, handing him an extra ten euros to let me go back, but no way was that going to happen, and he kept the ten. He was yelling at me in Greek and I was yelling in English and some Spanish, which seemed to apply—almost an international incident.

I was mainly angry with myself for getting ahead of Judy and knew she felt I had abandoned her to deal with all of this "new stuff"—certain she was going back to join her sister in the tram line. I was stopped on the trail, letting other riders pass, feeling badly. Suddenly, from around the bend on the trail below came a white mule—rider with a yellow hat and, yes, unbelievable, there she was and she was hauling.

As I sat there on my steed, she raced by with a big smile, shouting, "Blanco! Blanco!"

I couldn't believe it and was too stunned to take a picture.

I tried to catch up, but at the top she was waiting for me.

"What happened?" I asked. "I thought you were right behind me and then you took so long to get going."

"I wanted to ride the pretty white one," she answered.

I hadn't thought of that, but it made perfect sense.

Evidently, it was being reserved for heavy people, and she had to argue with the men to get it. Her white mule liked the shade and would pass others to get there first—I said mules were smart.

One of the handlers saw us talking afterward and came over, smiling, shaking his head, and said, "So this is your Madame, you are just like Madame, you two belong together!"

I had to agree.

Note: We dubbed this the Champagne Trail, so named because we spent an afternoon at a breathtaking, cliff-side restaurant, table for two, overlooking the bay, drinking champagne. The next morning we could not remember exactly how we got back to the boat, but we are sure it was not via Blanco.

Special Moments

After the excitement of the Parthenon, the Coliseum, Tuscany, Pisa, Rome, Athens, Venice and Cinque Terre begins to fade, there are some moments and snippets of conversation that linger. These remaining imprints are still vivid, for example:

- "Does it have, like, half legs?" came from a well-proportioned blonde gal observing a camel…legs folded under, with only large knee joints visible.
- "You must go back." An elderly Greek woman sitting in the doorway of her home offered this important advice as I was headed down the wrong side of the hill from the glorious Parthenon.
- "I'm listening" came from a very pretty Italian girl on the bus taking in some guidance I was receiving from my mate.
- "Under control," the cheerful response of the dining room receptionist from Croatia on the *Princess* to my inquiry, "How are things in Croatia?"
- "Give me the fire power and in one week I will take care of the Somali pirates. Any boat going beyond the twelve-mile limit into international waters would be sunk," from a retired Greek ship captain.
- "Anyplace, even Millwood, would look good after two bottles of this champagne" came from my darling mate while at a cliff-side restaurant discussing where we should live after our sailing adventure.
- "School children playing outside sound the same in any language in any country"—Judy's comment as we walked by a schoolyard of kids playing in Rome.

- "Blanco, Blanco!" This a shout for joy and excitement from Judy as she passed me like a veteran rider on her white mule on the steep trail to the village above.

- A desk clerk on the *Princess,* having secured us a room reservation in an already-overbooked hotel in Rome, said, "When you get there, you need to pretend you are rich."
  "How do I do that?" I asked.
  "You will do just fine," she replied.

- The instructor at a wine-tasting class on the *Princess* told the story of Napoleon designing the Champagne Saucer in honor of Josephine's magnificent upper body parts and her reciprocating by designing the Champagne Flute in honor of his lower body part.

- Our tour guide on the way to Siena, while speaking of the beauty and romance of the Italian language, quoted Charles V of Spain: "I speak to my priest in Spanish, my horses in German, my troops in French and my mistress in Italian."

- "They are on your head"—Judy's comment when I was agonizing over the loss of my favorite sunglasses.

Epilogue

These short stories were written shortly after each event, or at least roughed out. A couple of years later, while drafting the final document, it was harder to believe we did what we did. With time, that feeling of amazement increased as the details began to fade. The important point was we had done it, and while entering the fourth and final quarter of the big game. We had some medical issues, but we were still relatively strong and healthy. Equally important was that we had purchased a proven-seaworthy boat that covered our mistakes in what was to become an ongoing learning experience.

We also learned more about each other and ourselves. I still can't believe how my lovely first mate stepped up when needed most. Don't judge the capabilities of your mate before such an undertaking. These revelations about each other were ongoing and priceless.

Almost equally important was our realization that we are all in this together, only with different starting points in life. Irrespective of our starting points, we all have the same hopes and dreams. The little girl holding her doll while she studied us, the little boy clinging to his favorite toy, the proud parents nodding their approval, the sounds of kids playing in the schoolyard.

Cultural differences were important and amazing. Wherever we went ashore and traveled around, we were greeted with warmth and enthusiasm by the people. The wide range of economic success, measured by the accumulation of stuff, seemed to correlate inversely with happiness and enjoyment of life. A good lesson and a growing concern for our Western culture.

Many have asked us, "What was the highlight of your trip?"

Not an easy question to answer. Judy has several but always includes the time, after a quiet passage on a moonlit night, we approached a cove off Bora Bora as the sun was just breaking over the surrounding mountains. For me, surprisingly, it was while recovering from back surgery at a hospital in Malaysia at Christmastime.

Good news about getting older is that the accompanying lack of energy makes it easier to let the spirit of adventure slip away. We will not be buying another boat, but there is no doubt we did the right thing by selling our house and buying the *Nereid.* We also have a great story for the kids and grandkids. Our hope is that others will find some inspiration in what we did and maybe take a chance. It's not too late.

Wishing you fair winds and following seas in whatever you do.

Ray and Judy Emerson

Glossary

Aground – ship stranded on intertidal or sea bed

Backstay – cable supporting the mast from the stern

Ballast – weighted part of the keel for stability

Beam reach – point of sail with wind on the beam

Becalmed sea – a flat, quiet body of water

Bilge – the lowest area in the hull above the keel

Boom – the bar to which the main sail is attached

Broad reach/running – sail set to move down wind

Cap rail – seals upper surface of the hull

Close-hauled – sail set for sailing into the wind

Cockpit – in small vessels, a space toward the stern lower than the rest of the deck

Dinghy – small boat used to ferry people to and from shore

Draft – the depth of a boat from waterline to keel

Drogue – used to slow the boat in heavy seas

Following sea – assists the forward motion of the boat

Forestay – cable supporting the mast from the bow

Genoa – large headsail

Grib files – data base for weather forecasting

Headsail – any sail forward of the mast

Hove-to – parking your boat at sea without anchoring

Inverter – changes DC current to AC current

ITCZ (Intertropical Convergence Zone) – usually rough sailing area near the equator

"Jenny" – pet name for the genoa

Keel – fin on the bottom of the boat for stability

Line – term for any rope used on a boat

Logbook – a boat's record of activity

Mediterranean tie-up – using anchor off the bow with stern line to secured to the dock

Midship – the portion of the ship between the bow and the stern

Monohull – single hull unlike boats with two or more

Nautical mile – 6,080 feet or 1.15 miles

Passage – a route between two points or ports of call

Prop walk – factor to consider when docking

Puddle Jumper's Net – organized by *Latitude 38* to assist boaters crossing the Pacific

Reacher drifter – headsail larger than a genoa and smaller than a spinnaker, for light winds

Reefing – reducing the exposure of the sail to the wind

Roller furler – used to quickly rolls up the head sails

Running lights – safety lights for night sailing

Sea anchor – parachute setup to stabilize the boat in heavy seas

Sea Max charts – electronic navigational charts

Sea state – general condition of the surface of a large body of water

Seacock – part of the through-hull to control intake of sea water

Seafarer's Net – provides daily tracking of boats at sea

Scuppers – drain holes in the deck allowing water to run off

Slip – a place to park your boat in the marina

Spreaders – help support the mast

SSB radio – single side band radio for broadcasting and receiving while at sea

Stanchions – upright supports for the guard rail

Staysail – located between the main and head sail

Stern – the back or rear part of a ship or boat

Tacking – method of sailing into the wind

Through-hull – allows intake or drainage of sea water

VHF – radio for communication and emergencies

Wind generator – like solar panels, helps keep the batteries charged

Wind vane – a robust auto pilot, requiring no electricity, mounted on the stern

Windlass – a winch to move heavy anchor chain

Wing-on-wing – sail set for running downwind

Whisker pole – attached to the mast to hold out a head sail